D1559660

Practical Rules

Rules proliferate; some are kept with a bureaucratic stringency bordering on the absurd, while others are manipulated and ignored in ways that injure our sense of justice. Under what conditions should we make exceptions to rules, and when should they be followed despite particular circumstances that they ignore?

The two dominant models in the current literature on rules are the particularist account, which rejects the relevance of genuine rules, and that which sees the application of rules as standard. Taking a position that falls between these two extremes, Alan Goldman is the first to provide a systematic framework to clarify when we need to follow rules in our moral, legal, and prudential decisions and when we ought not to do so. The book distinguishes among various types of rules; it illuminates concepts such as integrity, self-interest, and self-deception; and finally, it provides an account of ordinary moral reasoning without rules.

This book will be of great interest to advanced students and professionals working in philosophy, law, decision theory, and the social sciences.

Alan H. Goldman is Professor of Philosophy at the University of Miami. He is the author of *Empirical Knowledge* (1988), *Moral Knowledge* (1988), and *Aesthetic Value* (1995).

CAMBRIDGE STUDIES IN PHILOSOPHY
General editor ERNEST SOSA (Brown University)

Advisory editors:
JONATHAN DANCY (University of Reading)
JOHN HALDANE (University of St. Andrews)
GILBERT HARMAN (Princeton University)
FRANK JACKSON (Australian National University)
WILLIAM G. LYCAN (University of North Carolina at Chapel Hill)
SYDNEY SHOEMAKER (Cornell University)
JUDITH J. THOMSON (Massachusetts Institute of Technology)

RECENT TITLES:
MARK LANCE and JOHN O'LEARY-HAWTHORNE *The Grammar of Meaning*
D. M. ARMSTRONG *A World of States of Affairs*
PIERRE JACOB *What Minds Can Do*
ANDRE GALLOIS *The World Without the Mind Within*
FRED FELDMAN *Utilitarianism, Hedonism, and Desert*
LAURENCE BONJOUR *In Defense of Pure Reason*
DAVID LEWIS *Papers in Philosophical Logic*
WAYNE DAVIS *Implicature*
DAVID COCKBURN *Other Times*
DAVID LEWIS *Papers on Metaphysics and Epistemology*
RAYMOND MARTIN *Self-Concern*
ANNETTE BARNES *Seeing Through Self-Deception*
MICHAEL BRATMAN *Faces of Intention*
AMIE THOMASSON *Fiction and Metaphysics*
DAVID LEWIS *Papers on Ethics and Social Philosophy*
FRED DRETSKE *Perception, Knowledge, and Belief*
LYNNE RUDDER BAKER *Persons and Bodies*
JOHN GRECO *Putting Skeptics in Their Place*
RUTH GARRETT MILLIKAN *On Clear and Confused Ideas*
DERK PEREBOOM *Living without Free Will*
BRIAN ELLIS *Scientific Essentialism*

Practical Rules

When We Need Them and When We Don't

ALAN H. GOLDMAN

University of Miami

CAMBRIDGE
UNIVERSITY PRESS

PUBLISHED BY THE PRESS SYNDICATE OF THE UNIVERSITY OF CAMBRIDGE
The Pitt Building, Trumpington Street, Cambridge, United Kingdom

CAMBRIDGE UNIVERSITY PRESS
The Edinburgh Building, Cambridge CB2 2RU, UK
40 West 20th Street, New York, NY 10011-4211, USA
10 Stamford Road, Oakleigh, VIC 3166, Australia
Ruiz de Alarcón 13, 28014 Madrid, Spain
Dock House, The Waterfront, Cape Town 8001, South Africa

http://www.cambridge.org

© Alan H. Goldman 2002

This book is in copyright. Subject to statutory exception
and to the provisions of relevant collective licensing agreements,
no reproduction of any part may take place without
the written permission of Cambridge University Press.

First published 2002

Printed in the United States of America

Typeface Bembo 10.5/13 pt.   *System* DeskTopPro$_{/UX}$ [BV]

A catalog record for this book is available from the British Library.

Library of Congress Cataloging in Publication Data
Goldman, Alan H., 1945–
Practical rules : when we need them and when we don't / Alan H. Goldman.
p. cm. – (Cambridge studies in philosophy)
Includes bibliographical references and index.
ISBN 0-521-80729-8 (hardback)
1. Ethics. 2. Rules (Philosophy) I. Title. II. Series.

BJ1031 .G67 2001
170'.42–dc21

2001023138

ISBN 0 521 80729 8 hardback

In memory of my father, Larry Goldman,
never one to follow rules needlessly

Contents

Acknowledgments

I first thank Jan Narveson and Christopher Gowans for helpful comments on the entire manuscript, as well as Jonathan Adler and Frederick Schauer for comments on parts of it. I am grateful to Ernest Sosa and Matthew Lord for expediting the publication of the book. I thank Helen Greenberg for excellent copyediting.

Parts of the book appeared in articles in *Synthese, Law and Philosophy,* and *The Southern Journal of Philosophy.* I thank those journals for permission to reprint sections of them. Portions of various chapters were presented in talks at the University of Auckland, University of Canterbury, University of Waikato, Simon Fraser University, and the University of Victoria, and I benefited from the discussions on those occasions.

Much of this material was written with the help of Max Orovitz Research Grants from the University of Miami, for which I am grateful.

Introduction

"A rule's a rule!" How many of us have been infuriated by hearing these words from some bureaucrat across a desk or government counter? How many have thought such an attempt at justification more appropriate for a robot than a human being? How many take this pat response as a cue to request a supervisor or higher-up who can look through and beyond the rules? On the other side, how many of us have resented administrators who took it upon themselves to ignore rules and make exceptions that we thought unjustified? How many have condemned those who adopt or acknowledge rules only to ignore them later or consider themselves above them? Can both of these reactions be right? That the former reaction is more common begins to indicate that the application of rules is not the norm in sound moral reasoning, at least in difficult or controversial situations. That the latter response also occurs begins to indicate that there are nevertheless circumstances in which agents ought to obey rules even when they regret the outcomes and believe they could do better. The question we face here is "Which circumstances?"

Most philosophers have remained oblivious to this mundane phenomenology. Most, despite the warnings of Aristotle, and perhaps influenced by such hoary texts as the ten commandments, by suspect interpretations of Kant and naive versions of utilitarianism, or by a once dominant picture of theory construction in science, assume that moral reasoning always consists in the application of rules to particular cases. More respectably, adherents to this view of moral reasoning believe that only the generality of rules can afford genuine reasons for particular moral judgments, or that only general principles can create or reveal the coherence within sets of particular judgments. I shall dispute this more respectable line of reasoning. The justification for and coherence of particular judgments do not require their support by universal rules.

Genuine rules state sufficient conditions for acting or refraining from acting or, in weaker versions, state conditions that always must be given independent weight in any circumstance in which they obtain. But there is a yet weaker constraint whose satisfaction suffices for consistency among judgments: We must not judge two cases differently without being able to cite a relevant difference between them (where relevance is relative to domain of discourse, e.g., moral or legal). Factors that are relevant must make differences in different conceivable circumstances, but not necessarily in all those circumstances in which they might be found. This constraint allows us to recognize differences or relevant factors that could not have been predicted, factors that are weighed directly against those that might be stated in rules and that therefore might defeat our ability to state sufficient conditions for action or universally sound rules in advance.

Reasoning by analogy and difference from settled cases under only this last constraint therefore differs from applying rules. But when this constraint is satisfied, judgments and actions that follow them are coherent in that they will not both pursue and defeat the same values in the same circumstances. I am tempted to call the weaker constraint the "difference principle," but since this might invite confusion, not to mention lawsuits, I will call it instead the "Kantian constraint." It might with greater accuracy be called the "Sidgwickian constraint,"[1] but this name would be less likely to ring a bell, and the requirement is, as I will argue, a charitable partial interpretation of Kant's fundamental principle of practical reason. It will figure centrally in my account of moral reasoning.

Many adherents to the view that moral reasoning typically consists in the application of rules would admit that the complexity of morally charged circumstances and the complex ways in which competing values can interact within them generate open-ended exceptions to any rules that might be of use in reasoning, exceptions that cannot all be predicted in advance. Here they seem to join forces with their opponents, those who deny the relevance of rules for these very reasons. What they do not seem to notice, as their opponents do, is that rules with open-ended exceptions, especially if the exceptions are determined by weighing opposing factors directly against those mentioned in the rules, become mere rules of thumb, reminders of factors that can be morally relevant.

They do no more than indicate certain paradigm cases involving those factors from which cases that could be exceptions must be differentiated. Rules of thumb contrast with genuine rules as characterized previously. The former become useless when we must weigh opposing relevant factors or values, precisely those situations that require serious moral reasoning. Genuine rules, by contrast, have independent weight in moral calculations. Breaking such rules is, other things equal, considered wrong in itself, independently of other reasons for and against the actions they require.

Particularists, the opponents of advocates of genuine rules, recognize only rules of thumb, which are dispensable in favor of the direct perception of morally relevant factors. For them, we simply perceive the morally relevant factors in each case and how they weigh against each other. Such relative weights can radically alter with the context. In the context of a doctor–patient relation, for example, not lying may be more important than not causing pain, while in the context of common courtesy, this priority is often reversed. Values can even change from positive to negative, depending on other factors in the context: The pleasure of a sadistic act makes it worse. Such shifting priorities and valences cannot be fully captured in sets of genuine rules, which state only a limited number of relatively simple conditions as relevant to decisions and which require stable orderings among the values they represent. Thus, particularists are right in believing that if recognizable and usable rules cannot capture the ways we order competing values in concrete contexts, then they cannot generally be applied to settle controversial moral issues in which interests do oppose one another. Since they will not generally capture our intuitive settled judgments, they cannot determine controversial answers that are most coherent with those judgments.

There are nevertheless two fatal flaws in the particularist position that must be remedied here. First, they have no alternative account of reasoning to the correct answer to difficult moral problems. They can point only to intuitions, however dressed up in new vocabulary, about the weights of factors in particular cases. But intuitions conflict, and I believe that reasoning can correct them and resolve these conflicts. In the final chapter, I shall provide an account of moral reasoning guided by the Kantian constraint that eschews appeal both to rules as the norm and to particularistic intuitions. Second, as noted, there are situations that do call for following rules even when ordinary judgment opposes them, and particularists have ignored such situations. The following chapters will attempt to specify when and how they arise in various domains of judgment and action.

Sophisticated defenders of rules these days, such as R. M. Hare, Joseph Raz, and Frederick Schauer,[2] do not claim that they capture all of our intuitive judgments or achieve perfect justice in application. They follow the implicit leads of Thomas Hobbes and J. S. Mill in defending rules as second-best strategies. Rules simplify reasoning so as to save effort and avoid errors from attempts to take all relevant factors into account in situations where such errors are more likely to occur than not. They remove authority to judge on ordinary grounds. Thus, where "no dogs are allowed" in order to prevent nuisance to patrons, a tiny, quiet, and meticulously trained poodle will nevertheless not be allowed on the premises. "A rule's a rule." A brilliant and mature twenty-nine-year-old cannot run for the United States Senate: The Constitution states necessary conditions here (sufficient conditions for impermissibility). We forgo the optimal mix of candidates or of animals and patrons because we do not think it can be achieved with reasonable costs in practice. The rules give us an acceptable second best.

According to Hobbes, we are prudentially better off following a strict rule to be moral because, while we might benefit on particular occasions from immorality, we cannot identify such situations with sufficient reliability to make them pay in the long run.[3] Thus we settle for the second-best pattern of behavior generated by the strict rule. According to Mill, we need a strict rule against paternalistic interference by the government because officials who would interfere are likely to get it wrong more often than not.[4] The optimal pattern of interference will not be achieved, and so we settle for the second-best solution of minimizing the errors by strict abstinence. In other contexts, rules state conditions that must be given extra weight in moral calculations, although they might not always override. Arguably, the First Amendment protection of free speech is a rule of this sort. We must not silence free expression simply when the ordinary weight of factors tells us to (when people are offended by speech with seemingly no positive value), but sometimes we must do so to prevent severe offense or greater harm. The rule tips the balance and corrects for our temptation to suppress offensive expression too often (without excluding all offense from counting).

There are two contexts in which rules are justified as second-best strategies. First, there is that in which errors seem more likely than not in each case. This might be so because of the complexity of the cases, because of the lack of epistemic resources for sufficiently investigating them, or because of stupidity or bias on the part of the investigators. These situations and justifications for rules have been emphasized by the aforementioned philosophers. The problem with this justification, however, is that it is easy to exaggerate the frequency of such contexts. Ordinary prudential and moral reasoning, even in the context of competing values and interests, need not be as overwhelmingly difficult as these philosophers make it out to be (this despite the fact that competing values resist permanent orderings). Despite Hobbes's argument, sometimes we can be quite certain that we can profit from wrongdoing, and so we are not always better off abstaining. Despite Mill's arguments, sometimes we *can* tell when paternalistic interference is justified on ordinary grounds, and so we do not need a strict rule against its occurrence. Then too, some agents are less prone to error than others. This explains why we are more apt to try to impose rules on others than to use them ourselves; it also explains why we expect the "rule's a rule" line from low-level bureaucrats but not from their supervisors (except in Miami). But in some contexts *everyone* ought to obey rules and not simply to be democratically minded. A more subtle justification is missing from the previous literature.

That more subtle justification will be emphasized here. The central cases involve individually harmless acts that have cumulatively harmful results. These resemble typical prisoners' dilemmas, in which prudentially rational actions leave everyone worse off than they could be, that is, result in collectively irrational outcomes, except that here morally permissible or required actions result in morally unacceptable outcomes. In these contexts there need not be any single-case errors when the collective result is unacceptable. Examples familiar to many readers of this book include teachers who base grades on the sad personal stories of their students or students who give test answers to their friends. Such acts may be morally right or permissible in light of the overall benefits produced in the individual cases (in the absence of rules), but cumulatively they may defeat the socially useful function of the grading system. Adopting rules in such contexts prevents the negative cumulative effects, as well as unfairness or free riding by individuals who correctly calculate the negligible harmful effects of their individual actions. Once such a rule is adopted, it is unfair to those obeying it when others do not do so (a useful tip on the first thing to teach in an ethics course).

Chapter 1, after classifying the types of rules and showing that genuine rules do not capture our ordinary moral judgments, will focus on the analysis of such cases, paradigms of contexts in which rules are needed. Like prisoners' dilemmas, they can be analyzed as coordination problems that generate collective-action problems whose solutions lie in rules as second-best strategies. The inability to coordinate so as to achieve optimal collective outcomes leads to the collectively harmful outcomes of individually correct decisions. Rules alter the moral status of these decisions. Individuals must follow such rules even when they perceive that they could do better in the single case by violating them. I shall isolate and describe such contexts in the public and private spheres and analyze the types of rules that are needed in them, as well as the type of wrongness involved in violating these rules. While such contexts provide the strongest justification for the adoption of rules, and while there are numerous examples, they remain atypical (the exception and not the rule).

Chapter 2 will compare justifications for using rules in prudential contexts, to further self-interest, with the justification for moral rules developed in Chapter 1. Prudential rules are said to be useful as a means to overcome weakness of will, as when we oppose the temptation of each opportunity to snack or drink martinis or (pick your favorite temptation) by adopting rules never to do so. The justifications for moral and prudential rules may seem similar in that the single snack or martini or other indulgence may be harmless in itself, and yet the cumulative result of overweight or alcoholism must be avoided. But there are differences as well, chief among them that we can more easily solve the coordination problem over time for our own actions than we can coordinate with the actions of others in the relevant moral contexts. This ability to coordinate actions over time allows the adoption of strategies to optimize instead of settling for the second-best strategy of strict rules. We can have the occasional snack or martini. More flexible and more profitable dispositions than those captured by rules are available to the prudential agent. Rules in this domain therefore not only reflect abnormal circumstances, as in the moral context, but also are needed only by abnormal (addictive or obsessive) individuals, those who cannot achieve the flexible dispositions available to others.

Second-best strategies are not rational when we know we can achieve what is optimal overall. This is compatible with the claim that sometimes we ought not to try to achieve what is optimal in a particular domain because of the costs involved in the attempt, the competing values that might be sacrificed. In Chapter 2 I will clarify the sense in which optimizing is definitional of prudential rationality, as well as the sense in which we should sometimes satisfice, settle for second best, instead of trying to optimize. In the former sense, optimizing is not an action-guiding rule; in the latter sense, rules are hard to come by. There are, once more, many interacting factors that might determine when to satisfice and when to aim at something better.

I claim that moral rules are more commonly justified than prudential rules. If morality reduced to prudence, as philosophers in the Hobbesian tradition claim, then there might be no such contrast. I shall argue that prudential rationality or self-interest can but need not include the interests of others. Moral behavior is therefore compatible with but not required by prudence. Those on the opposite side from Hobbesians, those who see an inevitable conflict between morality and self-interest, tend to think of narrow instead of broad self-interest (the latter including the interests of those one cares about), and they tend to think of one-shot encounters with those whom one can profitably exploit. Those who envisage a reduction of morality to prudence, by contrast, tend to advocate broadening one's concerns on prudential grounds, and they tend to think of continuous interactions in which one's dispositions will be found out. But both one-shot and continuous interactions are possible, and sometimes we know that we are in one-shot contexts. Furthermore, dispositions more flexible than those captured by rules (rules of the sort "Never exploit others" or "Always exploit others when you think you can profit by doing so") are once more available, psychologically more likely, but less likely to be completely discerned by others. Broadening one's interests has benefits as well as costs, and no rule seems to capture the optimal mix of self-regarding and other-regarding interests for all individuals. Some individuals can profit even in the long run from wrongdoing, but acting morally can also be an important and rewarding part of a good life. Chapter 2 concludes that no prudential rule requires morality; hence moral rules do not themselves reduce to prudential rules. The domains are separate (moral rules remain more often justified than prudential rules) but compatible.

Chapter 3, which focuses on legal rules, begins with a classification of legal norms, a clarification of which legal norms require interpretation, and an analysis of what such interpretation consists in. I will argue against legal philosophers who debate the question of whether law consists in a set of genuine rules that there is no right answer to this question. The same legal materials can be read as genuine rules or as weaker constraints specifying only paradigm cases from or to which others must be legally differentiated or assimilated (the legal version of the Kantian constraint). Although the way law is written can encourage or discourage its being read as rules, legal language does not force the issue. Alternative readings are available for the apparently broad standards of the Constitution, which certain interpretive strategies transform into narrower rules, as well as for apparent rules in statutes, which can be treated as broader and weaker standards (interpreted in terms of paradigm cases), as examples show. If some judges read legal materials one way and other judges read the same materials another way, then the normative question of how they should be read, whether or not they should be read in terms of rules, becomes prominent.

After critically examining arguments in favor of the widespread use of rules in law, I shall conclude that the criteria for justifiably framing the law in terms of rules are the same as those I defend more generally. We need legal rules when the cumulative effects of attempting to take all legally relevant factors into account directly – here directly attempting to differentiate cases falling within the plain meaning of legal norms – are worse than the imperfect justice of applying the rules. Examples will be provided from contract law, torts, and criminal law.

A most important example is the fundamental but unwritten rule of the legal system: that judges defer to legal requirements even when they disagree morally with their implications for particular cases. This rule fits our model since judges may correctly perceive that they could do better morally by following their own moral perceptions in particular cases in which legal norms require different decisions. But the cumulative effect of allowing such judgments would be to destroy the legal authority of legislators and of the law itself. Hence the rule that removes the authority of judges to decide cases on direct moral grounds is both itself a moral rule and a cornerstone of the legal system. Indeed, it will be a main paradigm in this discussion for the justification of rules. Its acceptance by judges does not imply that they must apply lower-level legal rules in making their decisions, however. They must do so only when our more general criteria are satisfied in legal contexts. Or so I shall argue.

Having shown that the application of rules is not the norm in moral or legal reasoning, and having clarified when rules are nevertheless needed as a second-best strategy in these domains, I leave it for the final chapter to describe in detail what the norm is. Particularist intuitions, I have pointed out, leave us no way to settle disagreements or to reason to correct answers once relevant factors have been identified but their competing weights remain controversial. Particularists can only insist that our judgments be properly informed and sensitive, but such judgments can still conflict or leave us uncertain. Beyond being informed and sensitive, we seek coherence in our practical appraisals so that actions based on them are not self-defeating, that is, do not both pursue and block the same values. If these judgments represent our values and not facts independent of them (as I shall argue), then we seek *only* coherence among our informed and sensitive judgments. They must represent a set of values fitting a rational life plan that can be consistently pursued. The correct answer to a controversial issue, then, is that which is most coherent with the base of settled judgments, that which cannot be differentiated from the closest analogous case in that base but can be relevantly distinguished from every case judged differently.

If coherence does not require subsuming particular judgments under universal principles or rules, it does require satisfaction of the Kantian constraint. This has two parts: We must not judge cases differently without finding relevant differences between them (or the same way when there are such differences), and these distinguishing factors must make differences in other conceivable cases. I shall defend the second requirement, the requirement of generality, against the particularist intuition that any right-making characteristic in one context might be found with defeaters or reversers in others. If it cannot be defended, then demonstrable reasons cannot settle disputes involving different weighings of competing interests or values. If it can be, then following the method of analogy and difference allows for resolution of disputes across incompatible moral frameworks. No dispute is in principle irresolvable, although some may in fact be if the disputants cannot find shared paradigms from which to reason.

Analysis, even in outline, of real controversial social issues will demonstrate the use of the method. It will also show once more that applying genuine rules in practical reasoning is the exception and not the rule. But it is an exception certainly not to be overlooked if we want to understand why certain kinds of action are wrong.

1

Moral Rules

I. OUTLINE OF THE TASK

My main task in this first chapter is to determine when rules are required for moral reasoning and when they are not, when, indeed, they are better dispensed with. The mark of a genuine rule is universal prescription. Such rules tell us what to do, or at least how to reason, in all cases to which they apply. Genuine moral rules connect natural or nonmoral properties universally to moral prescriptions. They tell us what to do whenever certain situations occur, situations that can be identified without moral reasoning.

Such rules can be broad or narrow. Their scope or range of application is determined by the extensions of the terms in which they are stated. "Don't torture kittens" applies to all young cats and orders us not to inflict severe pain on them. If we know the meaning of the nonmoral term "kittens," and if the term "torture" is used here to mean the infliction of severe pain (nonmoral terms), then we know what the rule unambiguously tells us to refrain from doing in all situations involving kittens.

Some expressions that appear to be rules, whose statements are universal or seem to apply to all things of a stated kind, can be reduced in practice (as they are actually used) to expressions without universal terms. Such expressions are not really universally prescriptive, although their form would suggest that they are. Despite their universal form, they do not in practice tell us how to act or reason in all cases that fall within their expressed scope, and hence they are not genuine (indispensable) practical rules. "Tell the truth," for example, in practice tells us no more than that whether a statement is true or false can be a morally relevant or decisive consideration for or against uttering it. Given the innumerable exceptions to the rule that we allow, given that a statement's being true can in some, even many, contexts count *against* uttering it, the apparent rule is not universally prescriptive. In order to distinguish these and other merely apparent or incomplete rules from the genuine articles, we will require a preliminary classification of different types of rules in Section II.

I shall then consider the broadest justifications for the use of genuine rules in the next two sections. First, in Section III, I shall consider the claim that they capture our ordinary perceptions of moral demands. It has been widely assumed in the history of ethics that morality lies in the obedience of a set of rules, for example the Ten Commandments or the Golden Rule. If this is so, then moral reasoning consists primarily in the application of rules to particular cases. More recently, philosophers usually called particularists have argued that moral contexts, situations in which morally relevant factors must be weighed in reaching decisions, are too fine-grained and too variable to be captured in a set of applicable rules. I will side with the particularists here and will review some of the reasons why they are right.

Particularists, however, have not generally addressed a more sophisticated defense of the widespread use of rules in moral reasoning. The central idea here is that rules represent second-best strategies (which are nevertheless widely needed) for maximizing the satisfaction of moral demands. Although they produce less than optimal decisions, their application is generally the best we can do, given our limited capacities and cognitive resources and the complexity of morally charged contexts that is emphasized by particularists themselves. In order to save time and resources and minimize errors, we must obey the simplifying rules, or at least give them independent weight (or allow them to replace other reasons) in our moral calculations. These cognitive limitations and moral complexities that are to justify the use of rules may be easily exaggerated, however, as I shall argue. Those who exaggerate them hold moral theories that themselves produce extreme difficulties in arriving at proper moral decisions. They also thereby underestimate the resources available to moral reasoning without rules, a subject for a later chapter.

Another common justification for the use of rules is to coordinate actions of different agents, or of a single agent over time, to provide information about likely actions of different agents or at different times and to render them predictable. This is an important and common function. In providing opportunities for coordinated actions such rules are not second best, as described earlier, but instead enable optimal behavior over time.[5] Here, however, the question I shall raise from the point of view of moral reasoning is whether such rules must be accorded independent weight in moral calculations. Normally the reasons that justify the adoption of such rules strongly motivate subjects to follow them. The question is whether, when there arise reasons to act otherwise, these should be weighed directly against the justifying reasons for the rules. In such moral calculations the rules drop out, by contrast to what I am calling genuine moral rules, which must be granted independent, if not absolute, weight in any moral calculations of opposing reasons. Such rules must make a difference in moral calculations, must alter the way that ordinary reasons get figured. Coordination rules typically allow the values that justify them, for example avoiding danger on the roads, to be realized. But they do not alter the weights for and against compliance in moral calculations. Or so I shall argue.

After dismissing claims on behalf of the widespread use of genuine rules in moral reasoning, I will offer in Section VI a narrower justification for using such rules in particular contexts. Although there is not the widespread need for efficiency and predictability in moral decision making that sophisticated defenders of rules suppose, fallibility, also emphasized by some defenders, does enter prominently into this narrower justification. As philosophers beginning with J. S. Mill have argued, we require rules to guide moral reasoning when such reasoning is more likely than not to produce errors in their absence. But the most interesting cases, on which I will focus, have not been explicitly noticed before. These involve a variant in the purely moral sphere of prisoners' dilemma cases, contexts in which individually rational decisions produce irrational outcomes on the collective or social level.

The model prisoners' dilemma case involves agents who act to further their own interest, where their prudential actions come to defeat their self-interest.[6] One solution to this dilemma involves their adopting a collective or moral point of view. Hobbes, however, famously argued that the decision on whether to accept moral restraints generally (in the absence of coercive power) is itself this sort of dilemma: It is in no one's but at the same time in everyone's interest to do so. I call these classic cases, in which prudential reasoning may give way to moral reasoning as a solution, "prudential-moral" prisoners' dilemmas. There are also cases involving single agents in which self-interest is self-defeating, but in which the solution requires not a moral viewpoint but the adoption of a longer-range prudential point of view.[7] I call these "prudential-

prudential" dilemmas. In contrast to these well-known prudential-moral and prudential-prudential prisoners' dilemma contexts, the case I will concentrate on first is that in which individually moral decisions and actions result in morally unacceptable collective outcomes. These are "moral-moral" prisoners' dilemmas.

After defining and contrasting these different types of cases, I will argue that the moral-moral context is the paradigm situation in which we require moral rules. Here there exists a radical fallibility not based on a remediable ignorance. In such contexts, there exists an optimal pattern of moral decisions on ordinary grounds and a threshold at which such decisions begin to result in cumulative harm. But the optimal pattern of moral decision making is unattainable, and the adoption of genuine rules allows us to achieve second-best or acceptable patterns of behavior. Recognition of the need for these rules and clarification of their use in various cases will ultimately require a modification in the original classification of rule types. The position I will defend differs both from particularism, which dismisses altogether the need for rules to guide practical reasoning and action, and from rule-based moral theories, which see the need for rules as the norm in practical reflection.

II. TYPES OF RULES: DISPENSABLE AND INDISPENSABLE

Moral reasoning must begin with nonnormative descriptions of actions or situations and terminate in moral prescriptions. If we begin instead with descriptions of situations that are themselves couched in moral terms, then we invite disagreement, and we must reason about whether these moral descriptions properly apply to the situations in question. We may perceive the situation directly in moral terms, for example perceive a fatal shooting, if we are so unfortunate as to do so, as an act of murder and not simply as a killing. That is, we may not initially infer that the victim is being murdered from the recognition that he is being killed, together with other facts. But someone with a different moral view of the matter will perceive it differently, and our moral perception that, together with the rule prohibiting murder, tells us that the act is seriously wrong, can be challenged. We will then have to reason about how the nonmoral facts of the situation justify our normative or moral description of it in order to defend our initial perception. Complete moral reasoning, then, must commence from descriptions couched in nonmoral terms, from natural properties that are held to be morally relevant.

13

If rules are to be indispensable in the arguments that such reasoning instantiates, they must be distinguishable from mere rules of thumb. Moral rules of thumb may remind us of factors that are often morally relevant. "Tell the truth" is a rule of this sort. Such rules summarize past weighings of reasons in favor of the conditions mentioned, for example, that a statement is false is often a decisive reason against uttering it. Sticking to them in normal conditions saves the time and effort of making moral calculations on each occasion. But they lack independent normative force in failing to imply even that the factors they indicate are always relevant in the same way and therefore must be taken into account in the instance at hand. The justifying reasons mentioned may or may not have force in the situation encountered, and when they do, reasoning in light of them will consist in weighing them directly against counterreasons, for which reasoning the rules themselves drop out. Other rules of thumb do not mention their justifying conditions, but substitute for them until serious counterconsiderations arise. Coordination rules that make one solution to a coordination problem salient, such as "Drive on the right," are often of this sort (I assume in this context that drivers are competent to determine when exceptions must be made).

Rules of thumb may be relied upon more or less heavily. One might, when in doubt, always reason directly in terms of background reasons, or one might simply follow the rule unless confronted forcefully by counterreasons. Which use is preferable will depend on the likely moral stakes on both sides. The crucial feature of rules of thumb is the fact that they make no difference to serious moral calculations, no difference beyond the reasons for and against following their counsel. Genuine moral rules, by contrast, do have independent effect (I leave open for now whether they do so by adding weight to the reasons behind them or by excluding those opposed).

Hence, while rules of thumb may provide or suggest materials for moral reasoning, the reasoning itself, if commencing from such materials, will consist in deciding whether and how they are relevant to the decision to be made. This reasoning will proceed by considering analogies and disanalogies to paradigm cases in which the factors in question are morally determinative. If the case at hand is more like those cases than like cases in which these factors are overridden by others, then the case at hand must be decided like the former. Such reasoning will be described in Chapter 4. It is not itself a matter of applying rules. Once such reasoning commences, morally relevant factors themselves can be recognized by thinking in terms of the cases or situations in which they are relevant instead of thinking in terms of rules. Rules of thumb are therefore entirely dispensable in moral calculations in favor of such direct reasoning by analogy and disanalogy.

Rules contrasting most sharply with rules of thumb are what I shall call "strong rules." These state sufficient conditions for doing or refraining from doing something. They are literal interpretations of rules as normally stated, that is, universal prescriptions. If usable, they will state a limited number of relatively simple conditions, linking nonmoral properties with specific injunctions for action. Rules in themselves determine proper conduct only if their moral concepts have sufficient conditions in nonmoral properties and if agents can readily recognize whether situations instantiate these properties. Strong rules determine proper action in advance of encountering particular cases.[8] They severely limit judgmental authority or the need for complex judgment, since their application is a matter of understanding the language in which they are stated and perceiving situations in ordinary nonmoral ways. Having a mandatory retirement rule, for example, removes the responsibility and the need for employers and employees to engage in complex reasoning, in weighing all the factors that might be relevant positively or negatively to the decision on whether to retire.[9] Requiring that presidents be native born eliminates the need to weigh possibly opposing loyalties of candidates from other countries. Prohibiting alcoholic beverages in a public gathering allows us to ignore pleas of those who claim to drink responsibly with no ill effects. (Numerous rules of this type show that we are not dealing with a straw issue in considering them.)

When a strong rule is to be applied, one need not decide which action will have the morally best consequences. Such rules, those other than the utilitarian principle itself, are not concerned with optimizing outcomes: They are not outcome oriented at all.[10] They have a grip on the mind independent of calculations of benefits that their applications might produce, even if their justifications must appeal to those benefits.[11] When we apply a strong rule, we do not look through the rule to the justification for taking those factors it mentions to be morally relevant. We do not weigh those factors directly against others with which they might compete in the context at hand, as we would do if we were using a mere rule of thumb.[12]

Those who emphasize that between the recognition of a rule and the choice of a morally proper act (or judgment of an act already performed) comes a complex judgment about the proper application of the rule probably have in mind rules of thumb. When using a rule of thumb, we must first decide whether the factor it mentions as often morally relevant is indeed relevant in the present context. We must then weigh this factor directly against others that might oppose it, for example being honest against gratuitously insulting someone. But when, by contrast, we apply a strong rule, we simply do what it says to do. If we treat a prescription as a strong rule, we will be literalists – we will be guided by its wording or the plain meanings of its terms. Such mechanical application may seem misguided or stupid in particular cases, but part of the point of such rules, in telling us what to do, is to curtail our authority to decide otherwise.

Nevertheless, in applying even strong rules, we may have to deal with vagueness at the boundaries of application for its terms. As H. L. A. Hart points out, there will be borderline areas in regard to any rule where it is not obvious whether cases fall within the extensions of its terms.[13] This "penumbra," as Hart calls it, does not negate the status of the rule as strong. The first real criterion distinguishing strong rules from rules of thumb is whether factors that oppose those stated in the rules' conditions of application are to be weighed directly against them (or those reasons that justify them), or whether the factors mentioned in the rules are always to be given priority when the rules clearly apply. In addition, strong rules must build in all exceptions in advance of encountering cases. At least all unanticipated apparent exceptions must be explained away as falling within the borderline areas and hence as not real exceptions. There can be no cases falling clearly within the meanings of the terms of a strong rule to which the rule is not applied. Exceptions to rules of thumb, by contrast, are typically open-ended.

In order to be directly applied, strong rules, I have suggested, must be stated in nonmoral terms. If instead rules are stated in purely normative terms, for example "Don't murder" instead of "Don't kill" (where murder is defined as wrongful killing), then the reasoning involved in applying them will consist mainly in determining whether the normative terms are applied appropriately – for example, whether a particular act of killing is murder, that is, wrong. Once more, reasoning by analogy and disanalogy will replace deduction from rules. We will need to decide whether the present case is more like clear cases of murder or more like clear cases of justified homicide. Genuine rules must therefore be distinguished also from what we may call "pseudorules." Genuine rules link nonmoral to moral properties; pseudorules refer only to moral properties.

Rules of thumb and even pseudorules can be useful as reminders that save cognitive resources. But since their statements typically invite confusion, it is important that they not be confused with genuine rules when it comes to weighing opposing reasons in moral deliberation. Since, as noted, their proper application depends on reasoning by analogy and disanalogy, it is important to dispense with them in favor of such analogical reasoning when real moral issues arise. If, to decide whether a rule is applicable, we must decide whether the case in question is more like cases to which it clearly applies than like clear exceptions, we should rather think directly in terms of the analogies and disanalogies between these cases. Thinking directly in terms of paradigm cases instead of dispensable rules makes it clear that analogies and disanalogies are what is crucial, that we must determine the moral distance between the present case and some paradigm in deciding what to do.

When rules of thumb are confused with genuine rules, the former may be treated as the latter, and faulty reasoning results. Moral rules of thumb are often stated in the same language as genuine rules: "Be honest" instead of "Often be honest" (whose connotation might well be taken as "Don't be honest now"). By being so stated, by specifying only certain conditions as relevant to moral decision while leaving others that might determine exceptions unspecified, such rules can encourage us to ignore those other conditions that might otherwise be seen as highly relevant. When it comes to strong rules, the constraint that factors not mentioned *must* be ignored can be turned into a reason in favor of adopting them; but from the point of view of full moral consciousness, it certainly appears to be a reason against doing so.

If one thinks of rules of thumb as universal and not as mere labor-saving reminders, one might be tempted to dismiss them when one encounters or thinks of counterexamples. In doing so, one might be tempted to dismiss the relevance of the factors mentioned in the rule to some case under consideration; but analogical reasoning from paradigm cases in which those factors are determinative might show that they are indeed also determinative for the case at hand. Thus, treating rules of thumb as if they were genuine rules can result in too casual an attitude toward both. I have known lawyers with such an attitude toward rules of law. The recognition of numerous exceptions to many rules leads us to treat too lightly the factors they legitimately emphasize. The remedy is to distinguish clearly between rules of thumb and genuine rules, and the best way to do that in practice is to think directly in terms of cases or relevant moral considerations instead of rules when these are really rules of thumb. The same is true of pseudorules, which can mask the real moral questions and make us too confident of our judgments.

Many of the rules that we ordinarily think of as normative are dispensable in moral reasoning in favor of their background cases and the reasons they instantiate. Examples are "Tell the truth," "Keep your appointments," and "Drive on the right side of the road." Calling these rules of thumb is not intended to downplay the importance of the factors they mention. The examples just mentioned range from the trivial to the all-important. Telling the truth, for instance, can be of the utmost moral importance when a person has a right to certain information pertinent to some vital decision, and driving on the wrong side of the road can be a matter of grave danger. But none of these norms rule out all other considerations when guiding behavior. They guide only in the absence of counterreasons that can defeat them, and not all such exceptions can be specified in advance. The crucial question for distinguishing types of rules is whether reasons against following them are weighed directly in the usual way against their justifying reasons.

In those situations in which reasoning might be required, in which we must decide whether or not to apply or follow rules of thumb, we must look through them to their rationales and weigh these against the counterreasons in context.[14] Such looking through and weighing in effect dispenses with the rules themselves in the reasoning process. It collapses the distinction between a rule and a morally relevant factor. In some contexts, as mentioned, being honest can be a crucial moral factor. But in others, we are dishonest for the most trivial reasons – for mere courtesy or simply because we do not feel like mentioning our ill health to mere acquaintances. In the case of a rule like keeping appointments, it is often only mere convenience that is barred from generating exceptions. Since any morally relevant factor will override mere convenience, the rule often does no more than indicate minimal moral relevance.

Other rules of this type may still appear to be more than moral rules of thumb, especially those conventions that solve coordination problems. Driving on the right is one such convention that coordinates people's driving patterns in a way crucial to safety. When in countries having a convention of driving on the right, we normally do not even consider not doing so. It certainly may seem counterintuitive to call this a rule of thumb, especially if we think that there is a suggestion in that term that it is permissible to break such rules for trivial reasons. I have explicitly denied such a suggestion, keeping the term to suggest dispensability and open-ended exceptions instead. It is important to emphasize that the

18

category here is determined by the role of the rule in moral reasoning, when reasons exist on the side of both following and breaking the rule. A moral rule of thumb implies that the weight of moral factors normally lies on the side of compliance. These factors may constitute strong reasons, as in this case, but the crucial fact again is that counterreasons are weighed directly against them.

In the case of a coordination rule, agents will have reasons for favoring the solution to the coordination problem that is made salient by the rule and normally no reasons against doing so.[15] Because they will normally be motivated by the rule's justifying reasons to follow it, they need not accord the rule independent weight. Such rules typically single out an optimal pattern of behavior and do not call upon agents to forgo an optimum and settle for second best.[16] I shall argue later that genuine moral rules, by contrast, are generally second-best strategies, and that their justification lies in a combination of coordination and collective action (prisoners' dilemma–type) problems. Here, in just those situations in which we might have to reason about the moral permissibility of not driving on the right, for example, we weigh factors that might not have been specifiable in advance against the normal reasons for doing so.[17] The latter might be completely defeated in context, in which case there will be nothing about which we need feel guilty or for which we need to make amends. The only thing that thinking in terms of a rule here adds to thinking in terms of a factor that determines a paradigm case is the nonnormative fact that the paradigm case is also very much the usual case. In regard to moral reasoning, this fact is insignificant, especially since such reasoning is required precisely in the unusual case.

One might dispute whether the ordinary case of moral reasoning is a conflictual one, as I just claimed. Aren't I distorting ordinary moral reasoning by focusing on the hard case, the case where opposing values or interests must be weighed in the balance? Isn't ordinary moral reasoning simpler, plausibly viewed as the application of a single rule to a case that clearly falls within its scope? And doesn't everyone admit that at least broader rules or general principles allow open-ended exceptions while still retaining their status as rules?

In reply to the first two questions, the context in which reasoning really is required is indeed that in which values conflict and priorities must be established. This is the interesting context for choice and the one in which I am interested here. If one insists that the application of a single rule to an uncontroversial context is a form, indeed the basic form, of moral reasoning, we can still speak indifferently in such a context of a single governing rule or a single determining moral factor; and previously I gave reasons why the latter is to be preferred. What determines the status of such a rule is its role in controversial cases where values conflict, whether the factors it mentions are granted priority or special weight. As to the third question, a rule, whether broad or narrow, that admits of opposing factors being weighed directly so as to generate open-ended exceptions simply specifies some relevant considerations, although, as I have noted, these may be very important considerations in certain contexts.

There is another distinction to be drawn between rules of thumb as characterized earlier and rules that specify conditions that always count for or against a particular type of action, although they may not always be decisive. Such conditions would then generate a third type of rule (called a "prima facie rule") between rules of thumb and strong rules. The difference is that here the factors mentioned are always relevant and continue to have weight even when overridden in context, leaving a moral remainder that rationalizes feelings of guilt and may require making amends, or at least avoiding similar circumstances in the future.

I do not take this distinction to be very important. In fact, it is merely theoretical, since the same considerations that defeat the widespread use of strong rules defeat the very existence of prima facie rules. Properties that we often take to be morally relevant are not always relevant in the same way or even in the same direction (for or against performing actions that instantiate these properties). But this will have to be argued, and many philosophers have thought prima facie rules to be the best candidates for moral rules having widespread use. The only use for such rules, however, would be to identify morally relevant properties, a use I have attributed to rules of thumb. That prima facie rules are supposed to pick out properties that are always relevant in the same way, that are never nullified or reversed, and that leave a moral remainder when overridden is not relevant to reasoning about what to do once these properties have been identified. It is the particular factors in question that leave a moral residue when they are overridden and not simply nullified. Prima facie rules, like rules of thumb, are replaceable by reasoning directly in terms of these morally relevant factors and analogies, the difference lying only in the factors always counting (allegedly) in the same direction (without being always decisive).

So far, the only rules we have identified as (possibly) indispensable for moral reasoning are those that state sufficient conditions, admitting of no exceptions not explicitly built in. The rules of that sort I have so far cited as examples – "No dogs allowed" and various institutional requirements – may not seem very significant morally. Later I will examine a strong, or nearly strong, rule that underlies the legal institution and hence is very significant morally. I will also describe genuine rules that are not strong, that have independent but not absolute or nearly absolute weight.

Certain moral rules with no exceptions, for example a ban on incest, may have this status because no strong interests normally oppose them.[18] Rules that are relevant to moral reasoning, however, establish priorities among (possibly) conflicting values. They often oppose or constrain what we ourselves want to do or values we want to pursue. If the interests they represent are instead unopposed in certain contexts, then moral reasoning is not required in those contexts. The questions to be addressed later in regard to strong rules, then, are, first, whether we can establish the fixed priorities among conflicting values they would require in order to be generally applicable and, second, whether they can function as second-best strategies. The second question will take us to weaker genuine rules.

I have argued that the sorts of rules we have so far distinguished from strong rules are not needed for moral reasoning, although they are often thought to be so. We may think of rules like that of keeping promises as required for moral reasoning because we think only of the paradigm cases to which they apply (ironically, the very cases for which reasoning is not required). Or we may think of acceptable rules as universal in this strong sense because we are thinking of pseudorules, those that specify conditions in moral or morally loaded terms. Murder may be always wrong, but that is only because justified killings are not considered murders. We cannot state a usable strong rule against killing other persons, for such a rule would have to settle such issues as preemptive self-defense, killing to prevent deaths of friends or strangers, killing a fleeing murderer, killing to prevent serious physical injury to oneself or one's family members, killing to prevent rape, killing in defense of home or property, capital punishment, killing civilians in wartime, and so on indefinitely. One might wish to prohibit all killings of nonthreatening, innocent persons,[19] but this would render virtually all modern warfare, including that against Hitler's Germany, impermissible and would leave various sorts of threats to oneself and others unresolved.

Rules such as "Respect other rational beings" or "Never treat others as mere means" are similarly nondeterminative as stated, since the question for moral reasoning here is always what constitutes respect or lack of respect, or what constitutes treating another as a means (e.g., in economic or sexual relations). When we buy a newspaper from the seller on the street, we use that person as a means, but there is nothing objectionable in the transaction. Consent seems to be the key here, but then sometimes we must treat people in ways to which they do not consent. Is the Kantian demand to universalize the maxims of our actions itself a usable rule? If we interpret it as a second-order rule requiring us to act according to acceptable (first-order) rules, requiring us to view our present conditions as morally sufficient conditions for our actions, then the demand is simply to act always according to strong rules. These, we have said, require fixed priorities among values and the ability to predict all the possible defeating conditions that, when added to present conditions, might require us to act differently (the plausibility of these requirements will be further assessed later).

If we attempt to avoid this problem by building into our universalizations a stipulation requiring the absence of further defeating conditions, then we get not determinative rules but a weaker constraint. The demand to universalize then reduces to the requirement not to act differently in morally significant situations without some morally relevant difference between them, a charitable partial interpretation of Kant's requirement that I have called the "Kantian constraint." This is the very requirement that guides analogical reasoning, and it is not the same as a requirement to act according to strictly universal rules, although these are sometimes confused.[20] The latter requires present conditions to be sufficient for moral justification in all other contexts; the former does not.

III. ORDINARY MORAL CONSCIOUSNESS

In this section we will see why ordinary moral consciousness cannot be cast in the form of genuine rules. I want first to take a closer look at strong rules. Despite the fact that it is easy to show that such rules do not reflect ordinary, full moral consciousness, that they do not capture our unfettered, reflective, intuitive judgments of rightness and wrongness, there are several reasons for beginning with this demonstration. First, as noted earlier, the literal, and therefore initially most intuitive, reading of rules as universal prescriptions interprets them as strong rules. If we are not to look through rules at all to their justifying conditions, then it seems we must accept them as simply telling us what to do. This is still perhaps the most common understanding of rules outside philosophy and, as we shall see immediately, still very much alive within recent philosophical writing. Common talk of rules as binding, as constraints or precommitments that tie down the future so as to render actions coordinated or predictable over time, also suggests this literal reading of them as strong.[21] Other weaker readings derive primarily from the realization that rules seemingly can conflict and that genuine conflicts among absolute rules generate contradictions. But, as indicated previously, the defender of strong rules can argue that exceptions must be built in, ordering the rules so as to resolve apparent conflicts.[22] The real question is whether it is possible to so order rules as to preserve their strength.

Recently, Scott Shapiro has argued that rules must be conceived as constraints and not as devices for shifting the balance of reasons for or against actions. If a rule is a constraint leaving us no choice but to follow it,[23] then, as noted, it is a strong rule. So Shapiro is arguing, in effect, that rules must be conceived as strong. He has three arguments that I can discern. First, he provides examples in which he claims that we cannot conceive of rules as shifting the balance of reasons. One of these involves an alcoholic who knows that there is already sufficient reason for him not to drink but who strengthens his resolve by adopting a strict rule against doing so. Another involves following a rule simply because it is a rule, for example a religious rule to eat only kosher foods. In the first case, Shapiro claims that the balance of reasons already favors following the rule on each occasion, and so it cannot be used to shift that balance. In the second case, it is not a matter of reasons at all, but of the acceptance of a constraint.

This argument and the analysis of examples on which it is based are, however, unconvincing. If, in the first case, taking each single drink is independent of choosing to take the others, the negative effect of each will be negligible, or at least outweighed by its benefits. If a rule is warranted to avoid the cumulatively bad outcome, it will be because it does shift the balance of reasons on each occasion (more on this case in the next chapter). If, instead, each drink causes the alcoholic to take others, as may be the case in addiction, then adopting a rule will be simply keeping in mind this connection as a way of overcoming weakness of will. Adopting the rule does not preclude choice based on reasons but brings those reasons to the fore and also perhaps adds additional force or weight to them. One need not shift the balance of reasons in order to add to them and thereby strengthen one's resolve by making that balance more clear. In the second case, one may indeed have reasons for adopting and following a rule of one's religion, whatever reasons one has for being religious or identifying with a tradition. The rule adds to these reasons when they are opposed on a particular occasion by some tempting nonkosher food.

My initial response to the first case, however, takes us to Shapiro's second argument. He thinks that, when the balance of ordinary reasons lies on the side of breaking a rule on a particular occasion and there is no intrinsic value to following the rule, it cannot be rational, that is, a matter of the balance of reasons, to follow it.[24] We therefore must conceive it simply as a constraint, as something that precludes further reasoning altogether. But, however plausible the first premise here seems, it is false. In rationally adopting a rule, we typically sacrifice local optima for a global improvement when opting for the optimum on each occasion has cumulatively worse results.[25] The rule then provides an independent reason for doing what it prescribes on each occasion. This reason may, but need not be, of the type that outweighs or precludes all others.

Shapiro's final argument appeals to the phenomenology of rule following. He argues that, while we may choose to adopt a rule, we do not then choose to follow it on each occasion in which it applies. We simply accept it as a constraint on further choice. But it seems to me that we do often choose to follow rules (often the rules are not themselves of our own choosing) after deliberating, giving the rules independent weight if we consider them valid in imposing obligations. Indeed, the notion of a constraint strikes me as a metaphor here, since typically nothing literally prevents us from following or not following a rule that we have freely adopted or that others have sought to impose. We follow it if we think it is rational to do so (or else we do indeed act irrationally, without reason[26]). Shapiro attempts to unpack or eliminate the metaphor by holding that the adoption of a rule creates a disposition that makes it impossible to break the rule for a reason.[27] But once more, it seems to me that, having adopted or accepted a rule, we are being irrational if we do not either (a) conceive the rule as a sufficient reason in each case of its application (strong in my, not his, sense) or (b) reserve the right to override or make exceptions when reasons for doing so outweigh the reasons behind the rule and the independent weight or effect of the rule itself.

Thus, while I do not agree with Shapiro's interpretation of strong rules or with his claim that we must conceive of rules as strong, I cite his arguments in part as evidence of the continuing pull to view rules that way. But the most important reason for beginning with the concept of strong rules is that the only possibility for a thoroughly rule-based morality would be a morality of strong rules. While, as I shall now argue, it is a contingent fact about how we value in different contexts that prevents strong rules from capturing the set of our intuitive moral judgments, it is conceptually impossible for weaker genuine rules to do so. If rules are genuine, that is, if they are not rules of thumb dispensable in favor of thinking directly in terms of reasons and the cases that instantiate them, then the rules must have independent effect on moral deliberation or independent weight. But then, if the rules are not sufficient to determine what ought to be done, that is, strong, this effect must be added to the weights of ordinary reasons: it is not ordinary itself. Hence only strong genuine rules could capture the set of ordinary moral judgments.

Let us then see why they nevertheless do not. Since, if usable, they state only a limited number of relatively simple conditions as relevant to decisions, they omit other factors that may turn out to be intuitively relevant. Decisions regarding actions must be made in very different contexts involving complex and multiple aims and interests. Such contexts may be too rich and variable to allow the prediction of all factors that might weigh against those conditions stated in genuine rules. In simplest terms, such rules fail to capture our full perceptions of moral demands because of the diversity of factors that may be relevant, the diverse values that attach to these factors, and the ways they interact in concrete contexts.

Others have pointed to these considerations before. I will briefly review and combine them to set the stage for later sections. First, morally relevant factors can interact in various contexts in ways that change their priorities and even their positive or negative values. Jonathan Dancy makes this point by noting that giving pleasure may make one act right and only worsen another.[28] If indeed factors that weigh in one direction in one context may be not simply overridden in others, but irrelevant, completely nullified, or even weigh in the opposite direction in others, this nullification or reversal defeats not only strong rules that build such factors in as sufficient conditions, but prima facie rules as well. Remember that prima facie rules require that factors always count morally in the same way wherever they occur, although they need not always be decisive.

It might seem that there is no way to tell whether a property that is positively relevant in one context is reversed instead of being simply overridden in another.[29] But examples seem to show that reversal does

25

indeed occur, along with an absence of regret that one would expect were a prima facie rule simply overridden. The pleasure of a sadist is not simply overridden by the harm to the victim; it makes the act worse than it would have been had no pleasure been derived from it. Certainly there is nothing to regret if the act, and hence the pleasure derived from it, is forgone. One might argue that the pleasure derived from sadistic acts reflects negatively on the actors as persons who enjoy inflicting harm on others, but it does not make their acts worse.[30] But it seems intuitive that a sadistic act of murder is itself worse than one committed with regret. We condemn the sadistic murderer more than his hesitant and regretful counterpart not simply because the former is more likely to repeat his act, but also because of the nature of the act, which must therefore be worse in itself.

Giving pleasure does seem to be a property that can take on all three moral values: positive, negative, and neutral. Contra some interpretations of Kant, taking pleasure in helping others does appear to make such acts better, while taking pleasure in their pain makes acts that cause it worse. And much harmless pleasure is simply morally neutral. Being true is a property of statements that seems similar in this respect. It needs no arguing that the truth of a statement is often a positive moral reason for uttering it. But the truth of some statement that reveals an embarrassing private affair to those with no right to know of it can make the statement more blameworthy in being more damaging. Likewise for the truth of a statement to a malevolent pursuer about the whereabouts of his victim. And whether one answers truly to a casual inquiry about one's health may be morally indifferent.

Of course, showing that there is no prima facie rule regarding pleasure does not show that there are no prima facie rules at all. It may be the broad scope of such properties that is at fault here. How about the property of killing a happy, healthy child – would this always count negatively toward the morality of an act instantiating it?[31] Even here I am not convinced. Suppose that the child were Hitler and we could predict the future; or, more realistically, suppose that the child were about to open fire with an automatic weapon in a school yard, and his happiness derived from contemplating the mayem to ensue. Suppose that the only way to stop him was to shoot first. One could claim that shooting the child would still cry out for moral justification or excuse and take this requirement as evidence for a prima facie rule being in effect. But I believe that the need for justification derives from the fact that killing a child is almost always wrong, not because it is always almost wrong. We might regret killing the child, but whether regret would be rational in the case of an incorrigible menace is another question.

We cannot narrow the property further by building all such conceivable exceptions into the statement of our alleged prima facie rule;[32] and even if we could, the rule would become so narrow or specific as to be of no use in moral reasoning. Furthermore, the property would not be the sort that we ordinarily take to be morally relevant, not the sort of property to which we appeal in justifying moral judgments or explaining the moral status of actions. We take certain actions to be seriously wrong because they involve killing, not because they involve killing except when . . . (where the ellipses represent an enormously long list). Remember that prima facie rules are intended to pick out morally relevant properties, a task that could not be accomplished by rules gerrymandered in the way contemplated here. Remember finally that such rules, like rules of thumb, are entirely dispensable in favor of direct consideration of morally relevant factors. Indeed, they drop out when these factors must be weighed against one another in moral reasoning.

Nullification or reversal of morally relevant factors is one problem for strong rules as well. Another problem for such rules is the number and complexity of factors that seem relevant to practical decisions. Factors that could affect how one should treat another person include not only the probable consequences to the person and to oneself of one's possible actions, but also one's past actions toward the person, past actions of the person herself, one's present relation(s) to her, her probable reactions, her needs, wants, interests, expectations, how one has treated other persons in similar contexts, how this context differs from those others, how others treat other persons in similar contexts, how others will perceive one's actions and how they perceive the person affected, the truthfulness or sincerity of one's actions. . . . Various such factors may interact in complex ways. Consider one relatively simple and trivial example. Should I, as a Little League baseball manager, pitch my son in the next playoff game? In deciding, I must consider how much pressure this will place on my son, the short-term and long-term effects of this pressure, how much pressure pitching would place on other players on the team, how much practice he and they need for later games, whether pitching my son constitutes favoritism or would be perceived as such by other players or parents, how such perceptions would affect my son and my ability to manage the team, whether the team is more likely to win with him pitching, what the effects of winning or losing will be, and so on. Is it likely that all these weighings even in this trivial and minimally morally significant decision will be guided by strong rules?

Later we will consider the argument that it is the very complexity of ordinary, full moral reasoning that leads us to adopt rules in order to simplify the reasoning process. I will offer several responses to this argument. Here it suffices to point out that no simplifying strong rules seem acceptable here. If I were to adopt the rule of always allowing the pitcher with the best chance to win the game (in my estimation) to pitch, for example, this would not only make for bad longer-term baseball strategy (I might need my best pitcher in a later game), it could also be seriously insensitive to more important needs of the boys on the team. If I came to recognize some such previously unspecified needs in the course of making this decision, I would immediately abandon my rule in favor of satisfying them, revealing the rule to be no more than a rule of thumb, the factor it names to be only one among others potentially more important and to be weighed directly against it.

If strong rules state sufficient conditions, if they tell us what to do (without further moral reasoning), then they must be exceptionless or have all exceptions built into them in advance of their application. The latter two requirements are equivalent. For each rule with an exception built in, there is another prescriptively identical rule in slightly different language with no exception. "Don't speed except in an emergency" is the same as "If there is no emergency, don't speed" or "Don't non-emergency-speed" (new term). (None of these, incidentally, is a strong rule, since "emergency" here means "overriding necessity opposed to the rule" or, more simply, "morally justified exception." Hence moral reasoning is required to determine whether a situation constitutes an emergency.) If all exceptions are to be built into the statements of strong rules, then they must be ordered lexically in relation to each other, or we must have a list of all contexts in which each overrides the others. The latter is a practical impossibility, so a lexical ordering is required.

Rules that link objective properties with prescriptions express the values of those properties; hence, if there is to be a fixed order to a set of rules, there must be a single ordering of the values they express in all situations in which they might apply. Such an ordering, if of diverse values, comprises either a highest value that always takes priority over all others, then a second highest, and so on, or it requires a common currency into which all values can be translated in order to be compared quantitatively. But neither possibility is plausible.

Values are diverse. If this is not immediately apparent, one way to see it indirectly is by thinking of the appropriateness of regret in some contexts in which we must choose between conflicting values. Regret is a misleading sign of prima facie rules, since it is not always called for when apparent values conflict. It is out of place where the dominant values nullify or reverse the others. But that it is sometimes appropriate even when morally required actions are performed shows the irreducibility of diverse values. If there were only one value, then we could not rationally regret acting so as to realize the most of it. Our only regret could be not having realized more of it. But sometimes we do regret having to forgo one good in order to pursue another, and what we regret is not simply our not getting more of the same.[33]

We can add to this a second argument, deriving from aesthetics but with some application in the moral sphere as well. Its first premise is that some people have better taste than others. This implies that they have different values: They value different things, and some of them are more intelligent or worthy of respect in what they value. If there were (ultimately) only one value, then better taste would be only that which could produce or appreciate more of it. But that is not the way we distinguish higher from lower tastes. Those with better taste are capable of appreciating and pursuing different kinds of value. These pursuits lead not simply to more or less pleasure, but also to qualitatively different kinds of experiences.

Among diverse values, there is none that always takes priority.[34] Hobbes's favorite candidate, avoiding death, is often more important than avoiding pain, but not always (e.g., in the context of a prolonged terminal illness). Most people would not relinquish all their autonomy (the candidate of the Kantians) for a life of constant pleasure, but most relinquish some autonomy in order to have children, enter contracts, and so on. That there is no highest value suffices to refute the idea of a fixed order among diverse goods, and we find the same sorts of variable trade-offs involving all kinds of goods. Welfare can be weighed in different ways against freedom, equality, desert, or justice; justice sometimes requires rewarding effort or contribution, sometimes satisfying needs. When we try to adjudicate conflicts among values by means of higher-order rules, for example utilitarian or libertarian ones, we find that these conflict and that each takes priority in some contexts but not in others.

Nor is there a common currency into which values cash so as to be compared. Welfare, as noted, must be traded off against other goods, sometimes taking priority, sometimes not. The most plausible attempt to find a common currency cashes these other values in terms of preferences for them, making preference satisfaction the common coin. But on the level of the individual agent, a rule to maximize preference satisfaction is not genuine or action guiding. There is no psychological reality to which it can be applied. We do not first note what we prefer and then choose to maximize or not to maximize what we have discovered as our preferences. Instead, what we call our preferences simply reify our choices among diverse and incompatible goods, choices in some contexts of x over y and in others of y over x. Talk about maximizing our choices, if it means anything at all, refers to something quite different – ensuring our freedom to choose or leaving our options open. Talk of maximizing or optimizing also contrasts with what is now called "satisficing." We sometimes satisfice instead of optimizing. But this is not a matter of choosing what is preferred less over what is preferred more, but of stopping the search for a best alternative at a certain point.[35] The gains from continuously looking for better possibilities for action or for better results must be weighed against the costs of doing so. But this does not imply that there is some common coin, preference satisfaction, to which the values of all potential results can be reduced.

Knowledge, for example, is of value. In my view (for which I will not argue here), it is of value because we value it and because it facilitates attainment of other things we value. But values, even if all ultimately subjectively grounded, need not reduce to one another or to some common kind of satisfaction in the subject. Pleasure, the earlier candidate for the universal value solvent, is at least sometimes psychologically real. It is also a matter of fact whether others or the world satisfy or frustrate our preferences among value alternatives. But we ourselves do not adopt and then follow a rule to find out our own preferences and then maximize their overall satisfaction, reducing all values or lumping them all together in the process.

On the interpersonal level, we do try to determine the preferences of others before acting. These are normally preferences among a limited number of alternatives that it is within our power to produce. Even if we have an accurate list of all such preferences of all those affected by our actions, and even if we can add or combine them (a notoriously contentious claim), there are different and conflicting ways of resolving conflicts between greater numbers of weaker preferences and lesser numbers of stronger preferences. We make some simplifying progress by recognizing rights to be correlated with those strong preferences that represent important interests, since we do not allow rights to be overridden by additions of values less centrally at stake in particular contexts. But here our old problem reasserts itself in the lack of a lexical ordering for rights. In some situations right A, for example a right to free expression, overrides rights B and C, for example rights against being offended or placed in danger of harm, and in other situations the reverse is true. It remains doubtful that these conflicts can be satisfactorily resolved once and for all by a fixed ordering of strong rules. In addition, if perfectionist ideals have some weight in some contexts, then preferences themselves can sometimes be overridden by values such as autonomy, which may not be fully represented in preferences, or by welfare, which may not reduce to preference satisfaction.

Values, then, are neither reducible nor ordered in a way simple enough to be captured in strong rules. It is true, as defenders of rules such as H. L. A. Hart and Bernard Gert point out, that, given human nature, there are certain things that all rational persons value, among them food and shelter, and certain things that all rational people disvalue or seek to avoid, among them painful injury and death. But, although all rational people value and disvalue these things sometimes or normally, they do not do so all the time. Equally obviously, they weigh these values and disvalues against each other and against other goods in different ways in different contexts. Given human nature and the nature of society, there must be some prohibitions of violence, theft, and fraud. In less fully normative terms, social cooperation requires that individuals develop dispositions against killing, taking others' possessions, and lying. But the scope of these prohibitions and dispositions can vary widely and once again need not be captured in strong rules as long as paradigm cases are clear in each society.

What holds for universal disvalues holds for positive values as well. In fact, one universal value, autonomy, provides an additional reason against imposing strong rules, at least if the earlier arguments to the conclusion that rules fail to capture the weights in all contexts of all conceivably relevant factors are sound. Being autonomous includes having the authority to find out all relevant factors and to act on one's full perception of their relative weights. Strong rules limit or block precisely this authority, which is why we normally think of them as imposed from without. In stating limited sufficient conditions, they preclude judgment based on fresh and full perception of morally charged situations. Those who would accept strict rules either mistrust their own autonomous judgment or lack moral imagination, that is, fail to envisage possible situations in which exceptions will need to be made.

If we have two values, such that one overrides in some contexts and the other overrides in others, how can we rationally decide their ordering in a controversial case? It might seem that the alternatives are ordering by rules or relying on intuitions in each such case, as particularists hold. If so, then we can understand the desire for rules to guide our ordinary moral reasoning. Once more, however, we can instead reason in terms of analogies and disanalogies to cases in which the ordering among competing values is clear. This is precisely what we do (if we are social ethicists) when faced with a difficult social issue such as abortion or affirmative action, in which opposing values and plausible claims or rights based on them are at stake.

Reflective reasoning aimed at resolving an issue like affirmative action will consider contexts in which compensation is owed to groups, in which compensation takes priority over further applications of distributive rules, in which claims of competence are overridden in favor of equal opportunity, in which diversity trumps merit, and so on. It will then compare the call for preferential treatment for minorities to the clearer contexts and test for relevant differences. By working out these analogies and disanalogies, we can arrive at positions coherent with our settled judgments and shared values. By contrast, the appeal to rules in itself gets us nowhere on such issues. Each side can trot out its favorite rules requiring rewarding competence, compensating wrongs, and so on. Reasoning begins when these rules conflict, the rules then playing only the role of identifying relevant considerations. That analogical reasoning (to be described in detail in Chapter 4) can succeed where appeal to strong rules cannot is a final indication of the irrelevance of rules to fully autonomous moral judgment.

IV. RULES AS SECOND-BEST STRATEGIES

Particularists might end the debate over rules here. For sophisticated defenders of rules, however, it is just beginning. For them, strong rules are not intended to capture fully autonomous moral judgment. From the point of view of full moral consciousness, they are both over- and underinclusive, as well as being inflexible. They are too strict in disallowing behavior that should be permitted in the particular case and too lenient in allowing people to take advantage of loopholes or technicalities. In addition to ignoring relevant features of the parties affected, they are inflexible in prescribing what agents must do independently of what others are doing. Nevertheless, despite these defects they can represent second-best solutions intended to prevent worse outcomes in the form of serious moral errors and social disorder. The point of such rules is precisely to block full autonomy or allocate decision-making authority away from certain agents. They aim to simplify the moral universe by intentionally blocking or overriding[36] considerations that might otherwise be relevant.

Philosophers at least as far back as Mill have argued that when serious errors are likely to result from autonomous moral judgment, or when there is some reason to fear bias, weakness of will, or abuse of power, we need strong rules to limit the power of potential decision makers. Other contexts calling for rules might include those in which there is a special need for consistency or predictability in some set of decisions, or in which there is no time or resources for discovering all information that might be relevant to a fully autonomous decision. In these contexts, it is held that a rule has force precisely when it requires a decision that diverges from fully autonomous judgment, even when the justification for the rule includes mention of those factors that normally guide autonomous judgment as well.[37]

Let us look at these justifications in terms of consistency, predictability, efficiency, and avoiding error or bias more closely and critically. Consistency in moral decisions consists in treating like cases alike and relevantly different cases differently. Not treating a relevantly different case differently is being inconsistent, since it is refusing to allow a value to make a difference in this case when that value makes a difference between other like cases. Consistency, then, cannot justify the use of strong rules, since they will involve violating this requirement. Any time we count membership in a certain class as sufficient for the application of a rule, we ignore differences within that class, so that we may advantage some of its members and disadvantage others. When we give all batters in baseball only three strikes, we favor the contact hitters, which, of course, is what we want to do. But not all such effects are so obvious or justified. I have trouble convincing my university administration that giving all faculty the same percentage raise favors the highest paid (and the unproductive), just as taxing persons at the same rate would hurt the poor and taxing all at the same amount would hurt them more. Whenever strong rules prevent treating cases differently by blocking recognition of factors that differentiate among cases like those under consideration, moral consistency may be sacrificed.

If moral consistency is not increased by rules that ignore relevant factors, efficiency and predictability nevertheless do increase with the application of strong rules. In regard to efficiency, the application of rules saves time, effort, and investigative and cognitive resources because of their simplifying function. When we apply a rule, we need not search for and investigate factors outside its scope. But for just this resource-saving function, rules of thumb or even habits of judgment can serve almost as well. These can save time without barring consideration of factors that become salient without searching for them, and without requiring that the factors mentioned in the rules be given weight beyond their ordinary moral merit. In regard to predictability of decisions, this is of value for honoring legitimate expectations, for giving advance warning when sanctions may be applied to undesirable behavior, and for making available information required to coordinate actions over time.[38]

Appeal to expectations in this context, however, seems to place the cart before the horse. Expectations themselves arise in relation to standing rules and practices, and their moral weight depends almost entirely on the independent moral status of these rules and practices. It is important that those who may suffer sanctions for their behavior have a right to adequate warning, the sort of clear warning that known rules provide. But this benefit is opposed by the right to argue that a present case is relevantly different from a previous one in which sanctions were applied, a right that strong rules might disallow.[39] And the right to advance warning might be met in the absence of standing rules. Warning can be provided by clear paradigm cases and the refusal to apply sanctions by distant analogies. As for the necessity of predictability for coordination, we saw earlier that this can be achieved by rules that are mere rules of thumb from a moral point of view, that the extra effect of strong rules is not required when agents are already motivated to follow the rules.

Thus, the goal of predictability alone does not seem to justify the use of strong rules when other factors are taken into account that may have to be weighed against it and when other methods of satisfying this goal are considered. Strong rules buy predictability at the expense of morally sensitive adjustments to situations. The only contexts in which we prefer predictability alone to adjustments to morally relevant differences are those in which the moral stakes are trivial. When they are not trivial, they will most likely be salient, and adjusting to them should normally cause few surprises. If ordinary moral sensibilities are shared, then ordinary moral judgments should be predictable also, except in cases in which controversial new factors arise, and then we may not want to lock decisions into the old pattern.

Beyond the need for coordination among actions of ordinary people, there may be a special need for predictability in certain contexts – legal or political, for example. If economic agents are to make those contractual commitments necessary to sophisticated economies, they require a legal framework in which officials can be predicted routinely to enforce the law. Later I shall consider the full justification for a rule to that effect applied to officials in the legal system. Here it suffices to point out that the need for predictability *alone* does not justify the extra weight given to a genuine rule. Even where the goals of predictability and stable expectations is central, it does not in itself justify preventing decision makers from weighing the effects of their decisions on the expectations of others and on future ability to predict outcomes. Even when these factors are of primary importance, they need not always override, as they must to justify in themselves the imposition of strong rules. Hence it appears that fallibility at least must be an additional factor in the justification for imposing such rules.[40]

Let us then consider the issue of fallibility more closely. An initial crucial point here is that rule makers are also fallible. In order to justify imposing strong rules on the grounds of proneness to error in autonomous judgment, those who would impose them must presume to be able to predict those factors that should guide decisions better than agents in the contexts in which the decisions will be made. Thus, there should be no rules when rule makers are especially fallible or when decision makers can be trusted in the absence of rules. Beyond this, in the absence of special reasons to suspect bias, ignorance, or some other special source of fallibility, the assumption by rule makers that they know better is indeed presumptuous, especially when the value of autonomy and the need for individuals to develop moral sensitivity are weighed on the other side. To accept rules as second-best strategies is to mistrust one's own autonomous moral judgment. (And yet one must judge in advance of encountering actual moral problems when one decides to accept a rule.) Since few people do mistrust their own judgment, most who reflect on the matter think of these rules as more suitable for others than for themselves. (I am not endorsing this asymmetry, but I think it typically reflects too low an opinion of others and not too high an estimation of one's own powers of judgment.)

Indeed, it seems that every reason offered so far for adopting rules generates a reason against doing so. In simplifying the moral universe, strong rules oversimplify; they leave out factors that should normally be overriding in certain situations. In reducing authority to act on full moral perception, they eventually desensitize us to morally relevant considerations; and they provide a facile excuse for not accepting responsibility. Finally, they buy predictability at the expense of adaptability to new claims of injustice.

We can attempt to mitigate oversimplification by building more exceptions and conditions of application into our rules, but this move defeats a main purpose for adopting them, namely, simplicity in application and in the reasoning that results, while still not capturing autonomous moral judgment in context. We cannot fully capture such judgment in rules as long as we cannot predict all warranted exceptions, and we have given strong reasons – the number of potentially morally relevant factors and the ways they interact to override, nullify, or reverse one another in context – for thinking that we cannot make these predictions accurately. If our purpose is to do what is best or what is morally required according to ideally sensitive judgment, then the adoption of rules in normal contexts represents a suspect and defeasible strategy.

If rules do not determine what is right, but reflect only a strategy aimed at approximating the right as defined by other factors, then, as in R. M. Hare's account, they break down in contexts of serious moral reflection.[41] When we must reason about something morally important, then it is important that our reasoning be correct and lead to the right answer. If rules do not determine that answer, then we ought not to use them in the reasoning. If they do not determine what is right, then it must be right to break them when one can do better, and knows one can do better, than by following them. What is right is what one morally ought to do in full knowledge of the situation and taking all relevant factors into account. Hence one knowingly does wrong when one follows a rule that prevents taking factors into account that one knows to be morally crucial in the context in question. Recognition of one's fallibility lacks force when one takes oneself to know all that is relevant in a given situation. (This point lacks relevance, however, in contexts in which one *cannot* know all that is relevant, contexts to be described later.)

Both Frederick Schauer and R. M. Hare imply that the difficulty of unfettered moral judgment is so great as to require rules most of the time, even though their use is clearly second best. In Schauer's case, this thought rests on the assumption that we "incessantly" encounter complex moral problems with which we must somehow deal;[42] and in Hare's case, it rests on the premise that full moral judgment requires full calculation of utilities and disutilities of all consequences of our actions. Earlier, I offered an example of an everyday decision (as a baseball manager) that illustrated the number and complexity of factors affecting the interests of others and determining how one ought to act toward them. If I took the number and complexity of factors to be a reason why rules do not capture our reasoning process in such contexts, can I now consistently deny that this same reason justifies the frequent adoption of rules as a simplifying second-best strategy?

The denial of such widespread use of rules is not inconsistent with the example and others like it. I believe there are two senses of "morally relevant factor," indeed two concepts of morality, each of which suggests a different answer to this argument for the common and widespread use of rules. In the broad sense, morally relevant factors include all those that affect the interests of others, all those that are relevant to how one should act in contexts affecting any of their interests. In this sense, all the factors mentioned in the baseball example are morally relevant. But, as was pointed out there, not only are all these factors not themselves capturable in a set of lexically ordered rules, it seems equally difficult to see how many of them could be eliminated from consideration in favor of acceptable simplifying rules. Which interests would these rules represent?

One possible answer takes us to the second, narrower view of morality. According to it, we act in morally permissible ways as long as we do not violate anyone's moral rights. From a narrowly moral point of view, we need not fine-tune our actions in Henry Jamesian fashion to all possible interests or desires of others; we simply must not trample those central interests represented by moral rights. Here, the first thing to note, however, is that narrow moral considerations do not exhaust those factors we must consider in deciding how to act. Acting in a morally permissible way may not be acting for the best or even as one should. In the baseball example, once I make sure that I do not violate the boys' moral rights by subjecting them to extreme pressure from teammates or parents, I must still decide how to weigh all the other factors in acting. Once more, rules do not guide me here.

But the narrower view of morality does obviate the widespread need for moral rules to which the arguments of Schauer and Hare conclude.

If avoiding immorality consists only in avoiding violating people's rights (as these are determined by the weights of relevant factors in various contexts), then the premises of these arguments are false.[43] Rights are not so numerous that we are constantly bumping up against them in unexpected ways. Even though their relative weights may vary with the context, they do not give rise to incessant complex calculations that would call for the simplifying function of rules. As to Hare's utilitarianism, it is no part of common moral thinking that we are under an obligation to maximize the sum total of utility. That something would give you pleasure in itself gives me no obligation to provide it, even if nothing else I can do would provide as much total benefit. Indeed, rights exist in large part to protect certain fundamental interests of individuals (especially those connected with moral agency or autonomy)[44] against aggregations of lesser interests.

But now another problem may seem to arise: If rights are given extra weight against collective lesser interests, this might suggest a correlation of rules with rights, since I have maintained that a function of rules is to shift extra (or, in the case of strong rules, absolute) weight to the factors they mention. If this correlation were to hold, if all rights had to be backed up by moral rules, then not only Hare's utilitarianism but any rights-based moral theory would entail the (implicit) use of such rules as the norm in moral reasoning. But rights certainly do not correlate with strong rules. Once more they are not amenable to the kind of fixed ordering that strong rules require. As pointed out previously, their priorities vary with the context in ways unspecifiable in advance. For example, sometimes the right to the truth takes precedence over the right not to be harmed and sometimes not. Rights are overridden by other rights in ways we cannot always predict, and the other rights are weighed directly against them. It might be said that rights should never be violated, although they can be overridden. But a rule prohibiting violations is a pseudorule (as defined earlier), since violations are *unjustified* overridings.

Later I will introduce a final type of rule that is genuine, but not strong or absolute. This type of rule again involves the idea of extra weight given to the factors it mentions, weight beyond what is normal for those factors. Such rules will necessarily be part of second-best strategies in relation to what is morally ideal or optimal (but in these contexts unattainable). Rights, however, are not normally second best or part of a strategy for achieving the second best when the best is probably beyond reach. The weight they have against lesser interests is not abnormal; in fact, these lesser interests normally have no weight at all according to the narrower conception of morality.[45] Some rights, nevertheless, will be shown to be supported by rules of this type. But not all or most. The right to have an agreement kept or to be told the truth, as well as rights against various physical harms, do not need extra weight against other rights or interests that might oppose them. They have sufficient moral weight in themselves. Thus, there is no general correlation between rules and rights.

If rules represent strategies for avoiding errors by fallible decision makers, then the desirability of imposing them for purposes of simplification would seem to depend on the decision-making abilities of particular agents. Relevant considerations would include temporary conditions such as the time and investigative resources available to the reasoner, but also permanent conditions such as intelligence. That differences in intelligence could give rise to different sets of moral requirements may not paint an attractive picture for the democratically minded. We therefore encounter a final argument for a more general use of rules in moral reasoning, an argument put forth by Conrad Johnson in a recent book.[46] It goes as follows.

If less than normally intelligent or strong-willed people require rules where others might not, and if, nevertheless, we want to impose the same publicly recognized moral requirements on all, then perhaps all should accept the same set of rules as a show of equality and, on the part of the more intelligent and less weak-willed, of respect and solidarity with their less gifted brethren. Such acceptance acquires here a symbolic value; knowledge that the same rules apply to all expresses mutual respect and equal moral status. According to this view, persons who obey communally accepted rules even when they disagree with their applications in specific circumstances are persons who can be better trusted by others, while those who claim discretion to break rules lack proper humility and fellow feeling.[47] Shared rules bind a community together and express its integrity as a community. Here rules are not simply a strategy for approximating the right as defined otherwise. In creating these values of equality, mutual trust, and integrity, they help to define the right for all.[48] Thus, what begins as a second-best strategy is restored to the level of first best.

One advantage of this argument, then, is that it does not require or allow agents to break rules when they know they can do better on grounds independent of the rules by doing so. The additional values that underlie the adoption of the rules as applying to all individuals in a community are to justify the refusal to break them when it would be otherwise better to do so. But the problem with this argument for adopting strong rules is that the equality to which it refers is that of the lowest common moral denominator of which decision makers are capable. Likewise, the mutual trust derives from knowing in advance that all will ignore otherwise morally relevant factors. To ignore such factors is, independent of the rules, to treat one another wrongly or unjustly. So, according to this view, we are to adopt universal rules so that we can treat each other in ways considered (prior to their adoption) unjust. Finally, the sense of communal integrity derives from being locked into what are otherwise considered overly rigid patterns of behavior. Rules require repetition of actions in contexts where such repetition is normally unwarranted or injurious. Is this what we mean by integrity?

Consider more closely the equality that derives from all obeying the same rules that are required for those who are unable to act on all morally relevant factors because of stupidity or weakness of will. It follows from the demand for this equality that if, for example, alcoholism is a serious problem in my community because of all those who drink excessively and need a strong rule to control themselves, it would be wrong for me, who is not tempted to excess, to have one drink in the privacy of my home. The implication is false. Similarly, mutual trust should derive not from knowing that all are ignoring relevant factors and behaving less than optimally, but from believing that most will give those factors serious weight in similar contexts. Public criteria of right can be implicit in such shared values rather than stated in the form of strong rules.

In order to earn the trust of others, we must act consistently and with integrity. The demand for integrity is genuine for both the individual and the community. For the individual, the unity of the self derives in part from coherent patterns of action in pursuit of articulable values. Actions that are inconsistent or out of character are self-defeating in relation to the values that define that character. The actions of a person with integrity, who can be trusted by others, flow from other actions that explain and project them, constituting an intelligible narrative structure. We loosely describe a person whose behavior defines a strong character as a person of principle. But we should not take this to imply that such a person acts according to strong rules. Action according to such rules is essentially repetitive. Narrative coherence, by contrast, requires only behavior that fulfills a set of context-sensitive nested aims and values. It does not require that certain expressed values override others in all conceivable contexts. Persons with integrity stand by commitments and, above all, do not yield to temptation at the expense of perceived duty. They have the will to act on reasons perceived as strongest in context. But they need not act as fanatics, that is, single-mindedly pursue certain values in all contexts at the expense of all others, as strong rules require.

Communities too are identified by shared principles and constituted in part by shared values. But once again, "principles" here may refer to shared reactions to certain sorts of cases, reflecting similar weighings of values in those situations, as well as adherence to the Kantian constraint not to judge cases differently without finding a morally relevant difference between them.[49] Americans largely agree, for example, that we should not silence speech in order to prevent mere offense, and we grant wide latitude even for potential harm from forms of expression; but we probably do not agree on all possible exceptions in advance. Hence the First Amendment does not represent a strong moral rule. We are willing to forgo complete predictability in order to allow that some forms of obscenity or other causes of offense will not be permitted. We might tell those who would avoid offense by silencing or censoring every conceivable cause of it that there must be a strict rule against yielding to such temptation; but we do not accept such a rule ourselves or expect our public representatives to do so.

When faced with a democratic argument to apply the same exceptionless rules to all that some seem to require because of proneness to error, we should remember that strong rules are typically antidemocratic in their real applications, disabling from fully autonomous judgment only those who adhere to them. The dismissal of universally applicable, strong moral rules as the norm does not imply that less intelligent or strong-willed people face a different set of moral requirements. Differences in morally significant contexts, not differences in agents, defeat rules as determinative of right. The same factors may be morally relevant for all, regardless of intelligence or will, but not all will be capable of the same level of compliance with full moral demands. Probably none of us is capable of right action all the time, and we differ in our ability to act rightly in various contexts, in part because of differences in moral perceptual and reasoning abilities. Strategies for approximating to right actions over time, including in some cases simplifying rules as second-best strategies, may therefore vary from person to person (although in the next section I will identify contexts in which all must obey them). It is not plausible to suggest that the morally more adept or sophisticated should harm people knowingly because others cannot do better (and may sometimes have to do less than best in order to avoid doing worse more often).

v. THE JUSTIFICATION OF RULES: STRONG AND WEAK

The case for widespread use of strong moral rules in ordinary moral reasoning by ordinary persons in the private sector looks bleak. Whereas the tradition has conceived of moral reasoning as the application of rules to cases, genuine rules are needed only when we mistrust agents to reason as they normally would and to act on the results of such reasoning. But we should not downplay the importance of such contexts, and we should understand why they occur. The lack of trust in normal moral reasoning that the imposition or acceptance of a rule signifies is not always a sign of blame or even shortcoming on the part of moral agents.

Perhaps the best place to begin looking for contexts in which rules are justified is in the public sphere, where many morally significant cases must be decided without adequate resources for investigating all conceivably morally relevant factors, and where any perception of bias, correct or incorrect, may be very damaging. An apt example briefly mentioned earlier is that of judges within the legal system. Instead of deciding cases on grounds of unfettered moral perception, we want judges to defer to the institutional constraints of law. We want them to accept a rule as morally binding that they will follow settled law in their decisions, even when they disagree with the outcomes. All the reasons mentioned earlier – a special need for predictability, the prevention of bias, and the lack of resources for full moral investigation of every case – apply here. In addition, there is the division of power with democratically elected legislatures. If judges can ignore legislative enactments and substitute their own moral perceptions as grounds for judgments, then they in effect nullify the political power of legislatures. In regard to the doctrine of legal precedent in the absence of statutory constraint, the fact that a judge must follow a prior appellate court decision even when she morally disagrees with it, this can be justified by the need for a stable social environment and the fallibility of the lower-court judge.

Nevertheless, even all these considerations together do not fully explain why judges ought to defer to the law in cases in which they clearly perceive that the moral merits lie on the other side. One alternative model would have the well-intentioned judge weigh the institutional considerations – the legislative right to influence decisions, the expectations of the litigants based on prior settled law, and so on – against independent moral considerations on the other side in each case. The institutional considerations themselves can vary in weight: for example, the case might be governed either by common law or by statute, or the judge can be in a trial or an appellate court, the former being less likely to influence future law. And there is a second alternative model between the one just described and the adoption of a rule always to defer to law. This one would have the judge consider not only the institutional values at stake, but also the value of following (or appearing to follow) a rule to defer to law in such cases. Yet this model, which we might call "quasi-rule-following,"[50] would not give the latter value extra weight against moral considerations at stake on the other side in a particular case, as actually adopting and adhering to a genuine rule to follow legal requirements would.

Why are these alternative models insufficient in this context? It will not do to answer that the judge is a representative of the legal system and so, of course, must follow the law. Jurors represent the legal system as well during the time they sit, and yet they are not held accountable for applying law in the way that judges are. The explanation instead appeals to a special kind of fallibility here, similar to prisoners' dilemma contexts, in judging the cumulative effects of individually rational or justified decisions. In the prisoners' dilemma, individually prudent decisions become collectively imprudent. In the contexts that are relevant here, individually morally correct decisions result cumulatively in morally inoptimal or unacceptable outcomes. Sticking for the moment with the legal context, consider the specific case of a bank seeking to foreclose on a house and evict a poor, elderly widow. The additional assets to the bank will have a negligible effect on its overall financial position, while the widow will suffer greatly if evicted. Similarly, a single court's decision on moral merits instead of law will have little effect on the stability or predictability of the legal system. The problem is that the cumulative effects of many judges reasoning only on these grounds could be disastrous to the legal and financial institutions (also. in our example, to the ability of widows to obtain loans). This special fallibility, the inability in the absence of a rule to take account of overall effects in the single case, together with the fact that morally minded judges will be tempted to bypass law on moral grounds in such cases, justifies the imposition of a rule requiring a legal decision according to law and not unfettered moral perception.

Let us look at this case more closely, since it will be our paradigm (we can compare it to typical prisoners' dilemma, coordination, and collective action problems). For each judge in such a situation, the moral cost of applying the law exceeds its benefit in the individual case. But the cumulative result of following this judgment is a social or collective evil potentially affecting all in society. Such evils must be avoided: Their avoidance produces a greater need for rules than does the production of public goods.

A second feature of such cases is that there is an optimal pattern, the best the group as a whole could do, which in theory they could achieve through coordination. In this case, the optimal pattern would consist in some percentage of widows spared just below the threshold at which cumulative damage to the legal system begins to outweigh the further good to individual widows. It may seem obvious that there must be this threshold, the point at which the marginal damage to society begins to outweigh the marginal gain to the widow.[51] However, this point may not be isolable if we grasp the harm in question only by a vague concept, if we cannot say precisely where or when the legal system begins to break down.[52] If there is no threshold, then it is, if anything, easier to argue that the contribution of each judge to the collective bad is negligible, so that each should be morally motivated, in the absence of a rule, not to enforce the law. If there is a threshold, then we have what we can call a "lumpy bad" (collective-action theorists speak of "lumpy goods" in cases where the contribution of agents becomes significant only at the point where the lump appears). We also have an optimal pattern of enforcement or nonenforcement just below the point at which the social evil manifests itself.

The optimal pattern could be achieved in principle in many different ways, by different judges performing the "enforce" and "don't enforce" roles. It would always be compatible with each judge doing her moral best given what the others are doing (i.e., it would be an equilibrium). But in order to achieve this pattern, each judge would have to identify it and cooperate with all others, or all would need to adopt a mixed randomizing strategy to approximate to it. There are then three insuperable problems blocking its achievement (hence defeating the rationality of attempting to optimize). The first is epistemic: an inability on the part of each judge to identify the optimal pattern or to know how close to the threshold of damage to the legal system he might be in not enforcing the law. One might respond that the chance of being at the threshold (assuming there is one) is low. But the negative consequences

44

of crossing it are enormous, and a judge can assume that, in the absence of a rule, she or one of her colleagues will do so.

The second problem is social: an inability to cooperate or coordinate so as to reach the optimal percentage of departures from law, even if that percentage could be known. This is a classic coordination problem – the existence of multiple equilibria (patterns from which no one can do better by deviating unilaterally), indeed multiple coordination equilibria (patterns in which no one could do better by anyone's acting differently), with different agents or judges occupying different roles, and a problem in picking out and achieving one such pattern.

The third problem is moral: Even if judges could identify the optimal pattern and confer on ways to achieve it, they could not in good conscience assign themselves the required different roles in regard to applying the law. This means that they could not adopt randomizing strategies to achieve the same effect either. If some impoverished people were allowed to keep their homes while others were evicted, these egregious violations of the fundamental principle not to treat cases differently without morally relevant differences between them would be as damaging to the legal system as would crossing the original threshold. The optimal pattern from a purely consequentialist viewpoint would soon be upset as citizens reacted to these considerations of (comparative) fairness.

Thus, the inability to solve the coordination problem in the judges' case leads to a generalized prisoners' dilemma–type problem from a moral point of view.[53] The adoption of a strong rule is clearly warranted as second best. The rule picks out a second-best pattern of behavior – that all judges apply and enforce the law – and makes it salient, eliminating the coordination problem. Given that a sufficient number obey the rule, the moral gains from ignoring it and attempting to optimize are not worth the risk of social harm from too many doing so.[54] That a rule is warranted as a second-best strategy means that it is not the one that produces the best consequences if all obey it (the rule utilitarian's criterion for justified moral rules); nor is obeying it the best each judge can do given the actions of the others (the act utilitarian's criterion for moral action). If this example is to be a paradigm, genuine moral rules are rather those that, if followed by a sufficient number, produce second-best results when the best cannot be attained in practice by individuals acting on their independent moral judgments.

Once the necessity for such a rule is recognized, there is little problem in instituting it and securing obedience. The motivation to obey such rules falls somewhere between that involved in obeying rules that solve pure coordination problems and those that solve typical prisoners' dilemmas. In pure coordination problem contexts, it is in everyone's interest to obey a coordinating rule once one is identified, and so there normally is no problem of motivation. It is normally in no one's interest to drive on the wrong side of the road, for example. In typical prisoners' dilemmas (at least one-shot cases), by contrast, self-interest calls for defecting or breaking the rule that maximizes the collective benefit. The problem of motivation is therefore acute: Imposition of a rule requires social sanctions to back it up or internalization, the adoption of a different attitude from the usual prudential one. In our case, the judge must forgo independent moral judgment in favor of obedience of the rule to apply the law, but self-interest is not at stake. The judge must impose harm on one person to prevent the externality of greater harm eventually to those not directly involved in her decision, and she shares the cost of forgoing independent moral judgment with all other judges. But she can recognize the moral need for the rule, and her professional reputation can be enlisted also on the side of its obedience. Self-interest therefore falls on this side as well, although enforcing the law can be unpleasant, and this motive is bolstered by the hierarchical division of the courts that facilitates monitoring. What is required is therefore simply an altered perception of moral demands, all things considered, and this is easier to achieve when unopposed by self-interest. The judge can recognize the rationality of sacrificing the local moral optimum for the global moral improvement (or to avoid the global disaster).

We must be careful not to conclude from this argument that judges are required to follow (first-order) *rules* of law. Legal institutional constraint from the side of common law can consist instead in the requirement not to judge a present case differently from a previously decided one without being able to cite a legally relevant difference between them. As is by now apparent, this constraint is weaker than the requirement to follow rules but here is distinct from discretion to judge on moral grounds. It requires judges to decide like cases alike without requiring them to judge unlike cases alike, as rules would. This argument establishes a rule only at the higher level, a rule requiring acceptance of this constraint. The second-order requirement constitutes a strong rule because judges are not to look through it except in the direst of circumstances that call the validity of the legal system itself into question. Thus we find here a strong rule that is of far greater import than such things as age requirements, indeed a cornerstone of the legal system.

We should also note, however, that although we need not construe the law generally as a set of rules, there are undeniably strong rules within the body of law. The just mentioned age requirements are among them. Although there might be good moral reasons for allowing certain mature sixteen-year-olds to drink alcohol or vote, or certain mature thirty-four-year-olds to be president, we rely instead on rules allowing no exceptions. Officials with discretion to decide such matters would lack the investigative resources to do so fairly, and bias and abuse of such discretionary power would be likely and even more likely to be perceived. Here simplifying rules prevent wasted effort and worse outcomes, *both* in individual cases and cumulatively. These examples reflect a simpler justification of rules than the previous one, since the source of errors to be avoided by the adoption of rules is more straightforward. In these cases, the symbolic value of universal rules is perhaps another consideration in their favor. I will address this topic of rules in the law at length in Chapter 3. Let us return to the topic of moral rules, keeping in mind that the rule that judges should apply the law in their decisions is both a cornerstone of the legal system *and* a moral rule, albeit of limited scope.

In the public sector and institutional contexts, such factors as division of authority and public image may seem crucial. But I argued that appeal to fallibility (and especially the special kind of fallibility noted in the judges example) is necessary as well for justifying the imposition of a genuine rule. I also argued that, in the private sphere, the chances of rule makers being less fallible in advance of normal individual cases than the agents involved at the time are slight. But the more subtle kind of fallibility in which individually correct decisions are cumulatively incorrect is different. If this phenomenon is sufficient for justifying the adoption of genuine rules, then we should find examples similar to that of the judge outside institutional contexts. And indeed some such examples are easy to come by.

Before generalizing this justification of rules to the private sphere, however, we should note some of its features more closely, lest we generalize too broadly. We must not think that every time the cumulative effects of many agents acting in a certain way are bad, we need a strong rule, even if many are tempted to act that way. The cumulative effects of everyone's breaking their appointments or of everyone's walking on the grass are bad, but we saw that needed moral constraints in these cases need not take the form of genuine rules. They do not take this form because when situations arise in which it might be the case that one ought to break a promise or walk on the grass, moral considerations in favor of doing so are weighed directly against the moral reasons against doing so. Genuine rules, we have noted, do not permit looking through them to their justifying reasons and weighing counterreasons directly against them.[55] In these examples there is no special problem of fallibility in moral judgment and so no need for rules as second-best strategies.

In order to generate a rule, the cumulative effects of everyone's weighing *moral* reasons directly must be bad. Agents must be tempted on moral *as well as* prudential grounds to cumulatively inoptimal behavior, or ordinary moral constraints must be too weak to require cumulatively right behavior when considered from the individual's point of view, as in the case of the judge. Errors must occur more often than not when ordinary moral reasoning is used. As noted, these errors can result either from obvious epistemic liabilities such as bias or lack of investigative resources, or from the more subtle kind of fallibility I have been emphasizing.

Even when we find only weak direct moral reasons against a form of behavior that is cumulatively bad above a certain threshold, we do not require a rule if most agents are not tempted to act in that way. We do not need a rule requiring people to vote (against not voting) as long as enough people desire to vote. They may desire to vote in order to express endorsement of the democratic process by means of participation or simply as a pleasant social exercise. If enough are participating willingly, then not voting is not wrong even though it is cumulatively bad if enough people do it.

Voting is often mentioned as a classic example of a collective-action problem under the assumption that it is in no one's self-interest to vote, given the very low probability of affecting the outcome (yet everyone is significantly worse off when none vote). It can be counterargued that the great difference made by the outcome of an election offsets the low probability of affecting that outcome, rendering it in the self-interest of each individual to vote. But this counterargument has limited application, being plausible only for certain elections, and certainly not for all in which we want a sufficient number of citizens to vote. The better answer, and better explanation of why as many people vote as do, appeals to the side effects of the activity, the fact that many people find it pleasantly expressive,[56] especially if they are granted time off from work to do it. If instead most citizens vote only from a sense of duty, then the case is different. A moral rule would then be in effect, and other citizens would be obligated to follow it as well. My point here is that we require a rule only when direct moral *and* prudential reasoning together produce cumulatively bad behavior.

In order further to distinguish contexts in which moral rules are needed and to provide more examples, it will be helpful to review again and further clarify the different types of prisoners' dilemmas and coordination problems to which I have referred. The typical prisoners' dilemma is what I have called prudential-moral. It is a context in which self-interest is self-defeating. Acting on self-interest leaves all worse off than they could have been. All are better off when none do action A, but A is the dominant strategy for each, that is, each is better off doing A no matter what the others are doing. The adoption of a moral point of view, acting for the collective interest, is a solution; but from the prudential point of view, the question of whether to adopt a moral point of view is itself a prisoners' dilemma. All are better off when all accept moral constraints, but no one seems better off accepting them personally. Whether, despite appearances, it is nevertheless prudent to adopt a rule to be moral, a question that has much occupied philosophers, will be addressed in Chapter 2. Here I want to point out that the adoption of a moral point of view as a solution to this type of prisoners' dilemma, the acceptance of moral norms or the recognition of morally relevant factors as overriding considerations of narrow self-interest, does not entail the acceptance of genuine moral rules.

What I have called moral rules of thumb (by contrast with genuine rules) – keeping promises, telling the truth, and so on – can all be seen as solutions to prudential dilemmas. All, for example, are better off when all keep promises when these are opposed only by morally trivial reasons, but each is better off if she can break them (in the absence of sanctions) when convenient. A rule to keep promises is nevertheless only a rule of thumb according to our criteria: Opposing moral considerations are weighed normally against it, and exceptions (as described in nonmoral language) are open-ended. Thus the prudential-moral prisoners' dilemmas do not in themselves justify the acceptance of genuine moral rules.

Another type of case, similar in certain respects to our judges' case (our paradigm of a moral-moral prisoners' dilemma), and widely discussed in the literature of social science,[57] is the collective-action problem relating to the production of public goods. Here the contribution of each agent to the production of the public good returns too little to that agent to offset her cost. But this nearly negligible contribution accrues to all, so that the collective benefit outweighs the total cost.

Public goods have the properties of being nonexclusive and nonrival: Once available, they are available to all, regardless of contribution, and no one's use lessens the opportunity for others to enjoy the good. Given these features, there is a free-rider problem – it is in no one's self-interest to contribute – amounting to a prisoners' dilemma, since all do worse when no one contributes. The equilibrium position is universal noncontribution, but it is not Pareto optimal. Social scientists attempt to explain how some public goods do get produced despite this dilemma, and the degree of likely contribution.[58]

The typical problem of this sort is, as noted, a prudential dilemma. It is not clear that the adoption of a (narrow) moral point of view, or the acceptance of a moral obligation, is a typical solution to it, since we are not in general obligated to contribute to the production of various public goods. We do and should, however, accept one more general obligation of this sort: the obligation to pay our fair share of taxes, from which the government provides certain crucial public goods. Does this obligation generate a moral rule? Yes, but only because of the addition of a further consideration.

Remember that we need moral rules (perhaps together with laws) only when required collective outcomes cannot be produced by individual agents considering the moral consequences of their actions. We need moral rules as solutions to moral-moral and not simply prudential-moral dilemmas (although the latter may often produce ordinary moral obligations). In the case currently under consideration, a person may correctly perceive that he could put his tax money to a morally better purpose, especially since his failure to pay taxes will have a negligible effect on the government's resources. He can personally know a person suffering hardship who can be rescued by his money, and without the expense of bureaucratic middlemen. But the cumulative effects of allowing individuals to make such judgments on ordinary consequentialist grounds would be disastrous. The government can far better coordinate the provision of public goods to the society as a whole.[59] We cannot effectively administer personalized systems in these areas, allowing only some individuals to decide on better uses for their taxes, for example. The best we can manage is random spot checks that people are obeying the rules.

Other examples involve not morally required or better (from the individual's viewpoint) behavior with cumulatively bad results, but harmless or morally permissible behavior. Here, there is typically not a failure to contribute to a public good, but a minimal contribution to a public bad. These cases include such areas of behavior as convenient waste disposal, saving resources, and cheating of various kinds. Single acts of most convenient waste disposal (e.g., throwing a candy wrapper in the gutter of a city) may be morally harmless. They do not affect the overall appearance of the city. But the collective effects of many individuals acting on their recognition of such negligible harm are not negligible or harmless. Hence a rule is in order. Using resources such as water or electricity during shortages constitutes a similar example. Once again, each benefits far more from using the resource than she harms particular other people, yet all suffer from the collective overuse. One might suppose that the market should correct for such overuse, but we all know from brownouts and other such phenomena that markets do not always react quickly enough to shortages.

Another example is cheating of certain familiar kinds. A student's smuggling answers into an exam may benefit him without appreciably harming other students. We think of such cheating as dishonest and clearly wrong. But much dishonesty, especially of the harmless variety, is not wrong, and single acts of cheating such as this do not produce harm (if grading is not on a scale). Their wrongness consists instead in violating a justified rule, justified as the solution to a moral-moral prisoners' dilemma. That this normative explanation is the correct one is indicated by the fact that we see little reason to obey such a rule when most other people are violating it; the rule then is not really in effect. This attitude differs from that which moral agents take toward actions that cause direct harm to others.

I have said that most moral rights do not correlate with genuine rules. But some do, depending on the centrality of considerations of fallibility, especially the inability to gauge cumulative effects of individual acts. The violation of ordinary rights produces nonnegligible harm of sufficient weight to figure properly in ordinary moral calculations. These include rights against various sorts of harm as well as contractual rights. Some rights, however, do require the protection of rules. One famously emphasized by Mill is that of free expression. Here censors are apt to overestimate the gravity of offense in the single case. More importantly, while each act of censorship might have a minimal effect on the level of discussion and expression in the community as a whole, the collective effect on motivations and expectations can make for a closed and stagnant society.

A slightly more complex example involves protection of those who begin from a disadvantaged position and might otherwise agree to exploitive relationships. Individual workers in conditions of unemployment might agree to work in unsafe or underpaid positions as opposed to not working at all, but collectively they end up worse off for making such agreements. We might think that such exploitive arrangements are amply opposed by rights to safe conditions or a decent wage. The problem with appealing to such rights as the sole considerations in these contexts is that we are normally permitted to waive rights voluntarily (this is part of their attraction). But it is precisely the voluntary waiving of these rights that lands workers in the prisoners' dilemma. Hence the rights need support from rules in order to avoid the collective bad. Hence safety and minimum wage rules are warranted. If society is justified in ruling against prostitution, it would be on similar grounds, but the question there is whether prostitutes are collectively worse off than they otherwise would be – whether, like the workers in the previous example, they would rationally prefer a rule to the apparent exercise of free choice.

Property rights are a yet more complex case. To political conservatives, protection of property is a paradigm moral right and among the strongest, approximating to a strong rule even in the absence of second-best considerations. To political liberals, appeal to property rights may seem little more than a transparent front for brute power. In my view, to be very brief, acquiring property in certain ways does in itself give one some moral claim to keep those possessions. But from an ordinary consequentialist viewpoint (even one in which morally relevant consequences relate primarily to rights), this claim or right can be overridden by far greater needs of others to those goods. From this point of view, stealing from the sufficiently rich to give to the sufficiently poor would be morally justified. The additional consideration, however, is that of incentive, the motivation to be socially or economically productive. Here once again the effect of each individual act of forced transfer will be minimal, but the cumulative effect of allowing such transfers may well be socially damaging. If so, the right to property will be supported by a genuine moral rule. This rule then supports inequalities we would not otherwise allow, but we hedge it in with other rules limiting what the rich can do or buy with their money. For example, we do not allow them to buy votes (outright, except in Miami), places in lines, or exemption from jury duty or military service (outright). While each such transaction might benefit the individuals involved, we do not like the picture of society that emerges from the cumulative effect of allowing them.[60]

Whether moral constraints take the form of rules may depend on the strength of more direct moral considerations, and there is room for differing interpretations in some areas. Sticking with the example of theft, if one perceives individual acts of shoplifting as morally benign in shifting goods to those more in need of them, one will probably nevertheless endorse a rule against shoplifting; while if one thinks that justified property rights generally render such acts wrong in themselves, one will see less need for a genuine rule. It may seem ironic that acts less seriously wrong in themselves require genuine rules against them, while those in violation of more central rights do not need additional moral force behind them. (The question of what kind of sanctions should back various rights or control various kinds of wrongdoing is independent of our issue.) This is a consequence of the overall account of rules as second-best strategies that I am willing to accept.

I have represented the preceding examples as moral-moral prisoners' dilemmas, contexts in which, in the absence of rules, morally permissible actions result collectively in morally unacceptable outcomes. Completeness would require representing them, like the paradigm judges case, as unsolvable coordination problems that generate prisoners' dilemmas. Considerations of fairness aside, we could imagine an optimal level of forced transfers from rich to poor below the threshold at which social incentive is damaged. But potential Robin Hoods have no way to coordinate so as to achieve this optimum. It is once more this combination of an insoluble coordination problem with a resultant prisoners' dilemma that warrants the moral rule.

Ordinary coordination problems in themselves do not warrant genuine moral rules, despite possible appearances to the contrary. These problems again involve the self-defeat of self-interest, but they differ from prisoners' dilemmas. Here the equilibria are multiple but Pareto optimal: it is in the interest of all individually to coordinate on one such pattern of individual actions out of the possible optimal combinations. But independent individual choice does not suffice to achieve one such pattern. Rules as solutions make one optimal pattern salient. Normally such rules require no sanctions, since it is in each person's self-interest to follow them once they are identified. Hence, normally they are not perceived as moral constraints.

One often cited example to which I have referred is a rule to drive on the right side of the road. I have pointed out that this is not a strong rule, since exceptions are open-ended (most being grouped under the normative categories "emergency" or "necessity"). It can nevertheless be considered a moral rule because of the importance of the interest in following it. Hence, in contrast to other coordination conventions, we do find sanctions attached to its violation (despite the fact that it is normally in the self-interest of all to follow it). Whether we see its moral status as a genuine rule (although not strong) or a rule of thumb depends on our estimate of drivers' fallibility in identifying warranted exceptions, our estimate of their ability to weigh opposing factors directly against the rule in practice. The presence of legal sanctions might indicate a genuine rule, but their frequent suspension when violations of the rule are supported by reasons indicates the opposite. In characterizing this as a moral rule of thumb earlier, I saw no special problem of fallibility, but pointed out that this does not imply that the interest at stake is trivial.

There is a different kind of coordination rule, far less common, that arises not from a problem in self-interested action, but from the need to coordinate moral actions themselves. In some contexts there is a direct need for division of moral labor or authority to act on independent moral perception. This is not an entirely separate category, since division of authority between judges and legislators entered the argument there, and since rules as second-best strategies always limit moral authority. But in the cases I have in mind, moral fallibility is not so much the issue as the need for immediate decisions and unified actions. Military and quasi-military organizations are the paradigm here. The rules here are coordination and not prisoners' dilemma rules, since they assign different agents different moral roles in aiming at optimal (not second-best) patterns of behavior. Orders from superiors in military organizations have extra, although not absolute, weight. But I believe that contexts that call directly for division of moral authority are rare, and I have argued elsewhere that we need to be generally suspicious of appeals to such a need.[61]

Let us return to the more common type of genuine moral rules, ones that prevent collective harm from otherwise morally permissible or required individual actions, as in the judge, pollution, resources, cheating, and tax examples. When those rules prevent the thresholds of harm from being reached, it may still be difficult to see what could be wrong with violating them when one can do better by doing so and knows one can do better by doing so. The wrongness involved in breaking the rules cannot consist, in these types of cases, in causing the nonexistent or negligible harms. We have seen that individual actions in these contexts have minimal negative effects and that these are outweighed by individual benefits according to ordinary calculations. We must, therefore, in the presence of justified rules change from ordinary consequentialist to deontological reasoning. When the consequences of a group's doing or not doing something are bad, then the group as a whole has a duty to prevent the bad outcome. When refraining from action that causes the collectively bad result is a burden, each member has a duty to do his or her fair share to prevent the harm. When the necessary means consist in following a rule, each has a duty to do so. This is implied once more by the basic constraint that people are not to be treated differently without a reason to do so.[62] Here, some people are not to have obligations that others without morally relevant differences do not have.

The obligation to obey a rule warranted to prevent harm that would result from everyone's ignoring it explains the force of the prohibition against actions that would be wrong if everyone were to do them. At least it explains when the reply "But everyone's not doing it" is cogent and when it is not. When most persons are not performing the action in question because they prefer to do something else, then the reply is cogent. The claim that the action would be wrong or have bad consequences if everyone were to do it in itself lacks force. But the reply to it is not cogent against the charge that one is being a free rider in the context of a rule warranted to solve a collective-action problem. The force of the initial prohibition does not imply that morality is normally a matter of rules. It's the other way around – the prohibition is sound only where rules are warranted. Thus, the wrongness of breaking rules from this point of view normally consists in free riding, a form of unfairness to those who are obeying the required rules out of a sense of duty.

VI. INTERPRETATION OF WEAK RULES

That there are moral rules against polluting or cheating does not imply that it is never wrong to break them, or even that one can break them only in the most dire circumstances (as in the case of judges breaking the law in their decisions), or that all such exceptions can be listed in advance. It means only that individuals cannot be trusted to weigh reasons directly for and against the behavior they require, that agents must accept rules and give them extra weight or independent effect in their moral calculations. Thus, as I have hinted, we must finally allow for stronger and weaker genuine rules, where only the former determine morally proper conduct in themselves. Weak genuine rules give extra weight in moral calculations to the factors they mention (or exclude others; see the later discussion).

The category of weak genuine rules is more problematic than that of strong rules, even if it is also more extensive in the private sphere. The problem is how to specify the notion of extra weight short of sufficient conditions. One way is to interpret the notion epistemologically. According to this interpretation, a weak rule raises the level of certainty required for justifiably acting against it. This may capture the function of rules in some situations in which error is likely to result from ordinary moral calculation in the individual case but not in the prisoners' dilemma–type contexts, in which judgments of individual cases may be quite certain while cumulatively bad. One may know perfectly well that a particular individual act will have net optimizing consequences (when calculated according to the individual interests or rights at stake), and yet the act may be prohibited by a genuine rule that ought to be followed.

A second interpretation views a weak genuine rule as barring agents from acting on certain otherwise relevant factors but not others. On this view, a strong rule preempts all those factors not mentioned in its statement. This is the way that Joseph Raz interprets rules in a series of influential papers and books. I do not believe that this analysis of rules works well for the central cases I have been emphasizing. Raz begins from a different sort of case, indeed not with an analysis of rules per se, but with the concept of authority, an analysis of when it is rational to defer to authority and of what that means. He then extends this analysis to that of (authoritative) rules.

Agents typically defer to authorities when they are wiser, less biased, better able to afford the costs, cognitive and otherwise, of deliberation, or when their judgments can make certain coordination equilibria salient. The normal justification for such deferral is that by doing so one will be able better to satisfy the reasons that already apply to one's individual actions.[63] The authorities are more reliable judges of those reasons. Their judgments then replace the reasons pro and con on which they were based as the agent's basis for action.[64] These are the reasons that are excluded by the authoritative judgment. Since the point is to rely on the judgments of the authorities and not to trust one's own, one does not add their judgments to the reasons one has prior to them and continue to weigh these augmented reasons oneself. The whole point is that one will do better by replacing or preempting one's reasons by their judgments.[65] The reasons excluded are those within the competence or jurisdiction of the authorities to judge. A soldier faced with a command does not add this to the reasons he has for acting in accordance with it and weigh the augmented reasons against those that oppose the action; the command instead preempts the ordinary deliberative process.

Raz views rules in the same way, as providing exclusionary or second-order reasons not to act on certain first-order reasons. Rules too remove or limit decision-making authority by excluding action on certain reasons that would otherwise apply. In addition to the analogy with authority (and the fact that authorities often issue rules), he cites as evidence for the exclusionary account the fact that we often feel ambivalent both toward following and breaking a rule in a situation in which ordinary reasons point one way and we feel bound by the rule to act in another. For Raz this reaction points to two levels of reasoning, one of which excludes reasons on the other as a basis for action.[66] If the rule simply added to the reasons that then override those opposed, Raz thinks we would simply condemn those who fail to follow it. Our ambivalent reaction would be inexplicable. It is explained by our feeling that the rule should be followed along with the realization that the balance of first-order reasons opposes the action it requires.

Raz supports this account of rules finally by appeal to their simplifying function and by an account of supererogation that includes another sort of exclusionary rule. Rules simplify deliberation not by adding to reasons, which would complicate it, but by excluding them.[67] This function of simplifying moral deliberation could not be accomplished unless his account of rules were correct. A plausible account of supererogation, Raz holds, requires appeal to exclusionary permissions, permissions to exclude certain reasons that would otherwise render the acts obligatory. Since performing a supererogatory act is highly praiseworthy, there must be strong moral reasons in favor of doing it. If the act is nevertheless not obligatory, there must be an exclusionary rule that grants permission to exclude these reasons. But if there are rules granting permission to exclude first-order reasons, it is more plausible that other rules preempt or require the exclusion of certain first-order reasons.

I shall briefly answer these arguments in indicating also why the Razian account of rules does not work well in the central cases that justify the imposition of genuine moral rules. First, in regard to supererogation, I shall not consider rules granting permission. But I do not believe that an account of supererogatory acts requires appeal to exclusionary permission. There may simply not be a general obligation to promote the good or prevent harm (as opposed to one not to harm), although it is praiseworthy to do so. We are not required to do what most benefits ourselves; we do not need an exclusionary permission to forgo doing so. The same may be true in the case of others. We can account for supererogation either by this lack of a general requirement or by a permission to give our own interests extra weight (not exclusionary).

Turning to the more central cases, there are important disanalogies between genuine moral rules and the commands of authorities. While in the case of authorities it is plausible to say that the reasons excluded are just the ones that they are competent to judge, or ones on which their decisions are based,[68] in the case of moral rules, where there is no question of expertise, it is not clear which reasons are to be excluded. In defending rules to keep promises, for example, Raz says that they exclude only certain counterreasons, but he does not specify which ones.[69] All that is clear is that the ordinary balance of reasons does not determine whether a promise should be kept, but this is true also according to an account in which rules add to the reasons in favor of following them. If all opposing reasons are to be excluded by a rule, then the rule is strong, and there is no practical difference between this account and that which holds them to state sufficient conditions or reasons. Such rules on either account do indeed drastically simplify deliberation. But if a rule excludes only certain reasons and we do not know which ones, then it cannot simplify. It could do so better by simply adding weight or independent reason on one side, slanting the decision in that direction and determining it in all but very unusual circumstances.

Another key disanalogy between my central cases and Raz's is that in my cases the rule is not to ensure better compliance with reasons the agent already has in the individual cases, but instead reflects a new kind of reason relating to the untoward cumulative effects of individual actions with the weight of reasons behind them. These individual actions continue to have the weight of reasons behind them even when their effects on general practices are taken into account. But this new and different kind of reason, which changes the ordinary balance, affords a different explanation for any ambivalence we feel when the rule requires an action that ordinary reasons forbid (in most cases, I don't believe we do feel ambivalent toward breaking valid rules even in such circumstances). The ambivalence derives from the fact that the rule introduces a reason not included in the balance of reasons for and against the individual act, from the fact that we may know that we could do better in the particular case, perhaps far better, as in the elderly mortgagee case, by breaking the rule even when we ought to follow it.[70] The individual judge in that case has no initial reason to change the situation to one in which he is not to judge on moral grounds.[71] But the legal system has reason to change the individual contexts and gives judges this reason in the form of a rule.

This difference between Raz's account and mine is perhaps best illustrated by his analysis of a miscalculation that he takes to be fortunate. If the point of a rule is only to exclude certain reasons, then the best outcome in a case in which the ordinary balance of reasons lies against following a rule occurs when the agent disobeys the rule without acting on the excluded reasons, even if the disobedience results from a miscalculation. According to Raz's account, the agent then lives up to what the rule demands, the exclusion of the preempted reasons, and also does what is best overall.[72] In fact, it would be best if everyone miscalculated in this way in such cases. Exclusionary reasons do not cancel other reasons; they tell us only not to act on them.[73] Therefore, such miscalculations are always fortunate; they result in actions in accord with the balance of all reasons. By contrast, in the cases I have been emphasizing, it is clearly not best if everyone breaks valid rules when the balance of reasons favors doing so in the individual cases. In such contexts, it is best (comparative fairness aside) if a small percentage of agents do so, but clearly better if everyone follows the rule than if all break it. Raz's analysis therefore does not work for this sort of rule, the most important kind.

According to Raz, rules exclude completely certain reasons from being bases for action, while those that are not excluded count in their usual way. Both claims may be wrong, even in Raz's central case of authoritative commands (or rules to obey them). If an authority makes a clear mistake, misjudging badly in calculating reasons within her jurisdiction or ordinary competence to judge, or if a literal reading of her command leads to absurd or extremely harmful results, then it may be right to override her judgment (unless the rule to obey is strong).[74] This means that reasons that formed the basis of her judgment are not entirely excluded. Any reasons that are centrally enough at stake might override a weak genuine rule (at least any reasons not stated in normative terms, such as "mere convenience" or "morally trivial concerns"), and so none seems to be completely excluded. When one makes a promise, to use Raz's example, personal hardship should ordinarily not excuse one from keeping it, but if severe enough, it may. Offense is normally not permitted to override free expression (if anything is excluded by the rule to protect free expression, offense is), but if severe enough, it may.

On the other hand, we may want a rule to count to some degree against all opposing reasons instead of granting nonexcluded reasons their usual weight. In the case of cheating, for example, there may be considerations in favor of doing so in a particular context that could not be anticipated when specifying a rule in advance, but we may still want the rule to have extra weight against them. If the purpose of rules were to exclude only particular reasons instead of encouraging compliance against all opposing reasons, it would be mysterious why they are stated as they are. Why not simply name the excluded reasons (as is virtually never done)?

I conclude that it is better to think of a weak genuine rule as simply adding additional weight or an independent reason to the reasons directly in favor of compliance. Or we can think simply of adding a certain amount of disutility to the breaking of the rule itself, which will be weighed against the reasons for doing so. The problem with this interpretation is that it seems to assume a common currency for comparing diverse values, an assumption denied earlier in this discussion. In the absence of a common currency of utility and disutility, it may not be clear how to quantify or weigh the disutility of breaking the rule against the possibly incommensurable reasons in favor of doing so. Of course, this problem may be seen to plague ordinary consequentialist reasoning as well. But in the ordinary problematic context in which conflicting rights must be ordered or prioritized, we can appeal to paradigm cases in which the order among those rights is clear. We then argue by analogy and disanalogy to the present context (the form of reasoning to be clarified in Chapter 4). The addition of extra weight to certain factors, those mentioned in or underlying a rule, upsets or distorts this ordinary reasoning process, and it is not clear how to incorporate this addition or replace the process.

I do not know a fully satisfactory solution to this problem for the understanding of weak rules. The problem is only theoretical, however. In practice we do have an idea of the weight of such rules, although it cannot be numerically specified. For example, when there is a rule against watering your lawn during a water shortage, this means that something much more substantial than your liking to look at its beautiful green color must be at stake to justify your making an exception, despite your not harming anyone by watering. Such examples seem to show clearly enough that some such rules are needed and that they do not reduce to dispensable prima facie rules or pseudo-rules, as defined earlier.[75]

At the same time, we should not think that weak genuine rules are much more common in the moral domain than strong rules, given the limited justification for both types. The rule consequentialist is right on my account less often than the ordinary consequentialist, although both capture part of the moral truth. One might think that even the limited presence of moral rules admitted in this section contradicts the generally rule skeptical position defended earlier. But it only confirms it in another domain.[76]

2

Prudential Rules

When we think of rules for conduct, we naturally think first of the moral or legal domains, of interpersonal rules, the topics of the previous and next chapters. But individuals sometimes adopt rules for their own conduct for prudential reasons, and I will address the need for such rules in this chapter. Robert Nozick has argued that intrapersonal or prudential rules play an essential role in persons' lives.[77] His argument is reminiscent in significant ways of the strongest argument for interpersonal rules. But there are important disanalogies that will be brought to light in this chapter. They relate mainly to the ability to adopt strategies to optimize, as opposed to settling for the second-best strategy of genuine rules. In view of these disanalogies between the intrapersonal and interpersonal cases, I will again reach a mostly skeptical conclusion regarding the need for genuine prudential rules, this time with only one exception.

I will then consider two special cases of higher-level prudential rules that have been widely assumed to be sound, and I will again question this assumption. The first is a rule to optimize, or maximize, the satisfaction of our rational preferences. I will clarify the sense in which this indeed defines prudential rationality, despite recent denials in the literature, as well as the sense in which it is not an acceptable action-guiding rule. The second higher-level rule to be considered is a prudential requirement to be moral. Here, I shall briefly review the strategies for homologizing morality and prudential rationality, and argue that they do not force us to accept this prudential rule. While acting morally is rarely prudentially irrational (in a fundamental sense of rationality to be specified), neither is it rationally required of all agents.

Let us first briefly review the strongest scenario for genuine rules in the moral sphere. Genuine and usable rules state a limited number of relatively simply identifiable conditions as relevant to decisions. The conditions they state must be taken as sufficient for doing or refraining from doing something, or they must be given such weight that they fail to be sufficient only in extraordinary circumstances. For this reason, the best case that can be made for the adoption of genuine moral rules does not include the claim that they capture our ordinary, full moral consciousness. Moral decisions must be made in contexts that may be too rich and variable to allow prediction of all those relevant factors that may weigh against those stated in usable rules. Morally relevant factors can interact in ways that change their priorities in different contexts, once more in ways that cannot always be stated in advance. Strong rules require a fixed ordering of values that is normally not to be had.

The argument of this chapter does not depend on the argument of the previous one for these claims. If moral rules are sound more often than I believe, this will not affect my argument concerning prudential rules. I am interested here only in the *best* case that can be made for moral rules, the case I made in the last section of the previous chapter, for this is the argument that is parallel to the one we will consider for prudential rules. Before noting the analogies and disanalogies, however, I should mention one further argument that attempts to convince us a final time that moral rules must be generally applicable. The response to it is relevant to our later discussion in reminding us of a crucial distinction drawn in Chapter 1.

The argument is that when we judge cases differently, there must be something to which we can appeal that makes them different, something beyond the bare intuition that one action is right and the other wrong – that one promise, for example, must be kept and another broken. That something must generally make a difference, and not just in this single pair of cases. There must be a reason why one promise is more important than the other in context, and such reasons must be general in the sense that just the same reasons must imply the same prescriptions for action. Hence it appears that there must be rules, which we could at least in principle state, that capture this generality. A reason cannot function as a reason unless it can do so in more than one conceivable context. Genuine reasons cannot be completely ad hoc. If reasons must be reasons generally, must not this generality be capturable in rules?

In response, we can first question again whether statements of such priorities (for example, among promises) that hold across all contexts would be simple enough to be usable as rules, or even to be capable of being produced by less than omniscient agents. But second, and more important here, I pointed in Chapter 1 to a constraint weaker than that of genuine rules that captures the requirement of same reasons, same actions. Strong rules require that when all the present reasons are present again, the same action must be performed. The weaker constraint requires that the same action be performed when the present reasons recur in the absence of any other defeating reasons; not all, but all and *only* the same reasons imply the same prescriptions. The former treats present reasons as practically sufficient conditions; the latter requires only that one not act differently without a reason to do so, without being able to cite some relevant difference between the cases or contexts. It is such differences that must be generalized in a way to be spelled out in Chapter 4, a way that does not equate with the existence of rules. Here, the distinction between types of constraints will figure in an argument regarding prudential rules.

To return to the moral sphere, we saw that the best argument for applying genuine rules there views them as strategies for achieving second-best cumulative outcomes when we cannot expect to be able to achieve the optimal. We apply rules in order to approximate as best we can in the circumstances to the satisfaction of full moral demands over time. In applying them, we allow for less than best outcomes in particular cases in order to achieve a cumulatively better state in the long run. We need to do this when serious errors are likely to result from the free reign of full moral judgment. Rules prevent such errors by simplifying the moral universe, by slanting decisions toward acceptable outcomes when these are unlikely to be achieved in the long run by weighing reasons against each other in the usual way. There was one particular kind of context that was most relevant to my previous discussion. In it we found a special kind of fallibility, typical of prisoners' dilemma cases, in judging the cumulative effects of individually rational or justified decisions. In the classic prisoners' dilemma case, individually prudent decisions become collectively imprudent; in the moral case, individually moral decisions become collectively inoptimal, or unacceptable, from a moral point of view. Such cases require rules barring individuals from making decisions based on ordinary full moral perceptions.

Recall some of our earlier examples. An individual may judge rightly that his tax money might be put to a (morally) better purpose. But allowing individuals to make such judgments has cumulatively worse results, so we need not only a legal but also a moral rule requiring individuals to pay their fair share of taxes. A judge in a trial court may reason correctly that enforcing a bank's right to collect a debt from an individual will have a devastating effect on the person and little consequence to the bank or to the legal system as a whole. But allowing judges to rule on such moral perceptions would have devastating cumulative effects on both the financial and legal systems, so we require not only a legal but also a moral rule that judges must defer to law in such contexts. What these rules do is to alter the direct moral calculations by adding additional disutility or negative reasons to the cumulatively unacceptable actions, thus avoiding that result. Breaking the rules is then considered a wrong in itself, a form of free riding when others are obeying. Rules require individuals sometimes to forgo what they perceive to be the morally best course of action (as judged by full moral criteria) by denying them the authority to act on those ordinary moral perceptions. I want to concentrate on this sort of case again as our paradigm because of the similarities and differences between it and certain arguments for prudential rules, to which I now turn.

According to Nozick (and others), prudential rules are useful for overcoming temptations or irrational desires of the moment, those that lead to long-term greater harm. Such desires are strongest only momentarily and not from a suitable temporal distance before or after; hence they are not stable preferences. We give in to them out of weakness of will. Weakness of will exists when a present desire overwhelms one's all-things-considered or reflective judgment about the best thing to do. It creates an incoherence among one's desires and actions, as the satisfaction of the momentary urge blocks the satisfaction of desires that are reflectively judged to be more worthy or important. Since the action that manifests weakness of will creates this incoherence, since it fails to follow the agent's stronger reasons, it must be judged irrational. (I shall have more to say about the requirement of coherence among desires and actions later.)

One way to overcome weakness of will is to bind ourselves in advance to alternative courses of action.[78] There are various ways to accomplish this, for example by making the object of temptation inaccessible. Another way is to adopt a genuine rule for oneself. If one knows, for example, that one has a tendency to overweight that is fed by fattening between-meal snacks, then one can resolve – that is, adopt a rule – never to snack between meals and stick to it. There are several significant parallels between this strategy and our paradigm context for the adoption of moral rules. The snacking example appears to be what I have called a prudential-prudential prisoners' dilemma case, as opposed to a moral-moral case. Here a prudential rule is proposed as a solution to the fact that self-interested action in the single case is self-defeating over time, while in the earlier cases moral rules solved the problem of individual moral decisions being collectively self-defeating or morally unacceptable. The structure of the problems and their solutions seem similar. (Later, I will consider again the better-known prudential-moral dilemmas, moral rules as solutions to other contexts in which prudence is self-defeating.)

Ordinary prudential reasoning on a case-by-case basis seems to be inadequate in the snacking example in the same way that ordinary moral reasoning is inadequate in the tax and legal examples. Nozick's example is not quite a pure case of weakness of will, as described earlier. In the absence of a rule, following the urge to snack in the single case is not clearly irrational in relation to one's other desires. In fact, it can be supported by sound prudential reasoning. Each single snack has a negligible effect on one's weight, just as an individual taxpayer's or judge's decision has negligible effects on the national budget and legal system. Nor, in the absence of a rule and of direct causal links between snacks at different times, does each snack necessarily increase the probability of a next one's being eaten. So there seem to be no significant negative consequences that ordinary consequentialist reasoning can seize on in any of these single-shot contexts. If the pleasure of a snack is not negligible and its negative consequences are, then ordinary prudential reasoning in each single case will favor indulgence. It will do so despite the fact, noted earlier, that the cumulative effects must be avoided (in the prudential context over time only; in the moral context, across different individuals as well). We saw in Chapter 1 that one way to avoid bad collective results is to add negative consequences or weight to each cumulatively bad act, and this can be seen as a function of genuine rules.

How rules fill this function, how they add negative consequences to the single acts, can seem more problematic in the intrapersonal, as opposed to interpersonal, domain. Interpersonal rules can be enforced against individuals by others, sometimes according to fixed and impersonal social mechanisms. Socially imposed sanctions are clear instances of additional disutility added to cumulatively undesirable actions. Personal rules are not normally so enforced. But this difference is not crucial or constant, since moral, as opposed to legal, rules, while equally interpersonal, often are enforced only informally or by individual conscience. A variant of moral conscience can produce feelings of guilt for infractions of prudential rules as well.

How negative utilities become added in the absence of social sanctions, or why these feelings of guilt should be considered rational when they occur, remains problematic. In the interpersonal case, when others are obeying a valid rule, breaking it is a wrong as a form of free riding, not doing one's fair share to avoid a cumulatively bad outcome. But one cannot free ride on oneself. (Some philosophers write as if one has different selves at different times, in which case free riding might be possible, but I shall argue that this view cannot capture the ways I relate to my own future.) So it remains to be seen in what way breaking a prudential rule adopted in circumstances such as the snacking example can be wrong. Earlier I said simply that breaking a rule in such contexts itself is taken to constitute a wrong, but on what grounds?

Nozick has a complex explanation. According to him, when we adopt a rule, each act that falls within its scope comes to symbolize all the other acts to which it applies. By this means, the negative consequences of all the separate acts (minimally real, even if negligible when considered singly) are added together and applied to the consideration of each act, tipping the balance against its performance. When one act stands for a group of others, the utility or disutility of all attaches to the one, and the cumulative effects come to be considered each time as if they all occurred at once. Thus, in the snacking example, one can come by this means to compare the disutility of overweight against the pleasure of the single snack. Since the former outweighs the latter, it would then be only irrationality or weakness of will to give in even once. But weakness of will is once more overcome by keeping firmly in mind the total disutility that adoption of the rule creates.

When pondering the rationality of this transference of value by means of rules, Nozick responds by pointing out, first, that much of the meaning and value in our lives is conveyed by symbolic meanings[79] and, second, that principles or rules must be judged by how well they serve their function and by how necessary or valuable their function is.[80] In the case that currently interests us, the function to be served is preventing the cumulatively undesirable result that may accrue from actions that are overall desirable when taken singly. That there are such cases is undeniable. But we can question both whether genuine rules serve the required function better than other decision procedures and whether, even if we grant that they do, the symbolic transference of utility is possible for rational agents. This possibility seems relatively unproblematic to Nozick, given how widespread he takes the phenomenon of symbolic meaning and value to be. And he simply assumes that we often require prudential rules in the sort of context that his example of snacking illustrates.

Regarding the symbolic transference of value, must this not constitute a kind of self-deception if the single act does not in fact have the disutility of all taken together? In the snack case, one snack does not in itself cause additional overweight by thinking of it as if it did. It is one thing to make an act symbolic by taking it to be expressive of some value one holds, as when one votes in an election to express one's endorsement of the democratic process or cheers at a game to express one's loyalty to a team. The act of expression itself then acquires a value as such. One enjoys feeling a sense of community with other voters or rooters and showing this connection to them. It is another thing to take a single act to have the value of all similar acts together by simply symbolizing them: This seems to mistake a symbolic connection for a causal one.

Or perhaps the idea is that a single violation of a rule symbolizes all violations, hence all similar acts, by destroying the universality of the rule in practice. One violation does this, as do many; hence one has the same disvalue as many or all, at least symbolically. But, to return from such abstractions to the concrete example, if the disvalue of snacking is overweight, then one violation of the rule not to snack does *not* have the same disvalue as many violations. The symbolization allegedly created by the rule must still function as a belief that there is a causal connection here, that one act of snacking will necessarily lead to so many others that overweight must result. The symbolization here is supposed to be action guiding; the agent who adopts the rule is to act as if the symbolization were literal or true. In guiding action, it seems to function here exactly as a belief. But, since belief is a functional concept, what functions as a belief is a belief, or at the least amounts to one. Adopting a rule, then, according to Nozick, amounts to forming a belief in a causal connection among acts that, by hypothesis, we know to be causally independent. This is what appears to require self-deception.

Before commenting further on this issue of causal independence and the symbolic transference of utility or value that Nozick ties to the adoption of rules, it will be worth our while to expand a bit on this notion of self-deception, to see whether it is an objection to Nozick's account that self-deception seems to be an unnoticed part of it. There is

68

a philosophical literature on the phenomenon that raises two questions: "What is it?" and "Does it really exist (is it even possible)?"[81] The latter question becomes pressing if the answer to the former is that self-deception is literally what its name implies, that is, just like the deception of one person by another except that here the perpetrator and victim are the same. When one person deceives another, she intentionally gets him to believe what she knows is false or lacking in evidential support. But it seems impossible for a person intentionally to trick himself into believing what he at the same time knows or believes to be false or lacking in evidential support. In our example, the would-be snacker is seemingly to trick herself into believing that one snack has the disutility of all when she must know that it does not. This again seems to be an impossible feat.

If self-deception were indeed impossible, and if Nozick's account of the way prudential rules are supposed to work nevertheless required it of agents who adopt such rules as solutions to prudential dilemmas like the snacking example (one could equally use smoking, drinking alcohol, not exercising, or other similar examples), then the argument against this account and the function of rules that Nozick assigns to them would be easy. But what goes under the name of self-deception is an all too common phenomenon in both fiction and real life, hence clearly possible. Jean Brodie appears to believe that she is helping her students to develop independence instead of recognizing that she manipulates them to fulfill her frustrated desires;[82] my rich old neighbor appears to believe that his young and attractive wife married him for love; my son's tennis coach, like many other coaches, always encourages him to "think positively," to believe he can win when all the evidence points the other way. All these are apparent cases of self-deception, fictional, actual, or encouraged. The trick for the analytic philosopher is simultaneously to explain both how such cases differ from ordinary two-person deceptions (so as to be possible) and why they nevertheless merit the title of self-deception. In our example, if we are to accept Nozick's account, we must explain how a rule user can seemingly believe that one snack has the disutility of all while also seemingly knowing that it does not.

Several explanations have been offered of the common cases of self-deception. One closely modeled on the two-person case divides the self, so that one part believes the troubling truth (e.g., that the wife is after money or that the other player will win the tennis match) and deceives the other part into believing the reassuring falsehood. One objection to such accounts is that, if neither homunculus here is to be identified with the self, this could not be literally self-deception. This objection is not cogent, since we have seen that we must depart from literal copying of the two-person account. A better objection is that the analysis is too complex as an explanation, that simpler analyses that do not posit suspect psychological mechanisms are available. These accounts avoid attributing contradictory beliefs and impossible strategies to the self-deceptive subject by denying either the anxiety-producing (true) belief or the reassuring (false) one, as well as denying an intentional strategy to hide the contradictory belief.

Kent Bach takes the latter tack. According to him, the self-deceiver believes something unpleasant, but avoids the thought of it, where this avoidance is motivated but not intentional.[83] Annette Barnes opts for the former line, according to which the subject believes only the falsehood that reduces anxiety produced by the thought of its contradictory. The anxiety produces bias in processing the evidence, a bias of which the subject is not aware (hence the absence of an intentional strategy).[84] The concept of self-deception applies here because the subject is deceived about the cause of his belief (although no one is deceiving him). When confronted with such a case, it is often so hard for us to see how the evidence could not produce the unpleasant true belief in a subject who is neither stupid nor ignorant that the motivated bias seems to us to be intentional. Furthermore, the seemingly willful ignoring of evidence often relates to the subject's anxiety about her self-image, reinforcing the application of the term "self-deception."

I prefer Barnes's account, since our attribution of self-deception depends on the agent's acting as if the reassuring false belief were true, that is, acting as if he held that belief. How would Barnes's account explain our example as a case of self-deception? In the example, the subject knows that if the utility of each snack is higher than that of not snacking, he will continue snacking. He knows that if he continues snacking, he will be overweight. The thought of being overweight produces anxiety, which biases him to ignore the evidence of causal independence between single acts of snacking, so that he can deny the antecedent of the first conditional (that each snack has positive net utility).

All this explains how the symbolic function that Nozick assigns to a prudential rule (if it is to be action guiding) is possible. Remember that the functioning of the rule as a symbol is necessary to explain why the agent does not see it as prudent to break the rule in each case, why it would be seen as wrong to do so. Here again is an important disanalogy with the interpersonal context for rules. There, as mentioned, the wrongness of breaking a rule once adopted consisted in free riding. But, barring a bizarre theory of the self or personal identity, one cannot free ride on oneself, or on oneself at a different time. Hence the need to make the disutility of each act somehow outweigh its utility, that is, symbolically do so, when we seem to know that literally it does not. But if the symbolic function is possible only by means of self-deception, then we may wonder how the subject gains in rationality by adopting such a rule. One form of irrationality is used to overcome another: self-deception, the overwhelming of evidence by anxiety, overcomes weakness of will, the overwhelming of a greater reason by a closer one. Not acting on one's strongest reasons is avoided by not believing in one's strongest reasons. It might be replied that what is gained here is not rationality, but precisely what is not gained, namely, excess weight. But, of course, once we recognize the self-deception for what it is, it is no longer possible, at least not for us. Does this mean that we cannot adopt prudential rules in such contexts? (Is the price of reading this book greater than its monetary cost?)

Perhaps self-deception is not required if valuing is more under our voluntary control than I have been assuming. Perhaps the values we attach to individual acts of snacking need not follow our beliefs about their causal relations. When it comes to values, does thinking make it so? Can we just willfully value the single act differently and so create a different value for it? Can merely describing it as breaking a rule alter its utility or rationally alter our preference? One might then regret one's weakness of will in breaking the rule one has resolved to follow, but the question is whether it is rational to adopt the rule and attach the additional disutility to each act by redescribing it in this way. Once more, there is no additional wrong such as free riding to which we can appeal here when the rule is broken.

One might object also to the assumption of causal independence among acts. One might hold that there is a causal connection here that underlies the symbolic one, in that one snack may indirectly contribute additional disutility by increasing the probability of further illicit munching. The clearest case of such causal connection occurs in addictions, but I want to put that case aside as an abnormality for the moment. In the more ordinary case, if prudential reasoning allows *this* snack because the pleasure outweighs the negligible additional weight, why should it not allow the next one, and so on? One's recognition that the same reasoning applies in each case might seem to tie the first action to subsequent ones.

71

The reply to this objection is that the context of each subsequent action will be somewhat different – one will have had more snacks over a given time period – until eventually one can recognize that one is approaching a threshold at which further snacks will cause unwanted weight gain. If one is monitoring this threshold over time, then a particular snack well below it need not increase the probability of all future ones. The same reasoning need not apply in the altered contexts; we can come to recognize that we should go easy on the snacks for a period after frequent indulgence. Vagueness in the notion of overweight, or the lack of a clear threshold, does not matter here. A vague or indistinct threshold suffices for knowledge that recent frequent indulgence is beginning to show where we would like it not to. Once a threshold, vague or not, is approached or reached, it may no longer be true that the utility of each snack outweighs its disutility. Here the connection in thought between further snacks and overweight can come into play to alter the true or rational preference, so that only weakness of will could explain further continuous indulgence.

This suggests, however, that Nozick can respond that once we near such a threshold, *then* we need a rule to have no more snacks.[85] (The issue has now become not whether a prudential rule is possible but whether it is needed.) My answer is that we need not ever reach or closely approach the threshold if we intelligently monitor our snacks over time, and so it seems we never need the rigidity of a genuine rule. How about a rule such as "Not more than three snacks a week" or "Never snack if you have done so within the previous two days"? Once more, we need not be so rigid. We can go over these limits occasionally and make up for it by following a stingier schedule for the time being. We must keep in mind that rules, even when defended in such cases, represent second-best strategies (i.e., strategies for achieving the second best when the optimum is not available). The best thing is to derive the pleasure from snacking in such a way as to not cause overweight. Realizing this, ordinary reason must abdicate to the rigidity of a rule when adopting or following one. But how can reason so abdicate without the motivation of external sanctions when it knows it is doing so and knows that the result is less than the best it could achieve?

Not surprisingly, the answer depends on whether the result is indeed worse or better than what would or could otherwise be achieved in the actual context. One might still argue that adoption of a rule is justified in achieving a global improvement while sacrificing local optima. And if the adoption of a rule is justified, then it must be rational to follow it.

Replying once more, however, if we can reason reliably in each context as it comes along and coordinate our actions over time so as to achieve an optimizing pattern of behavior, then it makes no sense to apply rules that are cruder than the calculations we can make without the benefit of such rules. We should not aim at what is second best when the best is available, as I have argued is normally the case in the contexts in question.

Following the rigidity of any specifiable rule will lead one to forgo benefits that one can reap as they unexpectedly arise while avoiding cumulative harm by then making further piecemeal adjustments. This is why genuine rules (as opposed to rules of thumb) are second-best ways to solve such coordination problems. These coordination problems are normally easier for an individual to solve than are those involving groups of individuals acting independently and without knowledge of each other's actions. Not only can the individual monitor her overall pattern of past behavior more easily, but she can also better predict her future behavior, not needing the rigidity of a rule to create predictability.[86] An individual can therefore adopt a flexible long-term strategy that may be impossible for a group to implement.[87]

Such a strategy will require one to be resolute on particular occasions in resisting the temptation to snack, for example, on those occasions. Resoluteness is most necessary when the harm from the next snack remains in itself negligible, but the agent must forgo some such snacks and has decided that this will be one forgone. Edward McClennen points out that an individual can coordinate her choices over time either by being sophisticated – that is, not choosing a plan that she knows will contradict her future preferences – or by being resolute. He interprets the latter, however, as regimenting future choice to an originally adopted plan,[88] which is therefore viewed as a relatively strong rule. But, as just noted, one can be resolute on particular occasions, and such resoluteness can be part of a flexible long-term strategy that can approximate to the optimum over time better than can a rule. Resoluteness on an occasion amounts to treating one's intention as an independent reason to follow it. This is close to Michael Bratman's view of intentions generally as similar to Raz's exclusionary reasons (see Chapter 1, section VI). While I believe that the need for resoluteness requires us sometimes to treat intentions as independent reasons, just as we sometimes ought to adopt genuine rules, I also believe that my arguments show that sometimes it is better to treat plans and intentions as provisional or flexible, more or less as rules of thumb to be followed if there is no reason to change one's mind.[89] I will not defend this view here, however, as it would take us too far from our topic of rules.

Thus rules, as opposed to resolutions, are rarely needed for the purposes of prudence. We must nevertheless explicitly distinguish two types of cases (I postponed doing so earlier), one of which is normal and the other abnormal or special. In the ordinary or normal case, we found a crucial disanalogy to the paradigm context for moral rules. In that social context we saw that individual agents cannot monitor the cumulative effects of their individual decisions. They not only have no power over others, but also no way of telling how close they might be to the threshold at which collective harm begins to set in. In the absence of a genuine rule, an individual trial court judge, knowing only that the effects of one decision on the legal system are minimal, but that decisions based on correct moral perceptions can be collectively damaging, does not know how other judges reasoning in the same way will react. In fact, in the typical case that also includes taxpayers and potential polluters, it will seem that, however others are acting, since one cannot influence them, one should follow one's own best judgment, even though, again in the absence of a rule, the cumulative results are disastrous. But the prudential context is normally different in this respect. As noted, the coordination problem over time for a single individual is normally not the same as the coordination problem across different individuals in the moral prisoners' dilemma-type cases. In the intrapersonal context, one can continuously monitor the collective results of one's behavior, keeping those results over time below the threshold of harm in the absence of strict or genuine rules. It is this difference that defeats the argument for prudential rules as second-best strategies in normal cases.[90]

The abnormal case is that of real addiction. I argued that in the normal case one snack now need not increase the probability of more snacks later in relevantly different contexts (how many snacks were recently eaten constitutes a relevant difference in context).[91] But in the case of addiction, indulging in the short-term pleasure once does cause or increase the probability of future indulgence, at worst leading inevitably to long-term disaster. I would define an addiction as the repeated inability to resist temptations of a certain kind when one knows it would be better in each case not to indulge, when this weakness of will is brought about by prior indulgence. Here the causal connection between earlier and later contexts does justify the adoption of a rule. The rule can be considered either a summary or a reminder of all the single occasions in which it is irrational to indulge (hence not a genuine rule) or as adding yet additional weight to the already overriding reasons to abstain. And that same causal connection, or its recognition, nullifies the need for any symbolic transference of negative utility in the resolve to adhere to the rule. Since one act really is connected to others, making later ones much more likely, and since their utilities are therefore really connected as well, there is no need for merely symbolic connections. Reason need neither deceive nor overcome itself, since indulging in the addictively harmful behavior even once is itself the overcoming of reason, which recognizes the connection between acts and hence the need for strict abstention, by other causal forces. Indulgence is always a form of weakness of will. Thus, in the only case in which prudential rules are needed, they need not work as Nozick claims.

The claim that genuine prudential rules are needed not only in abnormal cases of addiction, but in normal contexts as well, may result from a failure to consider flexible dispositions or strategies that fall between total abstinence and complete indulgence. As we will see in later sections of this chapter, this lack of imagination fuels several arguments for adherence to rules. Here, it may be pointed out in parallel fashion against my mainly rule-skeptical position that there are cases that fall between my characterization of the normal context of temptation in the snacking example and the context of real addiction. I have assumed that in the absence of addiction one's reasoning abilities remain intact in the face of temptation. But we might think of cases short of addiction in which the ability to calculate prudentially seems somewhat impaired.

If I am very fond of cheesecake, need to watch my cholesterol, but have trouble resisting when faced with a display of pastries and cakes in restaurants I frequently patronize, then I may fall into this category. I am not genuinely addicted, since my previous indulgence has not caused an overriding craving outside the restaurants in question. It's just that the aroma and sight of that pale yellow wedge, especially if topped by fresh ripe strawberries, tends to distance the thought of my blood contents from my mind. Wouldn't it then be prudent for me to adopt some sort of rule to offset this weakness of mine? Might this not be supported or expressed by an image in which each act of cheesecake gorging symbolizes a lifetime's worth, a veritable mountain of deliciously flavored animal fat? Shouldn't the causal inaccuracy of this symbol be nevertheless used to counteract the irrational causal influence in the other direction?[92]

It once more seems to me, even in this context, that I need not resort to the rigidity of a genuine rule, and that I will not do the best for myself over time by adopting one. If I am not addicted, then I can once more monitor my intake of delicious desserts over time, thinking of the cumulative effect of not being reasonable if I have recently indulged, instead of relying on a literally false or misleading symbol. Failing this strategy for self-control, I can adopt a rule of thumb, recognizing that I can and should make exceptions when, despite my usual deficiencies in prudential calculation, I know that I will be better off making the exceptions in these instances (when, in the cheesecake example, I know that their infrequency renders them coronarily harmless). The freedom to make exceptions based on ordinary calculations distinguishes rules of thumb from genuine rules that must be given absolute, or at least extra, weight in any practical calculations.

If I am unable to maintain an optimizing strategy or even a rule of thumb, but not because of addiction, then how likely am I to be able to adopt a strict prudential rule and stick to it? The knowledge that one is addicted, if one is, might motivate adherence to a strict rule better than the sort of weakness of will we are now considering. Thus, if a rule were needed here, it would be unlikely to be successful. In this respect, trying to convince this sort of person that he needs to adopt a prudential rule is like trying to convince a hardened, amoral criminal that he has a moral obligation to obey the law. (The cases are more broadly analogous as well, in that the person who might be convinced of a moral obligation to obey the law as such is worth more to society if she does not accept such an obligation. Her disobedience of certain laws on moral grounds can be a healthy input to the social system.[93] Likewise, I have argued that the person who might be able to follow a prudential rule is normally better off optimizing.)

I do not wish to deny that there may be a fine line between addiction and weakness of will short of addiction. But the fineness of this line may be matched for our purposes with the fineness of the line between genuine rules and rules of thumb. In all but extreme cases, I maintain that it is best to regard any prudential rules as merely rules of thumb. This attitude resembles what I believe to be a rational attitude for the utilitarian to adopt toward deontological rules (in contexts other than those I described earlier as justifying genuine rules). True utilitarians can adopt rules of thumb for occasions in which they doubt their own ability to calculate consequences, but they should reserve the right to make exceptions when they are confident that they know it is better to break these rules. Ordinary contexts in which there is such doubt must be distinguished from prisoners' dilemma-type cases. In the latter cases we saw that, absent the ability to communicate and coordinate, there is an irremediable fallibility, while in normal cases one may have knowledge of relevant consequences and know or confidently believe that one has such knowledge. Likewise, ordinary contexts of possibly weak will must be distinguished, however finely, from genuine addictions. Addiction may be thought of as irremediable weakness of will (once indulged), while the ordinary kind can be resisted or overcome.

Nozick finally suggests one other function of prudential rules, a function that lies on the border between the intrapersonal and interpersonal. In binding ourselves to act according to rules or principles, we assure others that we will do so. We then acquire a reputation for being persons with integrity, persons whom others can count on to act in particular ways in particular circumstances. Such a reputation is an asset. If others can trust us to act predictably, they are more likely to enter into cooperative agreements with us. The easiest way to acquire such a reputation is to accept the principles we avow.[94] In accepting them, we become persons of integrity in reality and not in appearance only: We give coherence to our lives and help to define our identities.[95] In earning the respect of others, we gain self-respect as well. Thus, for Nozick, a person with integrity is a person with principles, and a person with principles acts according to genuine rules as defined previously.

In responding to this argument, I must expand on my brief comments on integrity in Chapter 1. It is easy to see why acting with integrity is often confused with following genuine rules. Persons with integrity stand behind their commitments in the face of adversity or challenge. They follow through on their intentions to pursue certain objectives despite the obstacles that may stand in their way.[96] They defend these commitments and the values they represent against competing considerations. Persons who follow rules always place the values they represent ahead of other considerations. This may seem to be the strongest way to stand behind commitment to certain values. Nevertheless, the genuine demand for integrity is not only distinct from a requirement always or often to follow rules; it is incompatible with this requirement.

There are two reasons for this incompatibility. First, the concept of integrity refers to the wholeness or integration of the self over time.[97] This implies, as noted in the earlier discussion, that a person with integrity acts consistently. But, as also pointed out previously, acting consistently means *both* acting in the same way when there are no relevant differences between contexts *and* acting differently when there is a relevant difference. To fail to do the latter is to be inconsistent on a second level, to fail to generalize differences that differentiate cases elsewhere. It implies that what counts to distinguish one pair of cases does not count to distinguish another pair when there is no relevant difference between the pairs of cases. We have seen that following rules often involves ignoring what would otherwise be relevant differences between contexts. Hence, in many contexts it is incompatible with acting consistently. Hence, it is incompatible with acting with integrity.

Second, there are different kinds of integrity – for example moral integrity, professional integrity, artistic integrity, and so on. It is the moral variety, I suppose, to which Nozick refers and that therefore interests us here. A person with moral integrity is committed to doing what is right or morally best. But doing what is right entails finding out all the morally relevant considerations and weighing them against one another when they conflict in context. Rules allow or require us to forgo this epistemic obligation. Hence, once again, their regular use is incompatible with the demands of acting with moral integrity. The underlying reason is the same as in the previous argument: The rigid rule follower ignores relevant considerations in always placing certain values first when they are at stake. Persons with integrity, by contrast, will not forsake their values *without good reason* in the form of competing values that override.[98]

Two final points made earlier are again relevant in response to this argument for the adoption of personal rules: that rules are second-best strategies in relation to all the factors that might otherwise be relevant to our decisions, and that there is a weaker constraint that still captures the demand for consistency in actions over time. In regard to the first point, we may shift from the agent's point of view to society's. The following question is pertinent: "Do we really want to count on a person to act in the same way time and again when there is a good reason not to?" There will be a good reason not to when following the rule is only second best and when it can be recognized to be so by the agent. When factors not mentioned in rules override those that are mentioned, and when agents are capable of weighing these factors against the need for routine or mechanical predictability, why would we want to count on the agents to sacrifice justice or other moral considerations to the rules?

We have seen that moral action does not require an agent always to place certain values over others, or always to act in the same way when certain considerations are present, even though opposing considerations may be present in some contexts but not others. Persons with integrity, I pointed out, do not act inconsistently with their own values, that is, they do not act differently from one context to the next without good reason to do so. This means that they obey the weaker Kantian constraint defined earlier. They recognize morally relevant differences when acting differently in morally charged contexts. But we have seen that this is not equivalent to obeying genuine rules. Above all, persons with integrity do not yield to temptation at the expense of perceived duty (to themselves or others). But we have seen that genuine rules are generally not required to resist such temptations.

II. SECOND-ORDER PRUDENTIAL RULES: OPTIMIZING

First-order prudential rules refer to the objects of our preferences and tell us directly what to do or not do in relation to those objects. Examples of such rules are "Never snack between meals" and "Always brush your teeth after meals." As we have seen, we have real need of such rules only in abnormal contexts. Second-order prudential rules refer to our preferences themselves and tell us what to do about those preferences, whatever they happen to be. In this section I shall discuss the apparent rule "Maximize the satisfaction of your (informed and properly ordered) preferences." In the previous section, I argued that it would be irrational to settle for the second-best strategy of first-order rules if we can optimize instead. But if optimizing itself is not rational or rationally required, then that argument becomes suspect. Does my dismissal of first-order rules then commit me to this second-order rule?

Indeed, the requirement to optimize has been widely assumed to be a (or the) central demand of prudential rationality. Of late it has come under attack, most prominently and radically by Michael Slote,[99] but also by Derek Parfit and Stephen Darwall. I shall argue that these attacks are in large part misguided. Understood in one way, and with different kinds of reasons properly distinguished, optimization, doing the best one can or acting on one's strongest reasons, is indeed trivially equivalent to prudential rationality itself, but it does not constitute an action-guiding rule. It does not provide us with a decision procedure that can be opposed by some other rational procedure. Understood in a second way, there can be a genuine rule to optimize, and it can be opposed by other rational procedures or strategies; but neither a strict rule to optimize nor strict alternative rules are acceptable.

Slote offers a variety of examples in which he takes it to be rational to satisfice, to choose what is good enough but not best, instead of optimizing. A person passes up a snack or additional cookies when she would derive harmless enjoyment from them because she has no need of them. A person selling her house takes the first reasonable offer because it is satisfactory, although not the best she might receive. A person is content with the affection his wife shows him instead of always seeking more. Slote claims that the individuals in these cases may be rational independently of whether their satisficing choices make them better off overall or whether their choices are overall better from their perspective. The subjects here may be better off overall with another cookie, a higher price, or more affection, and they may know this and know that the better options are available, that they could do better, and yet still be rational to choose less than the best. There is an intrinsic rationality to choosing less in such contexts; the choices reflect moderate desires, and having moderate desires is more reasonable or better than greediness in itself.[100]

But the use of such examples to establish Slote's claim is unconvincing, and the natural use of the term "better" in the previous sentence creates a fatal tension in the argument. How else are we to understand the term "better" here except as better from the agent's rational perspective? If we do understand it in that way, then all these examples seem to be instances of rational choice only if the choices are better from that perspective. Indeed, desires for more and more snacks, or money, or spousal affection generally do not make one better off. They may compete with desires for other goods or, more important, they may become insatiable, incapable of fulfillment. The examples here seem plausible only because one is generally not better off overall always seeking more of these goods, despite Slote's saying that the subjects would be better off with more in these cases. By contrast, one is generally not criticized for always wanting more knowledge, for example. The reason is that, despite the literary example of Faust, having more knowledge generally facilitates the satisfaction of other desires instead of competing with or frustrating them. Slote contrasts choices of less than best with greed. "Greed" is indeed a pejorative term, but this does not show that optimizing is inherently wrong. We regard taking the best that one can get as greedy only when it in some way (perhaps indirectly) deprives others or leads to ultimate dissatisfaction. Then optimizing for oneself is unfair to others or shows an imbalance or incoherence in one's set of desires, justifying the use of a pejorative term.

Noting himself the weakness of these examples,[101] Slote offers another set involving what he takes to be rational constraints on optimizing imposed by the past. A person who has had a longstanding desire or goal is considered irrational to switch to what offers a marginally better prospect for enjoyment or satisfaction. If I have always wanted to visit Paris, then I may be irrational to pass up the chance for a slightly better hotel deal in London. A person who constantly alters goals or commitments at each such prospect is fickle, and fickleness mirrors greed as the inherently irrational vice of the previous examples. But the response to this set of examples is also similar. The satisfaction from fulfilling a long-standing desire is generally deeper than the enjoyment one derives from satisfying more immediate or fleeting desires. That is why a person who constantly shifts interests and pursuits is considered shallow. Thus again, what appears to Slote as a constraint on optimizing derived from past commitment is more plausibly interpreted as a rule of thumb (not a genuine rule) that indicates a typical means to optimization.

Slote likens the prudential to the moral sphere and sees the sort of responses I have been offering to his examples, reinterpreting his constraints on optimizing as disguised means to optimizing, as similar to the utilitarian who reinterprets every deontological constraint as a means to utility, or as similar to the egoist who claims that all apparent altruism is really the pursuit of self-interest. The utilitarian may recognize deontological rules or rights as constraints on first-order utility calculations, but she must view these as second-best strategies to maximize utility in the long run. (I have viewed moral rules as second-best strategies to maximize the satisfaction of rights or other moral demands not limited to utilities.) The argument against the utilitarian here is that these constraints are deeper: They apply even when it is known that they oppose ultimate maximization of collective utility. But it remains to be seen whether satisficing is, as Slote claims, more than a strategy to do the best one can over time given limited cognitive resources and competing desires. We have seen so far that his examples are plausible only when satisficing is viewed as such a strategy.

Slote also sees the interpretation of seemingly nonoptimizing choices as prudentially rational only when they really are better for the agent or from the agent's perspective as similar to the psychological egoist's interpretation of seemingly altruistic actions as really done for the agent's own good.[102] But here the arguments are not analogous. The egoist argues as follows: (1) When agents help others, it is because they want to. (2) If they want to, then they act for their own good (to fulfill their wants). (3) Therefore, agents always act only for their own good. This argument seems interesting only because it trades on an ambiguity in the concept of a person's own good. I believe there are two distinct concepts of self-interest that it is important to distinguish both here and in later arguments. The distinction mirrors one drawn in Chapter 1 between broader and narrower concepts of morality.

In the narrow sense, the concept of a person's own good contrasts with the concept of the good of others. The narrow sense is that in which people sacrifice for their children when they desire their children's welfare: What they sacrifice is part of their own welfare or own good. In this sense, not everything persons want, even when their desires are perfectly rational, are for their own good. Only a subset of a person's rational desires are those the satisfaction of which defines that person's narrow self-interest. This is the sense of self-interest according to which voluntary self-sacrifice is possible and can be accounted for straightforwardly.[103] A person's narrow self-interest is defined by her desires for herself or for how her own life goes, or by what persons concerned about her would desire for her.[104] They must be desires for states of affairs that make essential reference to the person herself.[105] Thus the satisfaction of my desires for my children's welfare does not contribute to my narrow self-interest; but desires that my children bring me pleasure by succeeding do contribute to my narrow good when fulfilled.

The broad sense of a person's own good, by contrast, is that in which, in desiring the good of my friends, I desire that their children do well, since that is an important part of my friends' welfare or good. In the broader sense of the concept, one's own good can include the good of others (if one desires that). Even doing my duty can contribute to my broad welfare if I rationally desire to do my duty. Here there need be no essential reference to oneself in the list of one's desires that define one's good. Hence, when the concept of one's own good is used in the broad sense, the previous argument by the egoist is sound but uninteresting. It says no more than that rational voluntary action is always in pursuit of some perceived good. When the concept is used in the narrow sense, premise 2 is false. People do engage in self-sacrifice to varying degrees, and their doing so does not serve their narrow self-interest.

This response to the egoist is not entirely new. What I want to establish is that it is Slote's position that suffers from a similar ambiguity in the notion of choosing what is less than best. The sense in which, contra Slote, it is never rational to choose what is less than best is that in which we refer to what is best *overall* among *available, known* alternatives. In this sense the claim is conceptually true, since the concepts of choice, reason, and goodness are closely linked here. Freely choosing an option is part of what it means to prefer it or think it better. Conversely, to evaluate an option as better is in large part to be disposed to choose it.[106] We can have no reason for choosing less than the maximum unless we think that in some sense this choice is better. (This allows for forgoing a local or short-term optimum for the sake of a global optimum or improvement, a strategy that has been prominent in our previous discussion.) Without a reason, even a potential reason, a choice is not rational.

We have noted that maximization of particular goods is often not best overall, even when one desires more of those goods and these desires do not compete at the time with others. There is often something to be said along Platonic lines for moderation or modesty, for maintaining control over our desires by restricting them. But our reason for restraint cannot be modesty unless in some sense we think that modesty is better than immodesty. Why cultivate modest desires if we do not think these are more easily satisfied, or will make us more cooperative, or in some other way better off (we can be modest or timid out of weakness of will, but that is not rational)? If we don't choose to be modest, but simply are, and not out of weakness of will, this still does not help Slote's position. If one's desires are moderate, then one is completely satisfied with less rather than more of what one desires. But then one is not better off with more. Slote's thesis is that one *is* better off (overall) with more and yet is still rational to choose less. His difficulty in providing a reason cannot be overcome by the appeal to modesty in desires.

We have now seen that we can view rationality in terms of choosing what is known to be better, or we can define goodness as what it is rational to desire in full possession of relevant knowledge. Other philosophers build the requirement of full knowledge into the concept of rationality itself, so that it is rational to desire only what one would desire if fully informed. There are several problems with this analysis. First, as Allan Gibbard has pointed out, an agent often has to choose a course of action or strategy based on limited information, and the rational choice may not match that which would be made from ideal knowledge of the situation. My best strategy for getting out of the woods in which I am lost does not take me where I would go if I knew the way out.[107] Thus rational desire (here, the desire to act on the best strategy) comes apart from goodness in the absence of relevant knowledge, as rationality comes apart from full information. Second, others have argued against the idea that goodness for an agent consists in what a fully informed counterpart would desire for that agent by pointing out that full information in the form of certain firsthand experiences or vivid representations can so change persons that they are then not open to

83

certain other sorts of experience or able to choose more rational alternatives. If I dwell on certain things for which I have a weakness or a strong aversion, this may terrify or harden me, biasing rather than strengthening my future choices. It is also questioned whether full information of various alternative lifestyles is even possible, whether the idea is coherent, given that the acquisition of such information would require adopting incompatible perspectives.[108] I might not be capable of knowing what it is like to lead certain kinds of life, for example that of a Tibetan monk, that might depend on not knowing what it is like to experience other lifestyles, for example that of a Hollywood playboy or analytic philosopher. Thus, the ideal of a fully informed person is both impossible or incoherent and irrelevant to both goodness and rational desire for an actual agent.

It remains the case that one seeks to improve one's desires, to transform them into reasons for action, by gaining relevant information, especially information about their origins and the consequences of acting on them. There is certainly a fact of the matter whether acting on particular desires will bring, or is likely to bring, satisfaction or frustration and a rational agent seeks to gain such knowledge. A person learns from experience, both negative and positive, as well as from other people what is good and bad for her. It might then seem that we could avoid the problems noted earlier that face the full information account of the good by requiring only such limited transformation of actual present desires.

Two considerations, however, block a definition of one's good only in terms of such piecemeal transformation of present desires. First, seemingly going back to the full information account of rationality and goodness, we must also allow for desires that an agent might acquire with more information when these new desires are not simply transformations of present ones. One might learn of possibilities not previously envisaged. How can we allow that the satisfaction of such desires is part of the proper conception of an agent's good while avoiding the previously noted problems for the full information account? It seems that we can do so only if we can stipulate that the agent's basic motivational nature will be held constant as these new desires are acquired. In that way, we might allow new and better motivations to be acquired without so changing the person as to make the new motivational structure irrelevant to her present good.

Second, people persist in their mistakes or continue to desire what they know has negative consequences. Irrational desires may persist even when false beliefs about the origins and consequences of acting on them are corrected. In the face of frustration and disappointment, agents may rationalize instead of adjusting or rethinking their desires. This brings us to the second requirement for rational desire and goodness if defined in terms of it. If people continue to be unhappy when they rationalize or persist in satisfying certain desires, or if knowledge of what it is like to experience certain satisfactions leads to overindulgence, for example in the case of addiction, this is because these desires conflict with others, producing tension and unhappiness when the other desires are sacrificed. If there are no such conflicts, then an addict may be better off continuing to indulge the habit. The presence or absence of such conflicts, given relevant information, is a matter of coherence.

Coherence requires that the satisfaction of lesser desires does not block that of greater ones, and that, on the second level, the informed subject desires to fulfill the desires whose satisfaction she pursues. New information that uncovers a motivational conflict, that reveals unacceptable consequences of acting on a particular desire, may not eradicate that desire. It may instead create a second-order motive not to act on the first-order desire. A rational agent maintains autonomy by giving priority to such second-order desires.[109]

Desires are more coherent when the satisfaction of some positively facilitates that of others, and when the subject later remembers with satisfaction instead of regret the fulfillment of earlier desires. These last points imply that rational desires must be coherent over time. We must, for example, discount present satisfaction by later regret and augment it by later pleasure in memory. We cannot derive the interest or welfare of an individual by simply summing the satisfactions of her desires as they occur because these satisfactions interact and are interdependent.

If we cannot hold a person's basic motivational nature constant while providing information that will make the person's good congruent with the satisfaction of her desires, if we cannot solve this problem facing the full information account of the good, then we might have to move to an objective list account of a person's good. We would then also move to an objective list account of rational desire, such that a person, if rational, must desire certain things. Support for this other kind of account might also derive from the claim that a fully informed and coherent subject might continue to prefer the "lower" to the "higher" pleasures. The full information coherence account answers that, if this preference is irrational or not in the true interest of the individual, this is because the higher pursuits afford deeper satisfactions. They do so because, as Aristotle, Rawls, and others have pointed out, people derive satisfaction from the full exercise of their capacities, and because satisfaction of more exalted desires connects with other satisfactions, conflicts with fewer, and provides pleasurable memories. By contrast, moving to an objective list account of the good or of rational desire ignores the fact that rational individuals seek to transform their desires not by checking them against some independent list, but by seeking to gain information about their satisfaction and coherence.

To return to the main argument against Slote, on either type of account of rational desire, we can continue to define goodness in terms of rational desire with full relevant information, or view rational choice and desire in terms of choosing or desiring what is best overall among known alternatives. The direction in which these definitions run is a pragmatic affair, a function of context and explanatory purpose. Whatever the direction, the connections between reasons, dispositions to choose, and evaluations are too intimate to allow the rational choice of what is known to be less than best overall among available alternatives.

Nevertheless, reasons, we should keep in mind, and therefore being best in terms of providing the strongest reasons, are relative to different domains. Narrow prudential and moral reasons can compete against each other or conflict, and I will argue later that neither sort is reducible to the other or necessarily takes precedence. Neither sort is necessarily best for an individual to follow. Hence there is no overarching rule telling us always to follow one kind or another. We can specify types of reasons more narrowly as well; for example, a person may have professional, legal, artistic, or familial reasons for doing what she does. Most of these narrower kinds can be subsumed under prudential or moral reasons for the agent in question, and I will therefore focus on them. There is also, however, the concept of an individual's broad interest, and this refers to what is best for the individual overall, those reasons on which it would be best for the individual to act, whether they be moral or narrowly prudential reasons. Derek Parfit adds to this list what he calls "present-aim" reasons.[110] Relative to this domain, what is best for an individual is what satisfies his (informed and ordered) set of present desires without concern for the future. I shall argue against Parfit that it cannot be rational to allow these reasons precedence over prudential reasons (this amounts to a demand for coherence over time among self-interested reasons), and so I restrict the list of reasons to those sorts mentioned earlier.

Reasons that define a person's interest derive from that person's desires, but only when these are properly informed and coherent. Desires do not in themselves constitute reasons. People can experience frustration and disappointment instead of satisfaction when their desires are fulfilled. Agents do not always act voluntarily in their own interest. They can be not only voluntarily self-sacrificial in relation to their narrow self-interest, but also voluntarily self-destructive in relation to their broad interest. There may be things that a person desires that are not in her interest, even broad interest, and things that are in her interest whether she desires them or not. While, as noted, the notion of best may be relative to domain – that is, what is morally best may not be (narrowly) prudentially best – the rational choice for an individual, when known to be available, is always what best satisfies her overall set of informed and coherent desires (if this account is preferable to the objective list account).

It might still be objected that the connection between something's being in my overall interest or best for me and my having a reason to pursue it is contingent, in that I have such a reason only if I have a concern for myself or for my own interest.[111] That something is in my interest in the future, for example, gives me no reason to pursue it now, it might be claimed, unless I am now concerned about my future. And I am no more rationally required to be concerned about my future than I am rationally required to be concerned about other people. This line of objection revives Parfit's present-aim theory. I have rejected that theory by requiring coherence among a rational agent's desires over time, but more needs to be said about the reasons for this rejection.

One more general initial question, however, is whether rationality requires concern for myself at all, even my present self. Intuitively, the answer is yes. A person with absolutely no such concern, with complete apathy toward himself, while possible, would be considered pathological. This marks a difference between self-concern and moral concern, or concern for others. While a person is considered pathological if she has no concern for any other person, one is not rationally required to be concerned about all those who might be affected by one's actions or one's culpable omissions. At least lack of such near-universal concern is not thought to be a mental illness. There is a connection, by contrast, between our notion of rationality, or sanity, and that of self-concern. In regard to concern for the future, a person with no such concern is a person without hope or fear – any hopes or any fears – and such a person would be barely recognizable as human. It is irrational not to fear certain occurrences if they are likely, especially if one fears other things; and it would be as bizarre to fear nothing as to desire nothing.[112]

One might object that the characterization of a person without desires, hopes, or fears for himself as pathological cannot be correct since this is an ideal of Buddhism, a major world religion.[113] But the claim that major religions can have pathological ideals should not strike post-Nietzschean philosophers as counterintuitive, no more counterintuitive than that they can advocate beliefs for which there is not a shred of evidence. I shall not argue either claim here. It suffices to point out that a person as described previously would lack self-interest instead of simply failing to pursue it. Rationality perhaps requires only that a person find some reason to pursue his self-interest if he has such. The good for an agent would be indeterminate if that agent lacked self-interest altogether.

According to Parfit, prudential rationality is unstable or vulnerable: If prudence is capable of overriding present aims, then it must give way to moral demands. The argument from prudence against present aims is that the latter are self-defeating. If one aims only at one's present good at each time, one does worse than if one sacrifices some goods now or endures some pains for the sake of greater goods or lesser pains later. But, Parfit holds, the same argument can be leveled against prudence by morality. If all pursue self-interest at the expense of moral demands, all do worse than if all respect those demands. I respond, first, that this does not imply that each person does worse by pursuing self-interest given what the others are doing. In the next section, I will explore whether a prudential rule to be moral is justified from the point of view of prudence as a solution to the classic prisoners' dilemma (and answer in the negative).

Parfit can answer in similar fashion that, from the point of view of the present-aim theory, I do better at each time by following it, although I do worse over time (worse at future times, perhaps at each future time, than I could have had I not followed it earlier). I respond that, since I am a temporally extended self, since I will be the same person who suffers a greater pain later to avoid a lesser one now, or who lacks a greater good later to obtain a lesser one now, this must be irrational. The present-aim theory can make no sense of weakness of will (since the considered judgment that the present urge overwhelms in such cases expresses a concern for the future), just as a broad notion of self-interest can make no sense of self-sacrifice. But, while the latter needs only to be supplemented by the narrow theory of self-interest, the former must give way to prudence, with which it directly competes.

Parfit's argument in the end depends on his denial of the ordinary notion of self-identity over time, the idea that I am an identical temporally extended self. For him, what can be salvaged from the notion of personal identity are only relations of psychological continuity that are a matter of degree, and that I can share with others to the same degree that I share them with my past and future selves. He therefore views the reasons for distinguishing between oneself and others as no different in kind from the reasons for distinguishing between times in one's own life. But in my own case, it certainly seems that I have more reason to prefer my interests to those of others than I have reason to prefer my temporally proximate concerns to more distant ones. All my futures while I am alive will be presents for me, while it is not the case that I will be all those other people whose interests I can affect. Furthermore, my projects extend to the future (the projected span of my life forms a natural boundary for them), to my future, and I have control over my intentions and plans in regard to them that I do not have over the similar states of other people. It is personal identity, indeed at bottom bodily identity, that makes the difference here, the sort of identity that Parfit dismisses as irrelevant.[114]

The upshot of this rather long digression is that the relation between optimizing prudence (in the broad sense, which may or may not reduce to the narrow sense for particular individuals in particular contexts) and rational choice is, and remains, conceptual, despite the objections of Slote and Parfit. The rational requirement of optimizing among known, available alternatives is compatible with the claim that we may have no coherent notion of our maximal good over a lifetime. Since our major life choices help to determine those later rational desires whose satisfaction measures our good, and since, as noted earlier, different life paths constitute different, incompatible, and seemingly incommensurable perspectives from which to judge personal welfare, we cannot always rationally rank these alternatives. Nevertheless, we can keep aiming at the overall best as we go along, either in local choices or globally, without ever knowing what could or would maximize our total good over our lives.

"If you are rational, you will choose what is known to be best (what is rationally preferred overall) among available alternatives." Does this tautology then correspond to a genuine second-order rule for ordering and following our preferences? The clarification of its status as a tautology, which was a primary motivation behind our consideration of Slote and Parfit, itself indicates a negative answer. Our rational choices themselves indicate what we take to be best among available alternatives. The tautology cannot generate an action-guiding rule at all. We can see this also from a related consideration mentioned earlier. We do not first note what our preferences are and then choose to maximize their satisfaction. Instead, what we call our rational preferences simply reify our informed and coherent choices among diverse and sometimes incompatible goods. Sometimes these choices are based on preexisting desires; sometimes they represent the discovery from experience of what is important or of what we like. Even when the former is the case, the choices are not collectively captured by rules for the same reason that our moral choices are not. In some contexts we rationally choose x over y and in others y over x, depending on a large and unpredictable variety of other interacting factors.

The three emphasized terms in our tautology (to be rational, choose the best *overall,* among *known, available* alternatives) leave much room for contexts in which it might not be best to optimize. When we are speaking of maximizing a particular good or kind of good (which may compete against others and not be best overall), or when we must search for or try to find out the best alternative that may not be known at present, it may well not be worth the cost to look beyond what is satisfactory and available (or to try to figure out when the cost of doing so begins to exceed the likely benefit). In such contexts we satisfice. We cut off the search for a best alternative when we have located a satisfactory one. In the real world we often do not know of all possible alternative actions; we lack full information about all their consequences; we must act within different time frames; and it may or may not be so important to achieve the best possible outcome in a given domain. In these contexts, both a rule to satisfice and a rule to optimize would be action guiding, a strategy that could be followed, but neither would be plausible in absolutely excluding the other strategy.

Could we then have a rule that tells us when to optimize and when to satisfice? Once more, the variety of relevant factors and the ways they may interact indicate a negative answer. The importance of having a better alternative, how much it costs to continue searching, how easy it is to find out alternatives, how probable it is that we can obtain or achieve a better one, how easily we are satisfied in the domain in question, whether optimizing in that domain will lead to less easily satisfiable future wants, whether it will compete with optimizing in other domains – all these factors are relevant, interact, and generate costs when we try to calculate them. Nor, finally, is there a rule available here as a second-best strategy to avoid serious errors in these calculations. Even the more reflective among us, I suspect, rarely make these second-order calculations. Our built-in and habitual mechanisms for doing what we feel like doing, or feel that we ought to be doing, at particular times may well work better for us over time than constant, deliberate calculation, whether rule governed or not. Such mechanisms might be predicted to work better in regard to self-interest than morality, which is not to deny the many potential causes of self-destructive behavior. Are these mechanisms themselves captured by rules? This question becomes irrelevant to the subject of practical reasoning, but I see no reason to assume a positive answer.

III. A PRUDENTIAL RULE TO BE MORAL

There is one other second-order rule that merits brief discussion. This is a prudential rule to act morally. It may be interpreted as a second-order rule because it tells us, at least in certain contexts, to count the interests or rational preferences of others equally with our own; that is, it refers to preferences themselves and not to their objects. Given the long tradition of philosophical argument on this topic, full discussion is obviously not possible here. But recognition of the relevance of our previous arguments regarding rules and of the different types of prisoners' dilemmas will throw some new light on the area. We will see why the main strategies for subsuming morality under prudence do not force us to conclude that prudence includes or implies a rule to be moral.

I argued earlier that prudential-moral prisoners' dilemmas generate mostly moral rules of thumb as their solutions. These are rules of thumb in that there are open-ended *moral* exceptions to the moral rules that solve the prudential dilemmas, and these exceptions are determined by the ordinary weights of moral reasons. Whether they are indeed rules of thumb or genuine rules has to do only with the form that moral requirements take. It says nothing about whether we can prudentially justify exceptions that are morally unjustified. The question now, by contrast, is whether there is a genuine prudential rule to accept moral requirements, whatever form these requirements might take. If there is a genuine prudential rule to be moral, then there are not open-ended *prudential* exceptions to this rule with reasons for them weighed directly against other prudential considerations.

A rule to accept a moral constraint on prudential optimizing seems to fit the paradigm for accepting genuine rules defined in Section I of this chapter. As Hobbes first noticed, this is a most important case in which individually optimizing actions result in a cumulatively inoptimal (according to Hobbes, disastrous) outcome. If each person pursues only her narrow self-interest in disregard for the interests of others, each does worse over time than if all accept moral constraints on such optimizing. The pursuit of narrow self-interest exclusively is collectively self-defeating. But this shows only that we collectively do better when we follow a rule to be moral, that is, that each of us is better off if all obey such a rule than if none do. As Hobbes also recognized, there remains the problem of individual motivation to follow the rule. The argument thus far does not establish what a prudential individual ought to do, given the behavior of others. Here the original prisoners' dilemma suggests that each is better off from the point of view of narrow self-interest trying to optimize, whether or not others accept moral constraints.

But this dilemma is defined only for single interactions, and the context is relevantly different when the same agents interact over time and can affect one another's future actions and reactions. Both Hobbes and contemporary decision theorists are interested in the latter context as closer to real situations in which we act. Within it they attempt to solve the problem of individual motivation by showing it to fit the definition of prudential rationality defended in the previous section. The Hobbesian tradition attempts to justify moral constraints along the lines suggested earlier for the justification of moral rules: as second-best strategies when first-best outcomes are unattainable. We will first look at Hobbes's argument and then at possible expansions or alterations of its premises. One question I will raise is whether the context of continuous interaction among agents is indeed the only relevant one. Another more troubling question is whether the rigid dispositions or strict prudential rules always to accept genuine moral constraints, or never to accept them when one can apparently profit from not doing so, exhaust the relevant choices facing real agents.

Hobbes's laws of nature tell us to accept moral constraints if others are doing so. His fundamental rules speak of seeking peace, accepting constraints on liberty if others do, and keeping agreements. His summary of all the laws of nature by the Golden Rule suggests their equivalence

92

to a fundamental rule to count the rational preferences of others on the same scale as our own.[115] But Gregory Kavka is correct in noting that Hobbes advocates only the weaker copper rule: "Do unto others as they do unto you."[116] This weakening of the Golden Rule makes it easier to justify morality by weakening its demands in relation to other conceptions, for example Christianity's, which calls upon us to turn the other cheek and love those whom we often can barely tolerate. Hobbes's fundamental rule does not only not ask us to turn the other cheek, but tells us to retaliate against violators (or even launch preemptive strikes against those who cannot be expected to behave morally). In this respect, it is probably closer both to that strategy to which biology predisposes us and to that advocated by contemporary rational-choice theory. This "tit-for-tat" strategy tells agents to cooperate with those who have not been known not to cooperate previously and to punish violators. Hobbes seems to intend something similar as the recommended prudential rule (although tit-for-tat calls for one-shot punishments, and Hobbes may intend something more severe).

For the sake of argument, and to make the proposal of a prudential moral rule more plausible, we may weaken the proposed rule still further. We can require not that individuals count the interests of others always as they count their own, but only that they not violate others' rights (who do not violate their rights). This modification is equivalent to a demand to count others' interests equally with one's own only when one's actions *strongly* affect them, and, as noted previously, when they can be predicted to act morally or to reciprocate. The question is why it would not be rational to violate this rule, or the rights of others, when one can predict benefit from doing so, given the optimizing theory of prudential rationality. We are interested here in the relation of narrow self-interest to morality. Later we will consider whether broad self-interest should include moral or altruistic motivations, that is, whether narrow self-interest is served by transforming itself in this way. For now, we want to know whether a person who does not desire to be moral for its own sake would nevertheless be prudent to accept moral constraints. Why should such a person not instead seek always to optimize, whatever others are doing?

Hobbes's two-pronged answer begins with his response to "the Fool" who asks the question we just posed.[117] While the Fool asks why a person ought not to violate particular agreements when he perceives it to be to his benefit to do so, Hobbes suggests a shift to a longer-term view. In contemporary parlance, we are to consider which long-term dispositions to develop in regard to keeping agreements or cooperating instead of considering only which immediate desires to satisfy. According to Hobbes, while individuals can certainly benefit on particular occasions by violating agreements or moral requirements, they cannot reliably predict that in the long run they will not be found out and excluded from further cooperative ventures, leaving them far worse off overall.[118] Thus, again in contemporary parlance, Hobbes is considering iterated prisoners' dilemmas without a predictable last encounter, and he recommends something like a tit-for-tat strategy within such contexts as likely to maximize expected utility or self-interest. Less technically, he argues along these lines that one is better off in the long run adopting a rule to be moral when others with whom one interacts on an ongoing basis can be expected to be moral.

His justification for this rule-bound strategy appeals to indefinitely continued interaction, the high probability of ultimate detection in wrongdoing, and the high stakes for being so detected. The last consideration might suggest to contemporary theorists that the best underlying strategy is not the maximization of expected utility, but a maximin or disaster-avoidance strategy.[119] Even in the absence of a state penal institution, the punishment that Hobbes envisaged, banishment from all future cooperative ventures, seems severe enough to warrant the adoption of a strategy that makes avoidance of this result the primary consideration. And adopting and following a rule to be moral implements this play-it-safe strategy.

Once more, it is the cumulative outcome (this time for the individual) of straightforward prudential calculations that is to be feared in the absence of a prudential rule. We should notice first, however, that despite this analogy, there is again a significant disanalogy with the paradigm case for genuine moral rules proposed in the previous chapter. Whereas in that context morally correct reasoning in particular cases led nevertheless to morally inoptimal outcomes, here the only fear is an eventual error in some single-case calculation. One must wrongly predict nondetection of some particular act for one to suffer the negative consequences. We may suspect right off, then, that the problem from a prudential optimizing point of view might be solved by raising the level of certainty (that one will not be detected in wrongdoing and excluded from future profitable interactions) that one requires before one breaks an agreement or acts immorally. From this point of view, this solution may seem superior to the adoption of a rule never to break agreements or act unilaterally in an immoral way.

A simple example. You are about to leave a restaurant where you have stopped to eat when traveling by car to a destination far from your home. It is raining hard, your car is parked in a distant lot, and you are recovering from a cold that might affect important business if it becomes worse. Near the door is a nondescript black umbrella that you happened to see a man leave there before he vanished into another room of the restaurant. You are very certain that no one will see you take that umbrella, certainly not its owner, and in the extremely unlikely case that someone will see and object, you can pass off the act as an innocent mistake. Assuming that you are a very forgiving person toward yourself and will not suffer pangs of guilt, that you do not easily form rigid habits, and that stealing umbrellas is not a habit of yours, can it really be against your narrow self-interest to take that one? Must you accept a weak rule and give the fact that the act is immoral extra weight if you are pursuing self-interest in this context where there is no real chance of sanctions?

The second prong of Hobbes's argument, of course, is the reinforcement that legal sanctions add against many forms of immoral behavior. For Hobbes, such sanctions not only threaten my own choice of immoral behavior but also, and perhaps more importantly, provide security that others will probably comply with moral and legal requirements. Only in the context of such security or expectation of reciprocation is moral behavior required in the first place. Together, these two prospects of social ostracism and legal punishment alter our natural short-term, purely self-regarding desires by adding negative utilities to certain immoral actions that would flow from them. The adoption of a rule based on the first consideration clearly represents a second-best strategy – gaining the fruits of cooperation by cooperating oneself when one cannot gain them in the long run without cooperating – but the addition of legal sanctions to immorality shifts it toward being first best in the particular case. Hobbes conceives the role of political institutions mainly in terms of these threats, but good social and political institutions can also encourage and facilitate moral, cooperative relations among citizens. Good social institutions should do both, thus closing further the gap between prudence and morality.

Nevertheless, given the costs of such institutions, often overlooked by Hobbes, they cannot close the gap completely. There will always remain antisocial or immoral actions from which individuals can predict benefit. These actions are either too costly to make illegal or, if they are illegal, too costly to punish at the level and efficiency at which expected utility from engaging in them is always negative. Many immoral actions are not illegal; many illegal actions go undetected and can be predicted to do so. Harms may also be imposed on victims with whom agents know they will not interact in the future. Thus Hobbes's first argument, the shift in focus from particular desires to long-term dispositions, remains the more important one.

The most serious problem with this argument, which infects contemporary versions as well, consists in the extremely limited list of dispositions that it compares. Given the choice only between always cooperating when others are or never cooperating when a utility calculation predicts benefit from defection, one may well be prudentially rational to choose or develop the former disposition. But this amounts to the choice between two strict or genuine rules; it ignores the possibility of behavior that is not rule governed, that is more context sensitive than genuine rules allow. The counterargument here parallels that in Section I of this chapter against the advocate of prudential rules to solve prudential-prudential dilemmas. There I pointed out that we need not choose between never snacking between meals and always snacking when the benefit in the single case seems to outweigh the negligible gain in weight. One can be more flexible and sensible in monitoring one's intake of snack calories over time. Similarly, one need not choose between always being moral when others are and always taking advantage when one can predict (bare) net benefit from immorality.

A prudential calculator may instead weigh many different factors when faced with such decisions: how much there is to gain from defection, how likely is future interaction, how certain is escape from detection, how important future interaction may be, how likely the ability to dictate the terms of such interaction may be, and so on. This may not be a straightforward utility calculation; as noted earlier, one may, for example, raise the epistemic standards or level of certainty at which one will defect, depending upon the combination of other factors. Given the possibilities of weighing and of affecting all these factors, even if the choice is limited to that between two dispositions that correspond to strong rules, the choice of morality may be prudentially justified only for those who cannot succeed in making their dispositions opaque to others[120] or for those who cannot nullify the capacity of others to retaliate. The stronger point remains that dispositions can be far more flexible than those considered by Hobbesians. While the latter are easily capturable by genuine prudential rules, the former are not.

The argument for the prudential rule is not yet defeated, however. It can be shored up with a third prong borrowed from Hume, specifically his suggestion that moral judgment as well as moral motivation builds upon our naturally altruistic sentiments.[121] If we combine this suggestion with the definition of broad self-interest to include one's interest in others, and with the fact that we can modify our desires so as to take a greater interest in others, we can see that a moral disposition need not be constantly supported by long-range considerations of narrow self-interest. It can instead become a natural expression of desire for others' welfare as part of one's broader self-interest. If such desires become nearly equal to one's self-regarding desires, then, especially when this possibility is combined with the two prongs of Hobbes's argument, it may seem possible to close the gap completely between prudence and morality. The question then shifts once more to whether it is in individuals' self-interest to seek to modify their initial desires in this direction.

Here it can be argued that the answer is yes.[122] First, when we broaden our interests to include those of others, we increase our chances of satisfaction and give ourselves more to live for. Many parents, for example, vicariously enjoy in their children's successes what they earlier missed themselves. Second, we can benefit from viewing ourselves as members of various communities, as genuine or valuable members not there only through the ignorance of the other members. By identifying with community causes and common interests, we again broaden the potential sources of our satisfaction. Third, self-respect is a major ingredient in a person's self-image, and persons with poor self-images are seldom happy. Individuals usually must gain self-respect by being respected by others, by meriting their esteem. To have self-respect we must see ourselves as earning it, and we earn respect first by our actions toward others. For all these reasons and more, as is well known, the most self-centered individuals, those who constantly seek only their own happiness, least often achieve it. Those who take an interest in the welfare of others and act to benefit them generally benefit themselves by doing so.

It is therefore a sound prudential rule of thumb to develop interests and concerns outside of oneself. Unfortunately, this does not imply that rationally one must adopt a genuine rule to be as impartial as morality (even a rights-based morality) requires. We need other-regarding concerns, but these need not extend to all those potentially affected by our actions; indeed, in order to contribute to our own well-being, they need not extend beyond our family, friends, and close associates. Few people count the interests of those beyond these circles as part of their own interests, and yet moral demands extend well beyond them.[123] Similarly, one perhaps needs to earn respect from those one respects, but not from all those who might be harmed by one's actions. The communities of which one is a member might treat outsiders badly while still contributing to their members' identities – mafia communities are (if one can trust Hollywood's image of them) among the most close-knit and self-reinforcing. We know from teenage gangs as well that respect within a group may be earned as easily by harming outsiders as by helping members. Depending on who one's peers are, peer pressure may operate for good or ill. Breaking agreements within one's community may cut one off from further enjoyment of its fruits, but one rarely conceives one's community as humanity as a whole, or even that portion of humanity that one may affect in some way or another. Conversely, making a personal commitment to be moral by adopting a strict rule may be one way to give one's life (more) meaning, but it is an unusual way, given the impartiality, indeed impersonality, of full moral demands, even when restricted to respecting rights, as opposed to commitments to family, friends, and personal projects.

I have been assuming that developing other-regarding concerns is prudentially wise, but the extent to which this is true can also be questioned. While increasing the range of our desires increases our chances of satisfaction, it also clearly increases our chances of frustration. We therefore find a philosophical tradition that argues for the opposite prudential strategy, for eliminating as many desires as possible, the satisfaction of which is beyond our control to guarantee.[124] The latter would include desires for the welfare of others whose welfare we cannot guarantee. When those we care about fare badly, this cannot increase our happiness. If our goal is to avoid suffering more than to achieve bliss, then the safe or maximin strategy would call for weakening affective ties to others. This strategy, then, would generally weaken other-regarding interests on prudential grounds.

The same considerations, however, would also call upon us to weaken desires for goods for which we have to compete. Competition, as Hobbes noted, is a major source of immoral behavior. Advocates of the prudential strategy currently under consideration would probably also view it as a major source of unhappiness. First, for those in very competitive situations, the agony of losing is probably greater than the thrill of victory, and the more competitive one is, the more difficult it may be to tolerate loss. More to the point here, competition means that success and the happiness that attends it are beyond one's control. If one's self-image is tied to such success, the risk is great.[125] The play-it-safe prudential strategy now being considered therefore advises avoidance of competitive contexts. If followed, it would thereby lessen violations of moral requirements as well, since intense competition often provokes breaking agreed-upon rules and acting in a hostile way toward rivals. Thus, while diminishing other-regarding interests may remove an incentive to moral behavior, it may also remove a major incentive to immoral behavior.

In sum, it is unclear which of these opposing strategies, augmenting or weakening one's other-regarding interests, is prudentially preferable. It probably depends both on one's initial psychological makeup and on the degree to which it is possible to modify one's desires in either of these directions.[126] Furthermore, as argued, it is unclear how adoption of either of these strategies would affect an individual's disposition to be moral. Regarding the first strategy, strong interest in the welfare of a few other individuals can, like self-interest, oppose morally required impartiality (in contexts in which such impartiality is required). It can also, of course, prompt moral sacrifice of narrow self-interest. Regarding the second strategy, there is the trade-off between weak other-regarding interests and weak competitive desires. While the overall effects of adopting either of these strategies on dispositions to be moral are unclear, it does seem clear that neither supports in itself the adoption of a genuine rule. It is prudentially wise neither to seek always to broaden our other-regarding desires nor to seek always to narrow them. Neither broadening nor narrowing them implies a requirement always to be moral.

Indeed, we can now conclude that all three prongs of the argument for a prudential rule to be moral do not obliterate the distinction between prudence and morality. I believe that experience and fiction both teach us that it can be more or less prudentially rational to sincerely accept moral constraints. Whether it is prudent to do so will depend on individual psychology, social institutions, and the particular circumstances of interactions from which benefits can be derived. Moral reasons cannot be reduced to prudential ones. It also follows, despite arguments on both sides to the contrary, that neither type of reason always overrides the other. While egoists have thought of rationality as narrow prudence, most ethicists have held that moral reasons by their nature override all others in determining what one ought to do, all things considered. I believe that both views are one-sided and incorrect.

One Kantian argument for the superiority of moral reasons runs as follows. First, a rational person is motivated primarily to act on her strongest reasons. She is so motivated not because they are *her* strongest reasons, but because they are her strongest *reasons*. A person so motivated will therefore also desire that other agents be rational, that they act on their strongest reasons. Since this desire is incompatible with narrow egoism, a rational person cannot be a narrow egoist. Second, fundamental rational principles, those that determine what counts as reasons, must be the same for all rational agents. So what counts as a reason for me must count as a reason for you in the same circumstances. Third, if I am rational, I must ignore irrelevant differences between persons, including irrelevant differences between myself and others. Reason is therefore impartial;[127] a rational agent acts on principles that are the same for all. When interests conflict, a rational agent therefore endorses moral principles as those that can be willed from an impartial standpoint. Such principles leave all better off collectively than they would be without them. Moral reasons express the impartiality of these principles and therefore reign supreme in motivating rational agents.

The answer to this argument focuses on the notion of a relevant difference. Relevant differences between individuals are, like reasons themselves, relative to domains. The fact that one person has red hair and another brown is not normally a morally relevant difference between them, but it is often an aesthetically relevant one. From the point of view of (my) self-interest, the difference between myself and others is very relevant. A rational self-interested agent acts on his strongest prudential reasons, while a rational moral agent acts on her strongest moral reasons. The former is not necessarily irrational *tout court* – from his point of view, the wants of others may not be reasons for him to act. As a rational self-interested agent, he is motivated to act on his strongest reasons because they are his, contra the first premise of the preceding argument. Most of us in fact are not motivated primarily to be rational; my wife, children, and even friends would resent that as my primary motivation for treating them as I do.

Intuitively, we recognize that a person is not irrational to take the difference between himself and others as relevant to his reasons. We do not react to immoral actions as we do to irrational actions. We are not baffled by the former; nor do we always attribute such actions to stupidity or ignorance. A fiend may be perfectly informed and coherent. Even a moral person, most of us will allow, may not be motivated to relieve all distress. She may not take the distress of persons very distant and unconnected to her to provide her stronger reasons to act than her own less urgent self-interested desires.

David Copp has recently agreed with the position I am defending here that neither moral nor self-interested reasons by their nature override. According to him, in order to determine that one type of reason overrides the other, we would need a third standard that is more important or central than either and that determines the priority between them. But we do not have this normative standard, according to him. And even if we did, in order to determine its priority, we would need a fourth standard, and so on.[128]

My argument is different. I believe that we do have a more encompassing, if not more important, standard, but that the priorities it establishes are relative to different individuals and different contexts. Remember again that both moral and narrowly self-interested reasons can be included in a person's broad self-interest. Broad self-interest can encompass not only the welfare of particular other people, but also social and moral goals of which the subject approves without direct benefit to himself. It then provides both moral and narrowly self-interested reasons and, in including both, can serve as our more inclusive third standard. Which type of reason overrides in a given context for a particular person depends on their relative strength within the person's broader set of relevantly informed and coherent desires. For a person who accepts both sorts of reasons, as most normal persons do, there is no set formula or rule for reasons which override. Priorities, where they exist, are captured not in some fixed percentage or rule, but in myriad settled verdicts reflecting which combinations of interests and values take precedence in particular contexts. The question of whether moral reasons override, then, can be answered only for particular agents in particular social contexts. Its answer for each agent is determined by whether she would choose, if informed and coherent, to be moral in that context.[129] Once more, the fact that morality leaves all better off collectively than they would be without it does not settle the question of whether it overrides prudence, which can conflict, for the individual.

The good news is that a general disposition to be moral is certainly compatible with prudential rationality as traditionally defined. It can be part of a good life, even the best life available for many individuals. For a morally motivated person, the question "Why be moral when your narrow self-interest opposes moral action?" is like the question "Why play tennis when you are forgoing other goods to do so?" Moral action itself can be among the goods a rational person desires. Morality seems different because its requirements typically oppose narrow self-interest. But feeding one's family or contributing to one's profession may also oppose narrow self-interest. It should no more surprise us that there are moral persons than that there are good fathers, good philosophers, or good tennis players.

It is prudentially rational in a narrow sense for me to become a moral person (shorthand for acquiring a set of different moral dispositions) if, when relevantly informed and coherent, I would see the benefit from doing so. Similarly, whether a moral solution to a prudential prisoners' dilemma is rational for each agent to accept depends on their psychologies and on the context – the likelihood of future interactions, the agents' relative powers, their self- and other-regarding desires, and so on. It is unlikely that acting morally would be irrational for a person. The moral choice itself would be evidence of his informed and coherent desires. For the action to be irrational, the motivations that prompted it would have to be eliminated by further information or coherence, or fail to match some objective list of rationally required desires, an unlikely outcome.

The bad news is that in real societies, with inevitably imperfect social institutions, no overarching moral rule can be rationally required of all individuals. For a rule to satisfy our optimizing criterion of prudential rationality, we must be unable to predict any informed and coherent aims that conflict with those of others with whom we interact, where the aims of others override from an impartial point of view, but we know that we can prevail without suffering overall negative consequences. But in fact, most of us are able to predict that we will encounter such situations on occasion. Collectively we must attempt to minimize them through threats, rewards, and social modification of self-centered desires. (Although in other contexts, a free market for example, such desires are seemingly to be encouraged.) But a rational person might want to resist the moral education that she advocates for others. And even a (mostly) moral person might treat a rule to be moral as only a rule of thumb or, more likely, a weak genuine rule (giving moral considerations extra, but not absolute, weight). That collectively and publicly we must advocate a strong rule that many individuals cannot sincerely accept as prudentially rational is the deep irony of moral education, indeed perhaps one of the ineradicable tragedies of the human condition.

With one exception, I have not in this chapter found a general need for genuine rules by which to direct our personal lives. There may be acceptable narrower second-order rules than those we considered, such as "Never place great stake in satisfying preferences that are highly unlikely to be satisfied." But even that one is only a rule of thumb, as is the rule not to adopt genuine prudential rules.

3

Legal Rules

In Chapter 1, I used as a paradigm context in which a strong rule is needed a judge's decision to enforce a bank's right to foreclosure despite unfortunate consequences in the individual case. The rule was supported by consideration of the cumulative effects on financial institutions and the practice of mortgage loans of judges acting on direct moral perceptions in such cases. I also suggested there that this sort of case could be generalized to a blanket duty of judges to defer to clear legal requirements even when they morally disagree with the outcomes of applying law in particular cases. Once again, while individual decisions on grounds of direct moral perceptions have minimal effects on the legal and political systems, the cumulative effects of allowing such decisions when opposed by law would nullify democratic institutions and must be avoided. Finally, I noted there that this fundamental moral rule for judges does not imply that the legal requirements to which they are to defer must themselves take the form of genuine rules.

Our questions for this chapter concern the extent to which legal norms do and should take this form. It is widely assumed, perhaps in contrast to the private moral sphere, that the need for uniformity and predictability in the legal system, and for limiting the power and discretion of those entrusted to enforce the law, means that legal requirements must typically be cast in the form of genuine rules. But, as we shall see, there are once more defects in rules and values to be considered on the other side. Before attempting to answer either the descriptive or the normative question in regard to law, I want to review also some of the initial classification of rules in Chapter 1 in order to compare and assimilate the usual classification by legal scholars of legal norms.

I pointed out initially that genuine rules, in the law and elsewhere, must be distinguished from mere rules of thumb and from what I called pseudorules. Genuine rules provide in themselves reasons for acting. At their strongest, they provide in themselves answers to normative questions. If the conditions for their proper applications are met, as this is determined by the meanings of the terms by which they state those conditions, then they tell us what to do in those contexts. Rules of thumb, by contrast, remind us of factors that are often normatively relevant. These factors must be weighed directly against others that may oppose them in given contexts, and the reasoning that takes place in those situations will consist not in simply applying the rules, but also in whatever that weighing consists in. We look through rules of thumb to the normative weights in context of the factors they mention and to whatever justifications there are for giving those factors particular weights. The rules in themselves do not add to these considerations. In the case of applying genuine rules, since such application in itself determines (or helps to determine) how to act or judge, we do not normally look through them to their justifications in order to give these justifying conditions their usual weights.

Genuine moral rules link nonnormative descriptions of factual situations to moral requirements. They tell us that if certain easily recognizable circumstances obtain, we should respond in a certain way, that is, certain moral requirements or consequences attach to our actions. Pseudorules, by contrast, are stated in purely normative and usually broad terms. In order to apply them, we must first decide whether perceived situations fit their normative terms, that is, we must interpret them as including in their extensions those factual situations.

I argued in Chapter 1 that both rules of thumb and pseudorules are dispensable. In indicating morally relevant factors (rules of thumb like "Be honest") or stating purely normative requirements (pseudorules like "Treat others with respect"), they both can be thought of as specifying certain core or paradigm cases or situations in which the value they represent can be taken to dominate (rule of thumb) and be clearly identifiable as doing so (pseudorule). Applying or deciding whether to apply these norms to other more controversial or ambiguous situations then consists in noting analogies and disanalogies to these implicit core cases.

Strong genuine rules do not require reasoning by analogy. They forbid us to make exceptions in cases falling within their stated conditions. They attempt to build exceptions (if there are any) into their statements of application conditions, or they are ordered lexically in relation to each other. Weaker but still genuine rules may be overridden in more or less extreme circumstances, but in themselves they still create a strong presumption of obedience and create reasons beyond those usually attached to the factors that justify their acceptance. If the latter condition is not met, then they collapse back into rules of thumb. We noted that the question of how this extra weight is to be granted to genuine rules that are not strong (in the sense of overriding or excluding all factors not mentioned in their statements) is a matter of considerable difficulty.

Frederick Schauer analyzes the extra weight of weak genuine rules, which he calls "presumptive rules," in two distinct ways (although he is not always careful to distinguish them).[130] First, he holds that decision makers operating under such a rule need take only a "quick look" at other factors to see if they might obviously overwhelm the rule in the present context. This understanding of "presumption" is necessary if rules are to serve the function of cognitive efficiency, simplifying the decision-making process; but in itself, it seems to allow contrary considerations to be weighed in the usual way once revealed. Schauer also speaks of the weight of reasons directly: We are to deviate from genuine rules only when there are strong reasons for doing so in the particular case. But repeating the requirement, or giving it a new name, as when the courts require "strict scrutiny" or a "compelling state interest" to override a rule barring distinctions based on race, leaves it problematic how decision makers will accord those factors that justify a rule more weight than they perceive them to warrant. That this problem is real in legal practice was evident in the *Bakke* case, for example, where Justice Powell held that racial diversity in university classrooms meets the test of a compelling state interest.[131] Finally, Joseph Raz thinks of rules as excluding certain reasons as bases for action. This account, however, infelicitously accords reasons not excluded their usual weight, allows excluded reasons no weight, and often leaves it unspecified which reasons fall into which class.

I have opted for the "extra weight" or "independent reason" account of the force of weak genuine rules, while admitting that it can be problematic to determine how this additional reason or weight is to be calculated. It will suffice here to allow that there can be weak genuine rules in the law and elsewhere. Rules are treated as such when they sometimes prevail even though decision makers believe it would be better in the particular case, all things considered (with all things given their usual weights), to make an exception, but when they are also sometimes overridden. Schauer holds that the First Amendment is such a rule because it protects the freedom of expression of speakers whom it would be better in the circumstances not to protect.[132] It also admits of numerous exceptions. It therefore is granted extra but not absolute weight, according to him.

Legal scholars do not often distinguish between weak and strong rules. They do, however, typically draw other distinctions among legal norms that roughly correspond to those I described in Chapter 1. Specifically, they now standardly distinguish between rules, standards, and principles. Rules are what we would expect – determinate and (ideally) mechanical in their application. They say that if certain routinely identifiable circumstances obtain, then a certain determinate response is required, or permitted, or that it will have a certain legal standing or consequence attached. Rules are once more opaque to their justifications; we usually need not look to the values that warrant their adoption in order to know when they are to be applied. Knowing their conditions of application involves knowing the meanings of the terms in which they are stated and how to verify the existence of certain uncontroversial factual situations. Examples are "No dogs allowed," "Stop at red lights," and "Two senators will be elected from each state." Both conditions of application and what is required in those conditions are clear in these examples of rules.

Standards, by contrast, are stated in broad, often normative, language, and the conditions of their application and/or the response they require, permit, or empower are often indeterminate, a matter of reasonable disagreement.[133] Legal standards, it is clear, correspond quite closely to what I have called pseudorules, except that they are explicit in the law and have legal consequences attached to their application. They indicate ends to be pursued and apply only when those ends can be furthered. Examples are "Exercise reasonable care," "Proceed with caution," "No state shall deny to any person within its jurisdiction the equal protection of the laws," and "No cruel and unusual punishment shall be inflicted." Like rules, standards explicitly promulgated in law must be followed when they apply, but their application is often a matter of dispute. Many cases are perceived as borderline when they arise, and standards must therefore be interpreted in terms of the ends they further in order to be applied to new cases.

Rules, by contrast, should have narrow borders. They may be over- or under-inclusive, but they should be definite and their application should be predictable.[134] They should rarely need interpretation. This claim contradicts a currently fashionable trend in legal theory to see all legal norms, including rules, as in need of interpretation and problematic in their applications.[135] But such rules as "Stop at red lights," "Presidents must be thirty-five years old," or "No dogs allowed" are not normally problematic to apply. Therefore, I claim, they need no interpretation. An interpretation is a certain kind of inference, an inference to the best explanation for certain (in this context) linguistic data.[136] We would need to interpret every rule, indeed every linguistic expression, if we always encountered them as meaningless marks or sounds to be explained by giving them meanings, or if we could never tell without reflection and inference whether perceived situations satisfied their stated conditions of application. But we do not encounter our native language or typical perceived situations in that way. In the case of rules like those just stated, we read their meanings straight off, and the natural ways we perceive situations normally tell us without the need for reflection whether they warrant the application of the rules. These rules are determinate in that there is normally no disagreement in practice about how to apply them to particular cases.[137]

This is not to say that we could not encounter hard cases in relation to any rule. Hard cases even in regard to clear and genuine rules can arise in three ways. First, there may be a degree of vagueness in all terms of a natural language, and hence, as Hart pointed out, there may be cases that fall within the vague borderline areas. (It would take some ingenuity, however, to find such borders for the three rules stated earlier.) Second, the application of a rule in a particular context that satisfied the stated conditions of its proper application might defeat or be irrelevant to the purpose for which the rule was enacted into law. Such is the case with Fuller's well-known example of a war memorial containing an army vehicle in violation of Hart's "No vehicles in the park" rule.[138] If the purpose of this rule is to maintain peace and quiet or to protect pedestrians, there seems to be no reason to prohibit the memorial that violates its literal meaning. But the case remains hard, because normally we are not simply to look through rules to their justifying conditions. The independent weight of a rule is to render those background reasons

108

more or less opaque (by making appeal to them less necessary) or to relatively weaken those reasons that oppose them. Third, the application of a particular rule might conflict with another value more important and more centrally at stake and protected by another legal norm. Such was the situation in the *Riggs* case, often cited by Dworkin, in which a grandson failed to inherit after killing his grandfather, despite the proper form of the will in which he was named the heir.[139]

In such contexts, rules require interpretation before being applied or withheld (narrowed or overridden). But well-designed rules minimize the occurrence of hard cases of all three types and hence the need for interpretation. Vagueness is to be narrowed or, ideally, eliminated; the aims behind the rules should be captured in their statements as far as is consistent with simple application; and conflicts among rules are to be resolved by exceptive clauses once discovered. In fact, all revealed counterexamples generate exceptive clauses, so that the ideal remains mechanical application. It is otherwise with standards, which often require judgment or interpretation in being applied. Since the conditions of their application are most often themselves conceived in normative terms, and since individuals, including officials within the legal system, disagree about the values or norms they accept and the relative weights they assign them, new applications are often contestable.

One point of emphasis and one caveat to the discussion thus far. First, not all rules will fail to be applied when doing so does not serve the purpose for which the rules were adopted. If no dogs are allowed and the purpose of the prohibition is to prevent irritation to customers, it still may be the case that a dog causing no irritation whatsoever will not be allowed. Applying the rule strictly and mechanically, treating it as a strong rule, saves time and effort in having to think about how to apply it to particular cases and, in the case of rules such as this one, errs on the side of caution if at all. (A seeing-eye dog might, however, be allowed because of the overriding competing value, but this exception should be built into the full statement of the rule.) If a president must be thirty-five years old, and the purpose of the rule is to ensure wide experience and mature judgment, an enormously experienced and mature thirty-four-year-old nevertheless cannot run for that office. These rules then contrast with Fuller's conception of the "No vehicles in the park" rule. This difference is a matter of the rule's strength or vulnerability to considerations relating to its justification. We can conceive of a continuum here, but if too many exceptions can be generated by situations where application is inconsistent with or irrelevant to the aim, the rule degenerates into a rule of thumb, a legally relevant factor that may always have to be weighed against others. The benefits of definiteness and predictability are best ensured by strong rules. It is often assumed in legal texts that rules will not be applied when the results are "absurd," but this is clearly not the case. Nor should it be, unless we want to grant to officials the kind of broad discretion that it is often a purpose of genuine rules to limit.

Second, it may be controversial how to fit certain legal requirements into the standard classifications. Consider the First Amendment prohibition of laws abridging freedom of speech. This is often thought of as a standard, governing core cases that involve political speech and extending to other forms of expression whose value will have to be weighed against competing values such as security or freedom from offensive displays. Under this reading, "speech" is conceived as a technical term or term of art, equivalent to a normative term whose core meaning refers to political speech. Or we can think of the requirement, as Schauer does, as a weak rule to be granted extra, but not absolute, weight against all competing values. Here we think of speech in its literal sense as any verbal, written, or, derivatively, behavioral expression, but view political speech as having the greatest value for upholding democracy and allow numerous exceptions when other forms of speech are at stake. The practical implications of these two conceptions may be the same, which would make it impossible to decide between them (except perhaps on grounds of consistency with our conceptions of other constitutional restrictions), but they remain different conceptions.

I have said that genuine rules rarely need interpretation but that standards or pseudo-rules typically do. What is it to interpret a rule or standard as a preliminary to applying it? One must first appreciate the core cases, real or hypothetical, governed by the norm. In the case of a rule, these will be cases falling under its plain meaning, and in the case of a standard, they will be cases in which its central value is clearly violated (e.g., in which equal protection or due process is clearly denied or reasonable care not exercised). One must then find a basis for extending or refusing to extend the norm from its core applications to the case at hand. When the legal norms result from legislative enactment, one way to do this is to seek the intent of the legislature or framers of the law. Here the explanation for the norm that the interpretation specifies lies in the intention that produced the norm. One can ask whether (a majority of) the legislators would have intended a particular result in the case at hand if it had occurred to them, or whether they would have intended the result if they had full knowledge of the intervening events and changed circumstances. These two questions may not have the same answer. Especially the second may be very difficult to answer, and the legislative history may not provide reliable evidence in regard to the first either.

Alternatively, one might ask what the purpose or aim of the norm is plausibly conceived to be, what value or values it best serves. One must then decide whether that aim or value is best furthered by applying the norm in the controversial case, and whether that case involves competing values that might override and therefore relevantly distinguish it from the core cases to which the norm applies. These latter questions are equivalent to asking whether there are relevant differences between the present case and the paradigms to which the norm applies, since relevant differences will consist in values attached to the new facts that nullify or override the value specified by the norm.

Looking for the aim or purpose behind the rule or standard is not, however, necessarily the same as seeking the intent of the legislature that enacted it. Consider as an example the question of whether the Civil Rights Act of 1964 allows voluntary quotas for minorities in training programs, whether its ban on discrimination prohibits all quotas. Legislative records might (contestably) indicate that a majority of legislators would at the time have opposed racial quotas of any sort. But if a major purpose of the law was to increase the representation of minorities in the economic mainstream, and if prohibiting discrimination without allowing quotas was not going to achieve the desired result, then one might answer the question differently by seeking purpose rather than intent. (If one instead saw the main purpose of the legislation as the ultimate creation of a color-blind society, one might answer either way on the specific question, depending on one's view of a very complex set of facts and hypotheticals.)

In the case of the common law, of course, there is no legislative enactment, and the question of intent becomes less relevant. One's view of legal interpretation thus becomes more uniform if one always seeks purpose instead of intent in interpreting legal norms for controversial application. But, as we shall see, there may be other reasons for seeking intent in the case of enacted legal norms. The issue of seeking intent as a means of interpretation will turn out to bear on the normative question of whether we should read the law as a system of rules. But we have other business to clear away before turning to that issue.

Having distinguished legal rules from standards (principles will be discussed later), let us turn first to the question of whether (American and British) law in fact consists mainly in genuine rules. Given our project, our main question in this chapter is whether we *should* interpret law in terms of rules. But given the prominence of discussion in the philosophy of law of the factual question of whether the law *does* consist of rules, there is good reason to address this issue first. Doing so will in fact better motivate our main investigation here, since my preliminary thesis will be that this factual question, lacking a determinate answer, naturally dissolves into the normative one.

The most prominent legal scholars disagree about whether law is best analyzed as a system of rules, although the dominant tradition has certainly been to so describe it. My answer will differ from all the prominent positions in the philosophy of law, and it may seem disappointing. It is that there is no right answer to the descriptive question, no conceptually correct answer and none that holds across time and across different styles of adjudicating, because the same laws can often be read and treated in practice as genuine rules or as somewhat weaker constraints. Although the manner in which the law is written can encourage or discourage reading it as genuine rules, it does not force any one treatment in practice. The normative issue will then become central. But let us first see how the most prominent legal philosophers have disagreed.

The taxonomy provided in Section I accords with the recognition of (early) legal positivism, in the theories of Austin and then Hart, as a picture of law as mainly a system of genuine rules. As defined by later defenders, the essence of positivism lies not in the thesis that law consists mainly of genuine rules, but in the thesis that law is identified by using a rule of recognition, a way of identifying law, that is itself a matter of social practice. This thesis implies that it is possible for law to be identified independently of other norms, and specifically of moral considerations.[140] Law so determined might or might not consist mainly in rules. But in Hart's theory it does, and there is a natural connection here. The connection consists in its being a natural way for the identification of law to exclude other normative considerations that law be a special set of rules (identified by their institutional pedigree), since rules by their nature override or tend to override considerations not mentioned in their conditions of application. If law consists in identifiable rules, then we need not look to political or moral considerations in order to apply it, since we do not need to look through rules to their justifications in the course of normal application.

Thus it is no accident that in the latest version of Hart's theory, rules collectively fail to determine legally correct decisions only in cases that fall outside their central cores or plain meanings. When a case does fall under the plain meaning of a rule, it fails to determine the result only when another rule applies and is judged to be more important.[141] And, of course, the validity of legal rules derives first from their pedigree, from their source in recognized legal authorities, and not from their content or moral justification. Thus rules in Hart's system are genuine. While not quite strong in the sense defined, rules are deemed by Hart to be "near-conclusive" and clearly to be contrasted with "variable standards as 'due care.' "[142] When legal rules apply, legally correct decisions are determined only by them and not by the morality of their outcomes.

Despite this connection between the main positivist thesis that law is a separate normative domain and its characterization of law as a set of pedigreed rules, the latter thesis, while sufficient for the truth of the former, is not necessary for its truth. The imposition of genuine rules (other than the rule to obey the law itself) is only one way to shield judicial decisions from the input of personal moral opinions. If, for example, we instead conceive the body of settled law in terms of settled cases – both actually settled cases and those core hypothetical cases uncontroversially determined by the apparent rules and standards of legislative and constitutional enactments – then whether law is independent of morality and other norms depends on the way the legal system allows contested cases to be distinguished from this settled core. If differences between contested cases and settled ones necessary for distinguishing the former derive only from values recognized or implicit in the law itself, then law remains a separate domain. If such legally relevant differences require even widespread social recognition or support, judicial decisions are shielded from the personal morality and politics of the judge.

Thus, while there may be a necessary connection between the theses that law is an autonomous normative domain and that there is a rule for identifying it based on institutional pedigree, it is a mistake to see a necessary connection between the thesis of autonomy and the claim that law consists mainly of genuine rules. Much other allegiance to the latter claim derives from similar mistakes. Several recent writers assume that the normative force of law itself requires that it take the form of rules, that facts in themselves can have no normative force, that they remain motivationally inert until or unless they are connected to rules or principles.[143] But, while Hume may have been correct (I take no stand here) that facts must be connected in some way to desires or values in order to motivate us, these values need not be captured in a set of universal prescriptions. As we saw in Chapter 1, our own values cannot be so captured, and yet they are what motivate us.

Other writers assume that the generality, impartiality, or predictability of law necessitates its consisting in a set of rules. Rules are general, impartial if they are formulated and applied as such, and they do increase predictability, but once more, they are not necessary for these purposes. Requirements are general if they are not aimed at particular individuals, but instead at all persons of a certain class. Requirements transmitted through analogical reasoning from decided cases satisfy this criterion as long as being a particular individual is not considered relevant to decisions. Relevant differences between cases need not themselves be captured by rules in order to be generalizable.[144] They can be generalized without being universalized (I shall have more to say on this in the next chapter), reflecting values that justify past decisions and statutes. Finally, in regard to the assumption that individuals' ability to know what the law is and to predict outcomes of legal disputes requires standing rules,[145] settled cases can again serve this function. Often only lawyers can predict legal outcomes, and they can know that some present hypothetical case will or will not be distinguished from a settled one without knowing sufficient conditions for determining outcomes.

At the other end of the spectrum from Hart on the question of whether law in fact consists mainly in a set of rules is Dworkin. In his early writings, Dworkin contrasted and characterized his own view of law as a union of rules and underlying, justifying principles, as if Hart had gotten the rules part right but had only overlooked the principles. In later writings, Dworkin made it clearer that for him rules apply in every case only because of the relative weights of the principles that justify them.[146] We always look through them to their deeper justifications, which is why British critics accuse Dworkin of "playing fast and loose with the law."[147] What these critics recognize is that for Dworkin there are really no genuine rules of law.[148] If we were required to look through genuine rules in this way and weigh their justifying factors ordinarily, then they could not serve their essential functions of simplifying the normative universe and limiting the judgmental authority of those who are supposed to apply them. Rules simplify and limit authority precisely because they normally determine judgments only according to the factors they mention. For Dworkin, not only do we always look through apparent rules to their deeper and more general justifications, but unstated principles always determine whether or not to apply the rules to particular contested cases. Such principles as that of legislative supremacy mandate that rules enacted by legislatures ordinarily will be applied, but such norms may always have to be weighed against competing principles in contested contexts.

There is therefore a deeper contrast between Dworkin's theory and Hart's than at first appeared (and this despite Dworkin's allowing preinterpretive law and Hart's granting that rules need not be strong). The latter remains a theory of law as genuine rules; the former, still in effect, denies that there are or even could be genuine rules in law. In my initial taxonomy for this chapter, I mentioned principles but did not characterize them. This is because they are peculiar to Dworkin's theory of law and because, in opposition to Dworkin, I do not believe that principles, as opposed to rules and standards, are a genuine part of the law. As now indicated, principles are supposed to be like standards in being formulated in broad normative language, but unlike standards, they are not normally stated in the law as written, and they are always to be weighed directly against competing principles. According to Dworkin, they are universal norms implicit in law as the justifications for past judicial and legislative decisions.

Dworkin views these principles as constitutive of coherence in the body of law, which is necessary for viewing the law itself as the expression of a genuine community and therefore as having genuine normative force. In his earlier writings, he saw them as the proper compromise between deference to prior institutional acts (since the principles must fit or imply most of the settled law) and moral adjustments necessary to achieve justice in the new individual case (since the relevant principles are the morally most appealing that fit), between adherence to the past and to democratic legislative decisions and fresh judicial input. Given the fallibility of judges, we don't want to grant them complete discretion, but neither do we want to lock them into past mistakes that generate harmful absurdities. In light of this justification for including justificatory principles in the body of law, the criticism that Dworkin's principles are neither morally pure or correct nor rules that are predictable in their applications is beside the point.[149] But whether coherence in law really requires Dworkin's principles, whether they are indeed what justifies enactments of rules and standards, and whether their relative weights determine which rules will be applied to particular cases are more pertinent questions.

Dworkin understands coherence in the body of law, as well as the justificatory explanations for rules that are necessary for interpreting them, in the terms of an older model in the philosophy of science, what was called the "deductive-nomological model." The ideal here was an overarching theory in which lower-level laws would be explained by being deduced from higher-level or more general laws until scientists arrived at the few most general and deepest laws at the top of the unified system. Similarly, for Dworkin, a normative theory of law specifies a series of nested aims, beginning with statutes and decisions as universal prescriptions that are explained by being deductively implied by more and more general universal principles, until (in our legal system) we arrive at the supreme principle, which for him requires equal concern and respect for all citizens. The higher levels of generality explain the lower by justifying them, and hence the former determine the normative force of the latter.

My picture is very different, not as beautiful perhaps but more true to life. I see rules and standards as indicating a set of core cases (which come closer to exhausting the normative force of rules). New cases must be assimilated to or differentiated from these by looking to the values expressed by the norms and at stake in the cases. I agree with Dworkin that at least one way to interpret a rule is to explain it by finding the purpose or aim behind it, the value it serves to protect. But this value once more need not be captured by a principle, with its misleading claim to universality. It is to be pursued or protected in the core contexts, and beyond them, depending on other values at stake and the orderings among them (once more as established by settled cases).

Dworkin's principles are then dispensable in favor of particular values and the constraint of not judging cases differently without relevant differences between them affecting the ordering of those values. When this constraint is satisfied, legal decisions are coherent. There need not be, and indeed there is not, a monistic system with a single principle at the top. Instead, the American legal system, reflecting a rich, diverse, and sometimes tumultuous institutional history, represents independent and often conflicting values. The system is nevertheless coherent when orderings among these values are preserved across contexts with no differences that generally alter them. Even single statutes can reflect such different and independent values, as when an exception to the protection of minority applicants is made in the Civil Rights Act for small-business owners in order to protect their freedom to hire, for example, their offspring. Even as individuals, we are unlikely to endorse a monistic, deductive system of values unless we are extraordinarily single-minded, and certainly not as a pluralistic society.

As to principles determining the application of rules, what determines whether strong rules should be applied is that situations fit the plain meanings of their terms. If we were always to look through them to their justifications, and if these justifications consisted in the hierarchy of universal principles envisaged by Dworkin, then it would be difficult to see why judges should not always apply the principle of equal concern and respect directly. What determines whether weak rules should be applied is the extra weight they add to particular values as these are normally ordered against competitors, as this weight is gradually specified in particular decisions.

We do, however, as Hart maintains, also have higher-level rules that guide us to the proper sources of law in their proper order. Some of what Dworkin calls principles, especially those that help to determine the application of rules (such as legislative priority or constitutional supremacy), are really metarules that determine priorities among legal sources. These rules are given extra, if not absolute, weight prior to the consideration of lower-level rules. Other so-called principles, we have seen, are dispensable. By contrast, when we interpret genuine legal rules and standards in terms of hypothetical cases in which priorities among values are established, we are not dispensing with them. As written into law, they create their own cores of (hypothetical) settled cases. Principles do not create such cases. They are exhausted by their supposed role in justifying past legal decisions, a role that is really played by particular legally relevant factors (thought to be universal only because of a misleading analogy with an old view of theory construction in science).

The normative force of law can derive from the rights of legislatures and judges to create and apply sanctions attached to their rules and standards. These rights derive from the need for social order. Beyond consideration of such threats, the obligation to obey laws can derive only from their moral content. It need not appeal to some Hegelian or Rousseauian conception of a community with a monolithic value system – a dangerous notion, I believe, even when its supreme principle has an individualistic ring. Absent the old model of scientific theories, coherence in the set of values embodied in a society's legal system does not require this kind of simple deductive structure.

The upshot of this discussion of Dworkin is, first, that we can no more say that the law cannot consist mainly in genuine rules than we can say that it must do so. Second, we need not expand our initial classification of legal norms into rules and standards so as to include unstated but implicit principles. The main descriptive question at this point seems to be whether the law consists mainly of genuine rules opaque to their justifications, as in Hart's account, or whether it reduces to real and hypothetical cases from which other cases may be differentiated according to further legally relevant factors. We have seen that for Hart, rules are typically almost strong, to be overridden in particular cases to which they apply only by other rules. If the ideal is to resolve all such conflicts by building in exceptive clauses, and if the borderline areas of rules, as opposed to standards, are to be as narrow as possible, then the model of law for Hart is really a system of strong rules.

More recently, Frederick Schauer has argued that judges generally treat law as weak genuine or presumptive rules. Law, according to him, generally consists in rules that have "presumptive but nonconclusive force"[150] (see Section I for his explanation of such rules). My thesis in regard to the descriptive question is that none of these theories is conceptually, or likely to be uniformly descriptively, true. Not only can't we claim that the law *must* consist or *must not* consist (mainly) in rules, we cannot even claim that (American) law *does* or *does not* consist mainly in rules. The reason is that writing and reading law as genuine rules is primarily a matter of jurisprudential normative philosophy and style, and such philosophies and styles differ among judges. If apparent rules can be read as genuine or not, the descriptive issue gives way to the normative. My second thesis is that the normative question of whether law *should* be treated as genuine rules should be answered in the same way as the broader question of when rules in general should be given normative force.

Before developing and defending these theses, I want to note a yet weaker stance toward rules than those that take them to be strong or presumptive (weak). The weaker stance is what Schauer and Gerald Postema call "rule-sensitive particularism." Here a decision maker will weigh all normatively relevant factors, *including the value of adhering to rules* in such contexts, but without giving the latter consideration extra weight. Postema holds that presumptive rules must collapse into rule-sensitive particularism, possibly because he believes it irrational to give rules extra weight beyond the value of having and adhering to them.[151] I shall indicate later why he is wrong, why in the primary context in which rules are needed, agents cannot be trusted to gauge these weights or values, and specifically the value of following a rule. There are once more contexts in which it would be better in the particular case to override that value (since one exception will not nullify the rule or its value), and yet the rule should be followed, that is, we should not trust agents to weigh values directly at all. The same description of that context will show why Schauer is wrong in claiming that proper adherence to or overriding of presumptive rules typically depends on the degree of injustice from adherence in the particular case.

It also cannot hurt to remind ourselves a final time of the weaker constraint that practical reasoning must follow in the absence of rules. This is the demand not to judge cases differently without being able to cite a relevant difference between them, now a legally relevant difference, a factor that generally makes a legal difference. Reasoning in accord with this weaker constraint is the same as reasoning from analogies and disanalogies to paradigm cases, and I have been emphasizing that such reasoning is different from applying genuine rules, which state determinative conditions in advance. The constraint is clearer in application, however, than rules of thumb or standards that simply state factors that must be taken into account and weighed against each other. This constraint makes it clear how factors that are determinative in some cases must be weighed. According to it, they will determine other cases in the absence of closer competing analogies or relevant differences between the cases in which they appear. In addition, a factor that overrides another in one case will do so in another absent a relevant difference between the cases. The distinction between this constraint and genuine rules cannot be overlooked.

III. THE DESCRIPTIVE QUESTION: SOURCES OF LAW

Given our account of rules, we have seen that we can ask both descriptive and normative questions of legal systems. The descriptive question is whether the law consists mainly of genuine rules, strong or weak. As noted, seeking an answer within the American legal system, where requirements that are or can be stated as rules can be interpreted as genuine rules or as weaker constraints, only leads to the normative questions of whether judges ought to view the law as a system of rules and ought to write decisions so as to encourage that view. While there are some uncontroversially genuine rules to be found in all the different sources of American law, whether other legal requirements, the preponderance of law, are viewed as rules depends on the style of lawmaking and even more on the accepted normative theory of jurisprudence that tells judges how to read these requirements.

It may seem instead that the main variable here is the particular source considered. We might think of legislated statutes more in terms of genuine rules than the Constitution or the common law. But there is once more leeway for different readings of law from all three sources. In all three sources we find some law that is written as if it were to be read as genuine rules, some law phrased as broad standards, and always the option to read law either as a set of settled cases to and from which others are to be assimilated or differentiated, or as mainly a set of genuine rules that are generally to be applied without looking through them to their justifications. I shall expand upon these claims separately in relation to the three main sources of law. This will require brief forays into political philosophy, since understanding the different political functions of these sources is relevant to how they should be read.

The Constitution limits the authority of the central government by dividing its branches, dividing its powers with the states, and reserving certain fundamental rights to the people as individuals. In the last function, it limits the power of the majority of people themselves through their elected representatives by written norms that protect individual rights. The federal courts, whose members are not elected, enforce these limits through judicial review. This aspect of constitutionalism derives from fear of the power of government, including democratic government. A main problem for constitutional theorists in the tradition of democratic political theory has therefore been to address the seemingly antidemocratic thrust of these limits.

A main tack has been to deny that they really are antidemocratic, despite appearances. One way to do so is to assimilate constitutional constraints in the protection of individual and minority rights to prudential rules by which individuals limit their own future power of choice. According to this analogy, the people themselves, or the majority of them, fearing that in a future time of weakness or temptation they will trample their own individual rights, or those of a minority of them, pass rules that severely limit their future ability to do so. This is not antidemocratic since, as in the case of prudential rules, the people here are choosing to limit themselves. The provisions of the Constitution that limit legislatures in order to protect rights are collective prudential rules according to this view.

There are many problems, however, with this argument. First, even if we accept the analogy, its force is not clear in light of the argument of Chapter 2. We found there that prudential rules are rarely needed, since individuals can often do better for themselves by monitoring their own yielding to temptation and making exceptions to the rule of thumb not to yield when the exceptions fall below the threshold at which cumulative harm results. We also noted in Chapter 1, however, that collectives may not be able to monitor their activities over time in the same way, and here we are speaking of a collective. But these points may not be of great relevance here because of the second and deeper problem with the argument: the failure of its central analogy.

The first disanalogy is that, while in the case of prudential rules for individuals, it is the same individual who will in the future be restricted by her present decision to adopt a rule; in the case of constitutional constraints, it will be different majorities who are constrained in the future by the currently adopted norms. Shifting the time frame forward, we may ask why a present majority that views present legislation as politically justified should be restricted by a different opinion of a much earlier majority in very different circumstances. The problem of time in itself might be solved by a conception of the American people as a continuous (self-identical) community over time. But even if some notion of identity over time can be relevantly extended to this collective, the problem for this way of holding democracy and constitutionalism compatible runs yet deeper. The present majority (or its representatives in the legislature) is restricted not simply by a previous one, but also by the opinion of an unelected aristocracy as to the proper interpretation of what the previous majority did.[152] The present majority may not be suffering from weakness of will, as in the paradigm case for prudential rules, but may simply disagree as to the legitimate boundaries between individual rights and collective interests.[153] They may disagree with the judges as to whether the present legislation is constitutional. The breakdown of the analogy here leaves us no reason to view the opinion of the small group of judges as the democratically endorsed one.

Dworkin has taken a more radical tack in attempting to evade the conclusion that the Constitution is antidemocratic in limiting the power of the democratically elected legislature. He denies the majoritarian conception of democracy, with its "majoritarian premise": that collective decisions must be those favored by a majority, even a rational majority. But the majoritarian conception of democracy is like the feline conception of cats or the unmarried conception of bachelors. One might deny it for rhetorical purposes, but then one's argument will not differ much from that of those who hold that certain fundamental individual rights are more important than strict majority rule, that is, democracy (although one important right to be weighed against others is the right to an equal say in political decisions, which only pure majoritarian democracy affords). Individual rights are not well protected by democracy per se (although they may be in the absence of a constitution by a strong tradition of protection). When a majority oppresses a minority, the fault is not that this action is undemocratic; the fault is in democracy itself.

When the majority of people lack control over officials, that is, judges, who make decisions that limit their representatives, this is antidemocratic, although it may well be justified by competing and overriding values. We in this society have never been pure democrats, although we have always recognized majority rule as one important political ideal among others. If we were pure democrats, we would have opted for direct democracy, which has certainly been technologically feasible for some time if it has not always been. But our commitment to certain individual rights is more fundamental; and if we do not view democracy as a competing value, we can view a limited constitutional democracy as the best means to protect those rights. As to the question of why an aristocracy of judges, and specifically justices of the Supreme Court, should be the ones to enforce constitutional limits on majoritarian rule, the answer is that they are both trained to do so and likely to be as neutral as any officials between the majority's representatives and the minority whose rights are at stake.

If we do view the Constitution as a source of limits on democratic rule, it may seem best that those limits be imposed in the form of strict or genuine rules. Rules by their nature limit authority, and if we must allow a judicial aristocracy to enforce the limits to democracy, we may want to grant them only minimal discretion in doing so, minimal authority to interpret constitutional provisions as they see fit. Genuine rules limit discretion in this way. Thus we might expect constitutional norms protecting individual rights to be in the form of rules. What we find instead when we look in the Constitution for rules are those that define the basic powers, functions, and makeup of the different branches of government, not those norms that protect individual rights by limiting legislative power.

The Constitution contains many rules specifying the structure of the three branches of government, requirements for holding office, for enacting federal laws, and so on. Many of these rules clearly prevent us from looking through them to their justifications. They are not only genuine but strong. That senators must be thirty years old is unjustified in relation to mature and brilliant twenty-nine-year-olds. But the framers of the Constitution did not want to give other officials or even voters the authority to judge the maturity of potential candidates under thirty. Such discretion might be difficult to exercise fairly and accurately and not worth the trouble, given the seriousness of errors here and the abundance of candidates over thirty. Thus a simplifying strong rule is in order.

In general, the framers could define the basic structure of government, the powers and functions of the different branches, and the criteria for holding various offices in terms of strong rules because this structure was intended to be permanent, or at least relatively unchanging. Stability, which is crucial here, allows few exceptions. Furthermore, such basic structural matters can be agreed upon by people with different values or substantive moral views, even views about which rights need protection when. Finally, it is not as important to be able to differentiate cases in a morally fine-grained way when norms are conferring powers instead of imposing constraints or burdens. It is true that power is limited at the same time that it is granted. But there is a difference between limits on jurisdictions and qualifications and limits in explicit protection of individual rights. The former once more can normally be defined by unchanging and relatively exceptionless strong rules.

This does not mean that all power-conferring clauses of the Constitution take the form of rules. The power of the federal government to regulate commerce is said to have been read in the nineteenth century narrowly as a rule, but is typically conceived more recently broadly as a standard.[154] But power-conferring rules and standards in the Constitution have not been the main subject of dispute in constitutional interpretation and theory. When philosophers of law and laymen alike think of the Constitution, they rarely think of such norms as typical (because legal cases almost never involve them). Constitutional law that probably comes to mind first consists in limiting norms in protection of rights stated in the amendments: the bans on laws imposing cruel and unusual punishments, restricting free speech, denying equal protection or due process of law, and so on. Even when such requirements are written in the form of strong rules ("Congress shall make no law . . . abridging the freedom of speech"), they are not read in that way (according to their plain or literal meaning). The important value of free expression is recognized in the First Amendment, for example, but exceptions not written into the Constitution have long been recognized as well. Some forms of speech are not protected at all, despite the literal meaning of the apparent rule as written, and other forms of expression may be curbed in more or less dire circumstances. Conservatives fond of strong rules in the law have never suggested taking this clause as one according to the plain meaning of its words.[155]

Such phrases as "equal protection" and "cruel and unusual" in themselves suggest that the norms containing them are broad standards or, in our terms, purely normative pseudorules that require interpretation to be applied analogically outside the relatively narrow core of cases explicitly envisaged at the time of their enactment. From the wording of these clauses, it seems as if the framers were deliberately delegating authority to the courts to specify the precise scope of rights that were to be protected over time, much as legislatures now typically delegate authority to administrative agencies to make broad law more specific. But, as we have seen in regard to free speech, wording is not the last word as to how constitutional norms are typically read. And there is at least one other way, not based on the literal meaning, of reading both free speech and such norms as equal protection as genuine rules with considerable strength:[156] according to the doctrine of original intent.

Intuitively, there are two ways in which one might understand the framers' intent as a guide to interpretation. The first is as indicated earlier, where intent picks out a core of hypothetical cases, and beyond that core, where intent is silent, the proper judgment is indeterminate, to be determined through analogies and disanalogies to the core. On this understanding, even though the framers of the equal protection clause did not intend to end school segregation or promote gender equality, it would be inconsistent not to do so if there are no relevant differences (as indicated by opposing values recognized in law) between these and the core cases.

According to the second way of understanding the force of original intent, if the framers did not specifically intend to extend the law to a particular area of behavior or to protect some proposed right, then that area remains free from legal interference or protection, to be considered by the legislature if it so desires. This is the way that the doctrine of original intent is now typically understood by friend and foe alike, and the way that allows interpreters of the Constitution to read apparently broad standards as genuine rules. Here we limit application of law to what the framers consciously envisaged and intended, or to what would have been understood to be intended at the time of enactment. The equal protection clause is so understood as clearly intended to protect African Americans against discrimination, especially against legally imposed burdens. Whoever was not explicitly intended at the time to be protected – women, gays, white males – is not included in the scope of the law. Here only political speech and expression directly bearing on political views are protected by the First Amendment; there is no question of protecting pornography, for example. More generally, whatever was not clearly intended in constitutional law is not included in its scope, leaving legislatures more future leeway and limiting the authority of the courts.[157]

In regard to reading laws as genuine rules, the effect of this theory of jurisprudence is to sufficiently narrow apparently broad standards so that it is no longer the case that moral factors not understood as intended in their statements must be weighed in determining applications to particular cases. If only African Americans are included in the scope of the equal protection clause, then judges need not consider morally relevant similarities and differences among other groups in applying this law. The doctrine of original intent need not be construed as restricting judges to the application of genuine rules, but, as typically construed, it enables seemingly broad standards to be read in that way.

Aside from the supposed benefits of construing law as genuine rules (to be assessed later), there are majoritarian or democratic arguments in favor of the doctrine of original intent in its conservative or narrow understanding. First, in regard to past majorities, it can be argued that the framers, and the majorities they represented, could have established only those legal norms that they understood as such at the time. They could not have established as law norms that they did not and could not have understood themselves to be creating.[158] Hence, if, for example, the framers of the Fourteenth Amendment did not understand themselves to be creating gender equality, how could they have done so? The will of those authorized to make law must be followed when they do so, and their will is equivalent to their specific intentions. What limits present legislatures are not simply marks on paper or even just words, but past institutional acts, and the framers of constitutional restraints only acted as they intended and understood themselves to have acted.[159]

Second, then, in regard to present majorities, it can be argued that if we accept undemocratic constraints on democratic rule (as I argued previously that we do), these should be construed narrowly. Since judges' values inevitably enter into adjudication in the absence of clear rules, we should not substitute these values for those of the majoritarian legislature. Even aside from the input of the courts, the problem of time, of why a past majority should have control over a present one, is at least less acute when the acts of the former are construed narrowly. It might be said on the other side that the doctrine of original intent exacerbates the problem of time, in that it is harder to see why we presently should be bound by what an earlier society could explicitly envisage in very different times and circumstances. But the idea here is that we should be bound *only* by that in order to allow democracy as much sway as possible within the framework of constitutionalism.

Other serious problems nevertheless beset this doctrine. First, if majoritarian arguments favor intentionalism in constitutional interpretation, then a rights-based moral or political theory might equally favor the power of the courts to protect individual and minority rights against majority intrusions. A narrow or rulelike interpretation of amendments such as the First, Ninth, and Fourteenth is not politically neutral, but rather complacent toward past or current realizations of moral rights in our legal system.[160] If we believe that we progress over time in our moral perceptions (some of the original framers owned slaves), then we should not want to limit our moral insight into constitutional norms to the specific insights of the framers.

Second, even if we accept the idea that the lawmaking authority of a past majority or their legislative representatives implies that we must defer to the latter's intentions, there are questions regarding which intentions are the relevant ones and how these are to be discovered. Intentions exist at different levels of generality, and it is not clear here that the narrowest intentions of the framers override the broader ones with which they may conflict in implications. The framers of the equal protection clause may not have specifically intended to end segregation in schools and would not have so intended if the issue had occurred to them *then*. But if they had had knowledge of all the intervening events and of the situation in 1954, can we say what they would have intended?

We can ask, then, why it is not more consistent with original intent to appeal to what the framers would have intended at present if they could have envisaged present issues and circumstances. A defender of narrow intentionalism might respond that it was for later lawmakers to prohibit school segregation, that it sufficed that the writers of the equal protection clause did not intend to do so that *they* did not do so. But we can reply that what they did enact into law was precisely what they intended to say, at the level of generality at which they *did* say it, not what they explicitly intended to cause in the way of consequences by saying what they did.[161] We can ask why they did not write these constitutional clauses as narrower rules if they so intended them to be interpreted in the future.

Why, for example, did the framers of the First Amendment not limit its protection explicitly to political speech? Why did the writers of the Fourteenth Amendment not specifically eliminate only those burdensome laws that they found morally offensive at the time? Why did they not specifically mention African Americans instead of all citizens if they intended protection only for the former? Robert Bork holds that the general language here indicates only that distinctions we draw among other citizens must be reasonable, but that answer to the question is ad hoc.[162] Why make the criterion reasonableness instead of "compelling state interest," for example? More generally, it seems that the broad normative language of the First, Eighth, Ninth, and Fourteenth Amendments reveals intent to state guiding values and to delegate authority to the courts to specify concrete implications by later interpretations made in light of changed circumstances.

In asking which collective intention is the relevant one for purposes of interpretation, I have been assuming both that the notion of collective intention is coherent and that the relevant collective intention can be recovered from the historical records. Both of these assumptions can be questioned as well. The legislative process is complex, often chaotic, and neither outcomes nor statements in the records necessarily indicate the intents of laws' framers or sponsors, let alone those of the collective majorities that enact them. Included in that process may be political bargains, logrolling, other strategic behaviors, public posturing, and the influence of an agenda or the order in which measures were considered and brought up for votes. Those in the majority may have had substantially different reasons for their votes. And, when it comes to recent enactments, the clearest way to discern even separate individual intentions is not open to the courts. Why, if the doctrine is meant to be of general application, does our legal system not require (or allow) judges simply to question legislators on their intentions when contemporary legislation needs interpreting?

I shall not press these questions and criticisms of the doctrine further here. Despite them, it may often be clear enough what past framers of constitutional clauses could not have had explicitly in mind. The framers of the First Amendment could not have had pornography in mind, given the context in which they conceived freedom of speech. And narrowings based on such inferences may be sufficient to make possible an understanding of these clauses as imposing rules whose core cases nearly exhaust their legitimate applications. Thus, there remains at least one way, taken seriously by some jurisprudentialists, to read even seemingly broad constitutional norms as genuine rules.

If the way legal requirements are stated does not determine whether they are interpreted as genuine rules, then the issue becomes not descriptive, but the normative one of whether they should be read that way. It might be replied that the descriptive question remains but that the evidence by which we can answer it is not as so far supposed. If the writing of legal norms does not in itself determine how they are to be read, we can still seek empirical evidence as to how judges in fact read them. I cannot attempt here to gather or even survey what evidence of this type exists. But I will indicate later why it is plausible to assume variations among judges of different philosophical inclinations. And the sometimes heated normative debate about how law should be interpreted itself indicates that there is no uniform answer to the descriptive question (except variation), once more bringing the normative question to the fore.

Although the way a law is written does not in itself determine how it should be read, styles of writing can nevertheless encourage narrower or broader interpretations. Thus the normative issue clearly extends to the writing of legislation and common law opinions. It also extends less obviously to the writing of constitutional law by the Supreme Court. I refer here not to the writings of the framers, but to the elaboration of constitutional standards over time through court decisions. The equal protection clause, as noted, has spawned through a series of decisions the distinction between legal differentiations among citizens that require the rationale of compelling state interest and those that require only weaker rationales. The term "compelling" once more suggests a standard, albeit at a level of generality lower than that of "equal protection" itself, but the specification of such distinctions through further decisions can again generate requirements plausibly read as genuine rules.

To take other examples, the ban on cruel and unusual punishments is clearly to be classified as a standard, given its formulation in normative language, but the Court's decisions on the death penalty over time can generate more-specific rules under this standard, such as the rule that death will not be imposed for rape but only for murder. Once such a rule is announced, it is no longer necessary for future courts to balance harm to the victim, culpability, and deterrence against harm to the offender in deciding whether death is a fitting or cruel and unusual punishment for rape. "Due process" too is a standard, but the legal right has become more specific, has come under the protection of rules granting a right to an attorney and to hearings in some contexts but not others.[163]

Thus standards can gradually evolve into a set of rules through elaboration in court decisions. They tend to do so when cases are likely to have repeatable relevant features. They are unlikely to do so when cases are likely to diverge in unpredictable ways, as in the many ways one can fail to exercise reasonable care in being negligent. As noted briefly earlier, the opposite course of development is not unheard of either (I noted, following legal scholars, the evolution of the clause granting Congress the power to regulate commerce from a rule into a broader standard). Even sub-rules that have been developed as ways of specifying standards over time may with further passage of time and changed circumstances be discarded and the process reversed. This may be happening now with the Court's levels of scrutiny for cases falling under the equal protection clause.[164] (See Section I in regard to the trivialization of the notion of compelling state interest.) While standards tend to evolve into rules when new cases make future ones more predictable, rules will tend to revert back to standards when many seeming exceptions force judges to look through the rules to their justifications, when the course of litigation proves to be less predictable than expected.

Whether a norm is treated as a rule or a standard is a matter of practice. As noted, its formulation in writing does not force either reading. It is possible to read even the seemingly most precise and narrow rule as a standard. One could with some ingenuity fudge the seeming rule that a president must be at least thirty-five years old by treating the requirement as a measure of average maturity in 1789, or in terms of a portion of life expectancy then, and so on.[165] But such a reading would be forced or perverse. Thus legislators and judges can write law so as to either encourage or discourage reading the requirements they specify as genuine rules.

This is mainly a matter of how broadly or narrowly requirements are formulated. The narrowest formulations, however, do not always encourage reading decisions as generating rules. If judges write very narrowly, citing all those particular facts of the case that might be thought somehow relevant, then they leave substantial room for other courts to distinguish future cases. But if they include only normatively salient facts in somewhat higher-level generalizations, then, especially if they are

129

higher court judges, they encourage lower courts to treat their decisions as creating genuine rules. The discretion of these courts is then more limited; they must be more wary of distinguishing cases that fall within the apparent scope of the rules.

To summarize, genuine rules must be stated at a sufficiently broad level of generality so that their stated conditions are likely to recur, but not so broadly as to suggest that they should be read as standards against which other factors may always have to be weighed. (There is also another way to try to write rules, namely, by trying to build all exceptions into detailed specifications designed to replace judgment and yet remain sensitive to different circumstances. This tactic attempts to have one's cake and eat it too when it comes to rules, to foresee widely different circumstances to which rules can nevertheless be applied without leaving out relevant factors. It is bound to fail in its purpose when unforeseen circumstances nevertheless arise, and it results in obscure regulations that defeat the simplifying purpose of useful rules.[166]) Since constitutional clauses can be read as rules but need not be, and since opinions that interpret them can encourage or discourage such readings, whether law is written or read as genuine rules is largely a matter of jurisprudential philosophy and style, so that no analysis of the concept of law as a system of rules can be universally correct (or incorrect). Before looking at some arguments for and against writing and interpreting law in that way, I shall briefly extend this point from constitutional to common and even statutory law.

Applying precedents from common law is often viewed as a matter of reasoning directly in terms of analogies and disanalogies to the precedent case, that is, reasoning only under the constraint of not judging cases differently without being able to cite a relevant difference between them. Judges deciding cases in this way are not required to state sufficient conditions for future judgments. It is important once more here to distinguish a metarule that requires judges to follow precedents from the idea that precedents themselves must generate or be expressed in rules. To treat a case as a precedent is to accept a reason to judge a future similar case in the same way independent of the content or of one's evaluation of the earlier decision.[167] To give a precedential case weight independent of ordinary moral considerations is to follow a rule that requires one to do so. Thus there is a genuine (meta-) rule that requires judges to follow precedent in their decisions, a rule that limits their authority to decide on grounds of direct moral perception and sometimes mandates less than morally best decisions. But this rule does not imply that precedents themselves are captured in rules. A present judge must recognize that her decision will constrain future judges, but not necessarily by creating a genuine rule that states sufficient conditions for future decisions or even gives factors in the present case extra weight when future cases can be differentiated from it.

The justification for the metarule is a matter of some controversy and misunderstanding. The crucial question is why a judge who believes that a previous decision is morally mistaken should nevertheless accept the precedent as a constraint on his present judgment. Perhaps surprisingly, we can answer this challenge to the doctrine of precedent neither by appealing to the fundamental principle that we should not judge cases differently without being able to cite a relevant difference between them, nor by appealing directly to the principle that we ought to honor expectations based on the prior decision. If the prior decision was indeed morally mistaken, then the principle of not deciding cases differently without relevant differences between them is likely to have been violated by that decision, and so the principle cannot call for conforming future judgments to it. In regard to expectations, they will be legitimately formed on the basis of prior legal decisions only once we have justified and adopted the rule of legal precedent, and so they cannot be used directly to justify that rule. Expectations can arise in the absence of a rule if behavior has been regular in the past, but here judicial behavior would not regularly follow precedent in the absence of a rule, and so expectations could not be based on their doing so. (Once other justifications are in place, the need to respect expectations can reinforce them.)

The initial justification for the constraint of precedent in law, similar to that of the rule to obey law itself, instead appeals to certain aims of the legal institution and to the place of judges, given the fallibility of their decisions, within the institution. The relevant aims relate to social stability, the creation of a social and economic environment in which stable expectations can be formed, useful ventures risked, and transactions conducted in an orderly and predictable way. For these purposes, the law must be knowable and hence judicial decisions predictable. They will be more predictable when judges adhere to earlier decisions of other judges, whether these are treated as paradigm cases or genuine rules. Personal moral judgment, even if only in the absence of legislation, is less predictable than adherence to prior decisions for which there is a public record. The conservatism of the rule, its tendency to maintain the status quo, is justified by appeal to the role of the judge vis-à-vis legislators and other judges. Radical change, it can be maintained, ought

131

to be introduced by legislators answerable directly to the electorate. And, given their fallibility and the constraints of time and resources for making decisions in cases before them, judges are more likely to introduce new errors by departing from precedent than to extend old errors by adhering to it, especially when the governing common law derives from whole lines of cases. Finally, fallibility as to cumulative results is once more central to the justification of the rule, since it is the reason we cannot rely on judges to gauge the effects of their individual decisions on the predictability of law and the ability of citizens to form stable expectations.

I have emphasized that precedents can serve the functions of stability and predictability without being formulated or treated as genuine rules. But legal analysts often do speak of applying rules established in prior decisions. Those who speak this way do not always refer to genuine rules, however, as is clear from the options they recognize as left open for later judges and the ways they allow or require judges to exercise those options. There is, first, the option either to accept the rule announced in the earlier decision (if there appears to be an announced rule) or to fashion a different rule that would equally imply the result reached in that decision. If the announced rule is accepted as governing the precedent case, then there are the options of applying it or extending it beyond its stated conditions, of limiting it by distinguishing the present case (even when it satisfies the stated conditions), or of overturning the prior rule.[168] If the choice among these options is governed by the perception of moral or legal support (from elsewhere in the law) behind the announced rule and/or similar grounds for distinguishing the present case, then once more this choice is constrained only by the weaker requirement not to distinguish without relevant difference. The judge looks through the rule in determining its application and proper exceptions.

In looking through the rule to its justification and to the justification for distinguishing the present case that falls under its plain meaning, judges no longer treat it as a genuine rule in deciding whether to apply it. Exceptions will be open-ended even within the core of the stated conditions. And the rule need not be given extra weight. On the other hand, especially if a rule has emerged from a line of cases and has an accepted canonical statement, perhaps with important distinctions or exceptions built in, courts, especially trial courts, may treat it as a genuine rule. Judges will then refuse to distinguish cases that clearly fall within the stated conditions of the rule, even when they think it would

132

be morally better to do so. They may still refuse even when the value at stake on the other side has support from elsewhere in the law (assuming that the support is not constitutional). They will accept the rule as overriding their authority to bring moral or even further legal judgment to bear on their decisions. Thus, once more we find both genuine rules and reasoning from the weaker constraint of analogy and disanalogy in the common law, and the possibility of reading the same decisions in either way.

Turning to legislative acts, we find that different statutes as well as different sections of the same pieces of legislation often contain wording suggestive of both rules and standards. Such normative terms as "restraint of trade" in the Sherman Act suggest broad standards to be developed into rules by the courts or applied interpretively in each new case. When instead we find apparent rules in statutes, the most salient difference in the context of the present discussion between them and rules derived from common law is the lack of an option for judges to reword or restate statutory rules (the first option discussed earlier). In addition, the principles of division of governmental powers and of majority rule and legislative supremacy make judges more hesitant to distinguish cases falling within the plain meaning of the conditions stated in statutory rules. Finally, while, as noted, we find both apparent rules and standards in legislation, statutes are more often written at the level of generality that encourages their interpretation as genuine rules. Legislators must limit the stated conditions for applying their laws, and they seldom address matters of principle as broad as those addressed in the Constitution. For all these reasons, of the various sources of law, it is most common to think of statutes as imposing genuine rules on citizens and judges alike.

When a case falls within the stated conditions of a statutory rule and the implied result is in line with apparent legislative intent and the purpose behind the rule, there is no question that the rule will be applied and that further interpretation is not necessary. Nevertheless, there are numerous examples, including those real and hypothetical cases originally cited by Dworkin and Fuller in response to Hart's theory (Section I), in which statutory rules are not applied to cases falling clearly within the plain meaning of their stated conditions, when such application runs counter to presumed intent, deeper justifications, or other legal rules.[169] The former rules are then not treated as strong. Whether they are given the extra weight of presumptive genuine rules may also be unclear when they are overridden.

In the *Riggs* case, for example, it may seem plausible that the justices would have given the fact that the grandson was named as heir in a proper will extra weight against the wrongdoing from which he would have profited, that it was only the extreme nature of the wrongdoing in this case that allowed it to override. But in Fuller's example, it would make little sense to give the fact that a permanently immobile vehicle is still a vehicle extra weight against the opposing consideration that banning the memorial would not serve the purpose of the legislation or the apparent intent of the members of the city council. Whether or not judges treat apparent statutory rules as genuine in giving their stated conditions extra weight, it is clear that, despite a general hesitancy, they will sometimes refuse to apply the rules to cases falling within those stated conditions. The degree of hesitancy will vary with the type of case and with the particular judge.

Equally important, even when the plain meaning of statutory rules coheres with presumed intent and hence determines an unquestionable core of application that may resist perceived lack of moral or (other) legal support, how far that core extends and, conversely, how broad the penumbra or boundary is considered to be may still depend on normative considerations. Thus a statutory rule may still be interpreted more or less narrowly, and how broadly it is interpreted may depend on its perceived justification. When it is interpreted very narrowly, it becomes more like a paradigm case to which later cases are compared for analogies and disanalogies. There remains considerable choice as to whether to treat apparent statutory rules as genuine.

I have pointed out that statutes contain both apparent rules and standards, and that apparent rules are not always treated as genuine. A final point here is that it may not always be clear from the wording of legislation whether a requirement is a rule or a standard. Title VII of the Civil Rights Act of 1964 prohibits discrimination by race in training programs. This might appear sufficiently specific to be a rule, and yet the Supreme Court in its *Weber* decision allowed voluntary racial quotas in training programs.[170] In so doing, it treated "discrimination" as a normative term referring to invidious but not "benign" preference. Part of what allowed this interpretation was another section of the act that says that preference is not required of any employer, without saying whether it is permitted. The justices then looked to the purpose behind the legislation in light of the fact that fifteen years had not appreciably improved the situation of African Americans such as those in the steel-workers union, instead of looking to the (probable) specific intent of

Congress at the time of the legislation.[171] The majority apparently felt that such interpretation in terms of realizing the purpose or value that justifies the legislation was the best way to enforce the rational will of the legislature. Different judges might well have used a different method of interpretation and thereby might have reached a different decision, on the grounds that looking to the assumed broader purpose behind an apparently specifically worded prescription is granting to its backers more than they were able to pass in the way of concrete legislation[172] or allowing judges to impose their own values.

Thus, as in the domains of constitutional and common law, there is once more much leeway to both write and read statutory law as genuine rules or as broader standards. One might think that, if we classify not by source but by subject matter, we will find areas of law where genuine rules are the norm. One might think first here of criminal law. If requirements are to carry heavy sanctions for violations, it seems that they should be simply and comprehensibly stated and strictly and routinely enforced. There should be clear lines between what is prohibited and what is allowed, and penalties should be well defined, so as to provide clear warning and knowledge of how to avoid punishment. But once more there are values on the other side, and sometimes a beneficial gap between public perception and actual practice. While the public might be led to believe that the criminal law consists in a set of strict rules, many officials learn to apply it selectively, sometimes treating its requirements as rules of thumb for the sake of justice, mercy, and even efficiency. The defense of duress and the practice of plea bargaining are prime examples. According to one legal scholar, the public is not aware of the degree to which this defense is allowed as an exception to criminal laws, and this lack of awareness is good in mercifully lessening the extent of brutal criminal punishments without significantly reducing the deterrent effect.[173] And, of course, the practice of plea bargaining produces convictions for crimes when these convictions are wrong according to the rules.[174] They do so for the sake of efficiency. In regard to justice, in the criminal law as elsewhere, strict adherence to rules can produce not only injustice in the individual case, but also the opportunity for evading the purpose of the law by shady exploitation of loopholes. Hence, it is no wonder that here, as elsewhere, rules are not always treated as genuine.

To take another domain as an example, in contract law legislators must choose between giving courts discretion to determine when understandings and agreements have been reached, and creating formal rules for writing and accepting contracts. The former allows courts to carry out the desires of the parties in cases where special needs are difficult to tailor to strict routines; the latter gives assurance that properly formulated terms will be enforced, perhaps reducing litigation. On similar grounds, judges must decide when to look through rules in order to avoid decisions that thwart understandings by adherence to technicalities. It is not my purpose at this point to mediate between these values, only to indicate why the course of legislation in this area too has sometimes taken one direction and sometimes the other,[175] and why some judges are likely to favor one approach and some the other.

Thus, although it is true that certain areas of law, especially those conferring powers or benefits, such as welfare law, are more willing to tolerate suboptimal results from the application of rules,[176] all areas of law can be written and read as genuine rules or as broader and looser standards. That law from any source and in any domain *can* be written so as to encourage or discourage its reading as genuine rules, and that it *can* be read either way in itself argues that the normative question is primary. But this freedom of choice does not in itself show variation in this regard among judges according to jurisprudential philosophy or style. There is, however, evidence to support this empirical claim. The cases that Schauer cites to support his claim that laws are generally read as rules with presumptive force seems to support better the claim that there is such variation. The evidence consists in a conjunction of cases, in some of which, such as those cited by Dworkin, judges override clear rules on (legally supported) moral grounds, while in others, they apply rules despite moral qualms about the results.

As Schauer notes, while Riggs's grandson did not inherit after killing his grandfather despite the proper legal status of the will, other unworthy beneficiaries did; while the signed document in lieu of other guarantees in *Henningson* did not determine its outcome, such documents often do.[177] As noted, Schauer takes this divergence to indicate that judges generally accept presumptive rules, rules that have extra weight but can be overridden in more or less extreme circumstances. But the lack of uniformity where we might expect it if judges were reading the law in the same way makes it more plausible to interpret the evidence as pointing to genuine diversity in jurisprudential philosophy. Some read rules as strong, others read rules as genuine but weak, and yet others read them as rules of thumb, referring only to paradigm cases from which others must be distinguished. This interpretation is further supported by the disagreements among judges writing on the same cases of the sort cited. If they were reading all rules as presumptive in the same way, then we would expect agreement in the application of the same requirements. Of course, we find disagreement not only among judges, but also among philosophers such as Hart, Dworkin, and Schauer.

IV. THE NORMATIVE QUESTION

Let us then turn to the normative questions. Before considering when the law should be written and read as genuine rules, we should answer another normative question remaining from the previous section regarding reasoning by analogy from precedent and interpreting standards. The remaining question regarding precedent concerns the grounds on which cases may legitimately be distinguished from earlier settled ones. Cases differ in innumerable ways, and grounds for legitimate differentiation must therefore be limited if there is to be any constraint at all. What constitutes a relevant difference? It must, first of all, be a difference that affects the values at stake in the two cases. But what kinds of values? Judges might distinguish cases based on their own moral values or perceptions of relevant differences, or on those values with widespread social recognition, or on those values recognized explicitly or implicitly elsewhere in the law.

I believe that the same grounds that justify the rule to follow precedent in the first place also justify choosing the third of these alternatives in a developed system of law. If judges are to follow previous decisions rather than using fresh moral perceptions in each case, then they are not to differentiate present cases from previous ones based only on their moral perceptions of differences between them. There is so much variation in the personal values of judges that a constraint that allows cases to be differentiated on that basis amounts to very little if any constraint, and once more would create instability and unpredictability in the legal system. Social morality, the second alternative, is a clear criterion only in a homogeneous society with a widespread moral consensus, not in a pluralist society with some social support for almost any view. Once more, a constraint that allows differentiation based only on such support amounts to little if any constraint at all. This leaves the third alternative, that cases are to be differentiated on the basis of values already recognized as legally relevant. An objection to this alternative might be that new values must be introduced into the legal system at some points in time, so that the method cannot be fully generalized. But we are speaking of the actions of judges here, and new values can be introduced by legislatures or by constitutional amendments. When a judge does distinguish a case from a purported precedent according to some value explicitly or implicitly invoked as the ground for some other legal act, she is claiming that this other source is more analogous or relevant than the purported precedent. Thus legally relevant differences are based on legally relevant similarities.

The same arguments that apply here to grounds for differentiating new cases from precedents also apply to judges interpreting standards from enacted law. I have argued that such interpretation is similar in that it involves the specification of core cases that clearly fall under the standard and the assimilating or differentiating of other cases from that core. According to Dworkin's latest writing, judges have no choice but to read broad moral principles (or standards) in the law in terms of their own morality.[178] It might indeed seem plausible that anyone seeking to understand what such principles or standards mean or imply must bring his own understanding to bear. But this is not entirely the case. In interpreting a standard stated in broad normative language, one can instead recognize the uncontested and uncontroversial core cases and values protected by that standard and then differentiate other seemingly similar cases only according to other values recognized in the law. Of course, this will still involve one's own understanding of the law, but one can recognize values implicit or explicit therein that one does not endorse. (Dworkin elsewhere recognizes the second clause here, and so the first clause may be all he means by the claim cited. It is certainly all he should mean.) Once more, unless such values constrain one's interpretations of standards, there is very little constraint at all. Constraint by legally recognized values can once more be seen as the best compromise in general between social stability and the perception of justice in the individual case. Thus, this is the alternative kind of reasoning by analogy and disanalogy, with this understanding of relevant similarities and differences, that we must weigh against reasoning by following rules in answering our main normative question, whether officials in the legal system should write and read law as genuine rules.

Once again, a major obscurity and equivocation in some arguments in favor of treating law as a set of genuine rules results from the failure to distinguish genuine rules from this weaker constraint of not judging cases differently without citing a legally relevant difference between them. Those who would argue that cases cannot be compared without appeal to rules (since all cases have innumerable features),[179] that without rules judges will be free to exercise their own unfettered moral judgment and hence will usurp the authority of legislatures or other courts, or that the law will completely lack consistency unless rules are applied are guilty of that failure. Cases can be compared in terms of their normatively relevant features without legislators or judges being able to list all those features in advance, as they must if stating strong rules. And they may be rationally unwilling to grant stated conditions extra weight against reasons that might oppose them, as weaker genuine rules still require. Judges can also be constrained by prior law under the Kantian constraint. Even if they distinguish cases on moral grounds (without being required to cite other legal support for their distinctions), this should not be an exercise of pure unfettered judgment as to morally preferred outcomes, and less so if the moral grounds for distinctions must have widespread social support (although I have argued that such constraint is in fact insufficient). And if, as I have argued, they ought to distinguish cases only on legally recognized grounds, the constraint is stronger and clearer still.

Obeying the Kantian constraint also renders decisions consistent over time, as I argued in Section II when discussing coherence. In fact, if consistency requires treating unlike cases differently as well as like cases similarly, then the law is more consistent under this weaker constraint, since the stated conditions of genuine rules will ignore relevant differences that might come to light later. When rules are applied, these differences will not be given their proper weight according to ordinary judgments of consistency or fairness, or according to orderings of values elsewhere in the legal system. Thus rules often generate inconsistency in value orderings, and hence inconsistency within a legal system that allows case-by-case reasoning as well.

When, in support of consistency, Dworkin argues against "checkerboard" solutions to social issues in the law, when he points out that the law cannot reflect the even split in our society over abortion by allowing only one-half of American women to obtain them (those born on odd days of months),[180] this is not an argument for rules, or even broad principles (as he believes), but only for not violating the weaker constraint. Neither cases nor persons can be treated differently unless there are normatively relevant differences between them. Odd versus even birthdays do not constitute relevant differences among those seeking abortions. Such differences are not morally relevant in this context, and they certainly do not represent values recognized in the legal system. Hence our Kantian constraint does not allow such political compromises.

139

Some purported reasons for adopting rules are therefore really reasons only for obeying the weaker constraint. Some of the real reasons for and against rules generally in the law were indicated in previous sections. What must be weighed is the discretion of judges to judge similarities and differences from hypothetically and actually settled cases versus limitation of that authority. The first method allows adjustments to the details of particular cases, allows them to be differentiated according to values recognized elsewhere in the legal system; the second creates uniformity (on the first level) and predictability. Those who oppose the first method see it as opening the door to judgments based on personal moral and political views. Those who oppose the second point to the inability of rule makers to predict differences in cases and changes in circumstances over long periods of time. Let us again look at these reasons for and against rules more closely, now in the legal context.

The strongest reason against treating laws as genuine rules is that such rules are (or become with time) instruments of injustice in particular cases. Legal cases and contexts will vary in too many unpredictable ways, normative considerations will be too rich and fine-grained, to allow prediction of all those factors that might ordinarily weigh against conditions stated in rules. The problem exists regardless of whether rules are framed narrowly or more broadly. If rules are specific, then they can be applied mechanically when their conditions of application are satisfied, without worrying too much that relevantly different cases will be treated similarly. But narrow wording allows exploitation of loopholes and risks having similar cases treated differently. Broadly framed rules tend to be treated as standards because they admit of many borderline cases and assimilate relevantly different cases, allowing or requiring them to be treated similarly.

Laws mandating certain treatment for the handicapped, for example, if written and interpreted as genuine rules, will deprive others whose interests may be more centrally at stake in certain contexts of needed resources, or they may work against certain handicapped persons who need to be treated differently from others. On moral grounds (recognized elsewhere in law) these requirements would need to be limited in certain cases satisfying their stated conditions; but genuine rules do not permit such judgments to be made, at least not without giving their stated conditions extra weight that is unwarranted on ordinary normative grounds.

Other regulations would need to be extended beyond their stated conditions on grounds of normative consistency. Early antidiscrimination advocates who framed the Fourteenth Amendment could not predict present controversies focused on women, gays, and white males who claim to be victims of discrimination. Reading the equal protection clause as a genuine rule in terms of original intent (narrowly) or plain meaning (broadly) gives judges no leeway to consider justifications for treating any of these groups similarly or differently from African Americans. But ordinary justice, both comparative and absolute, requires making these comparisons to determine whether other groups require similar protection and in what contexts. Rules, as I have emphasized throughout, are at most second best in promoting justice.[181]

In considering the other side of the picture, the reasons in favor of writing and reading law, including court decisions, so as to generate and obey rules, I shall turn to the arguments of Antonin Scalia in a well-known article.[182] One reason for doing so is the fact that he explicitly recognizes that rules as generalizations oversimplify and that we therefore cannot achieve perfect justice by applying them.[183] He thinks nevertheless that the arguments in favor of genuine rules in law override this acknowledgment of their imperfection. Some of his arguments are familiar in appealing to reasons for adopting rules generally – they apply to the moral sphere as well. Others are peculiar to the legal system and the need for genuine rules there.

His first argument falls into the latter category. He maintains that the appearance of justice and the satisfaction of the parties to the dispute, or their acceptance of the verdict, are as important as justice itself. Both sides to a dispute will feel strongly that they have the law on their side, and it will be easier to convince the loser otherwise if the court can cite a clear and firm rule.[184] The stability of the legal system and the tranquility of society are therefore promoted by the promulgation of genuine rules in law. Cases are more easily accepted as settled when their verdicts are implied by clear rules.

The second argument is more familiar and appeals to a general consideration in favor of adopting rules, but one with special applicability to the legal system, namely, the value of predictability. Citizens, especially lawyers, must be able to tell what the law is, must be able to predict the outcomes of potential suits, and the applicability of a rule certainly makes decisions more predictable. Judges, once more, cannot be trusted to gauge the cumulative effects of decisions opposed to rules on expectations and on the predictability of law. This gain in efficiency from following rules has been argued by others to be a gain in justice as well. Knowledge of law and the ability to predict outcomes prevent costly conflict that may result in injustice that application of law after the fact cannot fully correct. Hence, if standing rules are more easily grasped than sets of case decisions, more injustice may be avoided by applying rules even when their application itself is not perfectly just.[185]

Scalia's third argument appeals to division of decision-making authority, once more a typical reason for adopting genuine rules. As I have emphasized, rules severely restrict authority to make decisions based on one's own perceptions of situations. Besides promoting predictability, we may want to limit such authority for epistemic reasons, because we think it difficult for the decision makers in question to gather sufficient evidence for accurate judgments, or because we have reason to be wary of bias in the unfettered judgment of each case as it occurs. Scalia emphasizes the last reason in applying such considerations to the legal system. Writing decisions in the form of rules, especially Supreme Court decisions, restrains judges in future cases, including Supreme Court justices themselves. Committing oneself to a general rule prevents favoring one party in a future case only because of personal political preferences.[186] Once more, the problem that rules are to solve here is that of fallibility, proneness to error because of lack of epistemic resources or bias.

Finally, Scalia notes that judges sometimes need to stand up to popular opinion and render an unpopular decision that protects some legal right. An example of this is when they free an accused criminal on what the public considers a technicality, when the requirement actually protects the right to due process. He argues that judges will have more nerve to do their legal duty in such cases when they can stand behind firm rules. Such rules, in limiting the authority of judges, also limit their responsibility for unpopular decisions in the public's eyes. Hence they reduce pressure to render more popular but legally and morally incorrect decisions. Here we have an argument that is once more unique to legal systems.

I shall criticize these arguments in the order in which they were stated. The first appealed to the appearance of justice and the satisfaction of the parties involved in a case. There is, first of all, the question here of why parties to sophisticated legal cases should be fooled by the appearance of justice when their lawyers presumably know of other methods of adjudication. Disputants are capable of distinguishing between legally final and morally just outcomes, and a morally unjust application of a legal rule is unlikely to leave the party on the short end feeling satisfied. Second, and perhaps more to the point, the acceptance of verdicts might be an open question and therefore an important consideration in more primitive or unstable political and legal systems, in which verdicts might be openly disputed or resisted by extralegal means. But the American legal system is not of that sort, leaving losing parties little option but to accept the verdict of the final court of appeal. Our higher courts are therefore safer in aiming at genuine justice instead of its appearance. They need not fear extralegal resistance to final verdicts. Hence there is no disease here for which rules would be the cure.

Scalia's next argument appeals to predictability, perhaps the most widely cited justification for rules. Here again, we can raise two lines of questioning. The first acknowledges the gain in predictability to be achieved through application of standing rules, but asks whether that gain is worth the cost in terms of fairness or justice in particular decisions. It was noted earlier that avoidance of conflict through knowledge of law might avoid the injustices that conflict often makes inevitable. This gain still needs to be weighed, however, against the injustice involved in devaluing factors not mentioned in rules being applied. The argument in itself does not seem to justify the extra weight given to genuine rules, as opposed to the adoption of a rule-sensitive particularist stance on the part of judges. And the value that this stance would accord to rules based on greater predictability would vary with the degree to which decisions according to rules are more predictable. This brings us to the second line of questioning here.

The second line asks whether decisions in the absence of genuine rules must be so unpredictable as to leave the identification of law often in doubt and hence encourage conflict and superfluous litigation. Here Scalia seems guilty of the fallacy emphasized earlier, that of ignoring the force of the weaker constraint in arguing for the stronger. Indeed, the following quotation indicates his assumption of a dichotomy between being bound by a strict rule and having complete discretion to decide a case based on perception of all the facts:

it is no more possible to demonstrate the inconsistency of two opinions based upon a "totality of the circumstances" than it is to demonstrate the inconsistency of two jury verdicts. Only by announcing rules do we hedge ourselves in.[187]

The falsity of this dichotomy means that Scalia's predictability argument in part attacks a straw man. Lawyers can predict outcomes of cases from precedents without genuine rules if the grounds required for distinguishing cases must have support from other areas of law. Precedents and grounds for distinguishing cases from them are publicly knowable, and so there need not be any surprises or ex post facto judgments when they are applied. On the other side, most laymen must consult lawyers to find out rules of law, and lawyers can be expected to know precedents as well as rules. This is not to say that rules do not make the law more predictable, but the gain here is not as great as Scalia represents it to be.

One could, of course, be skeptical about the force of the weaker constraint and the degree of predictability it generates by believing that judges can always find some ground for distinguishing a later case from an earlier one when they disapprove of the earlier outcome. But one can equally be skeptical of the force of rules when they can be limited in later decisions. It is true that lower courts feel more rule bound than higher courts. But if a lower court will be wary of disregarding a rule announced by the Supreme Court, it will also be loathe to distinguish a case from a precedent set by the Supreme Court without solid grounds anchored in law for doing so. When there are such grounds for distinguishing a case falling within the stated conditions of a rule, we can ask whether lawyers can predict with confidence that the rule will nevertheless be applied. One might hope not if the legal system is to aim at justice.

A similar response can open the rebuttal to Scalia's third argument in favor of limiting the power of judges to rule in a biased way without the constraint of rules. Judges will be constrained by earlier decisions in the absence of rules if they can find no legally accepted grounds for distinguishing the cases before them. The absence of genuine rules will not leave them free to exercise personal morality or politics (unless they feel free to do so even in the presence of announced rules). While a lower court will be wary of drawing a distinction that is inconsistent with a Supreme Court decision whether or not that decision announces a rule, the Supreme Court itself will not hesitate to overturn an announced rule of a lower court as well as its decision. Thus constraint need not be enforced by means of rules, and it will not be unless the weaker constraint would be obeyed also.

Scalia argues that judges limit not only lower courts, but also their own future discretion to express political preferences, when they commit themselves to standing rules. But in order to want to limit judges in future cases by imposing rules on them, one must presume to be able to take the truly relevant factors into account in advance of the cases better than can the later judges who have the cases before them. This is often a highly questionable epistemic assumption. Once more, the fallibility of on-the-spot decision makers must be weighed against the fallibility of rule makers. The latter is normally insignificant only when future cases are likely to involve only one dominant value, or when the rules settle procedural or structural matters on which people can agree despite disagreeing in substantive value orderings.

In regard to limiting one's own power to inject political ideology into decisions, ideology can intrude in the act of framing a rule as well. When it does, the consequences are more serious, since courts may then be more firmly locked into the ideology of the rule. Notorious examples from both the right and the left are not difficult to find, among them the rules announced in *Plessy v. Ferguson* and *Roe v. Wade*. Such cases remind us again that, although conservatives often support rules in order to narrow the scope of such standards as equal protection and due process, rules in themselves can support either conservative or liberal causes, depending on their content. Rules banning interference in abortion decisions, limiting or banning the death penalty, or protecting all speech are among the many liberal examples.

Scalia's final argument appeals to the desirability of shielding judges from popular opinion to facilitate their performing their duty of protecting individual rights. What mainly shields federal judges, of course, is the fact that they are appointed, not elected. Whether the formal niceties of written opinions that the public never sees also serve this function is highly debatable. If they did see reports of legal decisions and noticed whether these decisions took the form of announced rules, one might imagine that they would disapprove more strongly of the prospect of blind application of genuine rules than of the attempt to be sensitive to differences among cases as determined by social morality or prior law. Standing behind unfair or unpopular rules is unlikely to make judges any more popular, although it may bring legislators into equal contempt. But again, given the stability of our legal system, federal judges at least need not feel popular in order to feel secure in doing their judicial duty.

My normative conclusion to this point is that, on balance, support for a general policy of writing and reading law as genuine rules is hard to come by. Nevertheless, we have noted that the law does and should contain some genuine rules. I believe that the criteria for deciding when rules are beneficial in law are those we should use generally to decide whether rules should guide normative reasoning. We need rules when the cumulative effects of direct reasoning that takes all normatively relevant factors into account are worse than the imperfect justice of the rules. This can be so for either simple or more complex reasons. The simple cases are those in which wrong decisions occur more often than right ones in the absence of rules, or in which getting it right more often is not worth the cost, time, or effort involved. As pointed out, errors may occur more often than not because of lack of epistemic (evidence-gathering) resources or because of bias. In such situations, we want to delegate authority to framers of rules with more resources or objectivity. As noted earlier, to justify the imposition of rules on these grounds, we must justify the assumption that the framers of rules will make fewer errors in advance of encountering particular cases than will agents involved in those cases when they arise. This is a strong assumption, but it can sometimes be justified. Furthermore, all three reasons – epistemic disadvantage, inefficiency, and possible bias – may combine to support the impositions of rules, as in the aforementioned case of age limits for high federal offices.

The more interesting contexts are, once more, the more complex ones, in which individually correct decisions, involving no errors in reasoning, can nevertheless have cumulatively bad results. Earlier, we considered the case in which a court enforces a foreclosure on the home of a person impoverished through no fault of her own. Here there might well be grounds in socially endorsed morality and in values recognized elsewhere in law for distinguishing this case from other foreclosures. This person will be homeless and suffering pitiably, while the extra money in the bank's assets will be negligible in its overall financial position. Then too, a decision by a single trial court will have a negligible effect on the law and the financial markets affected by it, but the decision might buy the person precious time. Nevertheless, the cumulative effect of all judges reasoning in this way, taking all normatively relevant facts into account, warrants the adoption of a rule, given a threshold of unfettered decisions beyond which negative effects set in and an inability of single judges to estimate how close to that threshold their decisions might be. The law must therefore impose a rule that overrides other relevant factors in all cases and thereby limits the discretionary authority of judges.

This type of case is certainly not unique in the legal system. Contracts and legal agreements generally, once determined to have been properly entered into, should be enforced for similar reasons, even when in hindsight the enforcement is seen to unfairly burden one of the parties. Even if this general rule is not strong, it appears to be genuine, the fact of legal agreement always to be given extra weight. In tort law, various contexts in which the imposition of vicarious or strict liability appears justified fall into this class as well. Most enforcements in particular cases may not only appear but be unfair to the party held liable without clear moral responsibility. But the cumulative effects of such enforcement in increasing precautions and lowering risks and actual injuries may warrant the rule that overrides ordinary considerations of responsibility. Once more, individual judges will not be capable of gauging whether they can safely make exceptions of their cases in the name of justice for their defendants.

All these cases show why Schauer is correct in his argument against Postema that presumptive rules (with extra weight) do not collapse into rule-sensitive particularism (although Schauer does not appeal to cases of this type). The latter strategy is justified when decision makers can accurately estimate the value of having a rule in the area in question, the effect of their decisions on others, and the competing values. But here the collective action problem creates a kind of endemic fallibility that cannot be factored in by the decision makers themselves. Hence it makes sense in these contexts to give rules extra weight.

At the same time, those cases that provide the strongest justification for the acceptance of genuine rules render Schauer's criterion for over-riding them inapplicable. The degree of injustice that might occur in the individual case, the severe harm to the person evicted and homeless in that example, does not seem sufficient for overriding the rule if the cumulative effects of applying this criterion are far more harmful in the long run. And the extra weight to be given the rule cannot be unpacked in epistemic terms, since there is no additional knowledge regarding the present case that would tell a judge to override the rule. If Schauer's criterion were the correct one, it would seem that rules should be applied only when the moral stakes are relatively trivial.[188] But this is not the case, and I doubt that he intends it to be.

In the context of justified rules, judges must instead think in terms of cumulative effects, of all judges acting in the same way, when thinking of making exceptions. None of these justified legal rules could be effective, however, without a more fundamental but unwritten rule operating as background. This is the most basic requirement that judges defer to legal standards even when their personal morality opposes the legally right outcome of a case. All the reasons offered in favor of imposing rules generally can be used to justify this fundamental rule of the legal system.[189] First, the law in general would certainly be less predictable and hence less knowable if judges appealed to their own moral sense instead of legal rules and paradigms that allow cases to be distinguished only on grounds of other law. While the effect of each decision based on personal moral perception on the predictability of law might appear minimal, the cumulative effects of such decisions would be disastrous, generating both unpredictability and inconsistency. Second, we want to divide authority for shaping the law and making it congruent with moral perception between judges and legislators. Indeed, legislators are more likely to reflect social morality in their judgments, being answerable to the majority, as many judges are not. Judges must therefore defer to statutory rules and paradigms. If they always used their own moral sense in deciding cases, legislators would in effect lack power altogether. Third, courts sometimes lack the epistemic resources to find out all the morally relevant features of the parties to disputes, and the law may then simplify the universe of decision making.

For all these reasons, even if the exercise of direct moral judgment by judges would not result directly in moral errors more often than not, the total effects of allowing such judgment would be most unwelcome, undermining the entire legal system and the democratic form of government. Hence there must be a rule requiring deferral to law. This rule is both fundamental to the legal system and genuine. It is genuine because judges are not to look through it to its justification in attempting to identify legitimate exceptions. They can ignore recognized legal requirements only in the direst circumstances. The rule to defer to such requirements implies that law is a "limited domain," that it is distinct from the complete moral framework of any decision maker. But this is a thesis not only of positivism, but of Dworkin's theory of law as well (since for him only those moral principles that justify settled law have legal status). Both, however, focus on how law is to be identified, taking for granted the normative rule for judges that I take to be fundamental. It is certainly not to be overlooked that its justification fits the general pattern defined here in Chapter 1.

In closing this chapter, I should emphasize one final time that obeying this fundamental metarule of law does not entail that judges always follow first-order rules in law. Whether the law consists in rules is not a fact independent of how judges ought to treat legal norms. And whether they should treat particular legal requirements as genuine rules is determined by the usual (but not usually conceptualized) criteria for deciding when rules should guide and limit normative reasoning. The satisfaction of these criteria is still the exception and not the rule.

4

Moral Reasoning without Rules

A reader might have predicted that this final chapter would be titled "Practical Reasoning without Rules." But there are good reasons for focusing on moral reasoning here. As hinted in Section II of Chapter 2, I do not believe that much prudential reasoning actually occurs, at least not of the complex and interesting variety that will be the target of explication here. When faced with conflicting self-interested motivations and pondering what to do, we typically simply summon the various considerations before our minds and await recognition of their relative weights. At least this is what we do after critically informing our desires, if necessary, as to their origins and the consequences of acting on them. This description is similar to the particularist's account of moral reasoning, which I will challenge. Moral reasoning is instead similar in structure to legal reasoning, although the databases from which these two types of reasoning proceed are different.[190] Not being a lawyer, I will concentrate on moral reasoning here for my examples.

In Chapter 1, I argued that ordinary moral reasoning does not consist in deducing particular prescriptions from rules. Rules cannot capture our ordinary moral judgments. The reason emphasized there was the complex ways that numerous morally relevant factors interact in various contexts, reversing priorities among them and sometimes their positive or negative values as well. There are no sufficient conditions that tell us, for example, when not lying is more important than not causing harm and when not causing harm is more important. It depends on other values at stake as well in various contexts, values that might not only morally require lying, for example, but might even give it positive value itself (a lie to a potential murderer might be better for being a lie). A related reason why strong rules fail to capture intuitive judgment is novelty. New circumstances arise that generate unpredicted exceptions, which therefore remain open-ended.

Less strong rules were also shown to be inessential to ordinary moral reasoning. Rules of thumb or prima facie rules that simply remind us of factors that may be morally relevant are useless and dispensable when those factors come to be weighed against one another. Weak genuine rules, which do not state sufficient conditions but indicate factors that must be given extra weight in moral calculations, do not figure in ordinary moral reasoning either, since, trivially, extra weight is not or-dinary or normal. Such rules are essential to second-best strategies when these are the best available or are needed to avoid worse outcomes. But these rules are not part of ordinary reasoning that does not need to settle for second best.

As just noted, Chapter 1 also claimed that, while rules are not the norm in moral reasoning, they remain not only useful, but essential as a second-best strategy in contexts in which errors are more likely than not in their absence, especially contexts involving collective action problems in which morally required or permissible actions from the individual's point of view cumulatively produce morally unacceptable results. These collective action problems themselves result from coordination problems that prevent the achievement of optimal patterns of individual actions. Obedience to rules then produces not optimal but acceptable results. In ordinary contexts, however, we can aim to do better by reasoning in the ordinary way. Having clarified the uses of rules in other contexts in Chapters 2 and 3, we turn finally to ordinary moral reasoning itself.

I. THE INADEQUACY OF PARTICULARISM

If such reasoning in the face of problematic conflicts does not consist in the application of rules to cases, do we instead simply "perceive" the proper weights or priorities among conflicting values in problematic contexts? That is pretty much what particularists like Jonathan Dancy say, following W. D. Ross and the older intuitionism. According to Dancy, some analysis is possible: We need not simply intuit our moral obligation directly when confronted with a concrete, morally problem-atic situation. Instead we perceive certain factors to be relevant ("sali-ent") and also see that they constitute a certain "shape" to the situation, an order that determines their relative weights in that case.[191] This account is similar to that of Ross, except that for him we know general (prima facie) rules to the effect that certain factors always weigh in the same direction.[192] Our particular moral perception is limited to determining priorities among them when they are in competition in concrete cases. For Dancy, we must in addition determine in each case which factors are relevant and in which direction; we cannot tell this from previous cases. I shall disagree with both Ross and Dancy: Factors do not always count in the same direction, but we can tell their priorities from previously settled cases.

The particularist account as it stands leaves us no way to reason to a correct answer in a problematic case. Nor is any reasoning available to resolve disagreements or to check intuitions or immediate moral perceptions. According to Dancy's account, persons trying to justify their moral judgments to others or to themselves are like art critics (although he does not explicitly draw this analogy). They do so not by argument, but by pointing to certain features of the situation in question, calling attention to relevant properties and relations that might have been missed. They then hope that their opponents will perceive the situation in the same way, that the same gestalt and the same reaction to it will emerge for them. But if uncertainty or disagreement persists, that is presumably the end of the matter. As in art, we will have to admit ultimate differences in taste or moral sensibility if parties to a disagreement recognize the same features of the case but continue to disagree in their overall judgments (in the moral sphere, they disagree about the relative weights of the relevant factors).

I do not want to deny that there are some moral disputes that in some sense (to be clarified) cannot be rationally settled. At some point some moral arguments may break down, leaving the disputes unresolvable. But I want to push that point much further back in the metaethical story than do the particularists. And just as important as the matter of disagreement is the matter of uncertainty, of searching for the right position on a difficult moral issue, of trying to reason one's way through it. Dancy's reasons, factors that are perceived to be morally relevant, do not function logically as reasons, as items of use in arguments. We simply see them as having a certain shape or set of relative weights in context. But when we are uncertain what to do in a problematic situation, and remain so even after we have decided which factors are morally relevant, our uncertainty reflects the fact that such factors do not come labeled with relative strengths.[193] Strength just is the tendency to outweigh other values and to be perceived to do so. Our uncertainties in these cases cannot be resolved by simply looking more closely, as the perceptual model suggests. We do not just wait for a gestalt to emerge, as in trying to see the duck when we see the rabbit or a meaningless two-dimensional shape. Even when we think that a gestalt has emerged, even when we are not uncertain, even when we have a gut feeling as to which value should take priority in a particular situation over another value that in other contexts has priority over it, we cannot always trust to such feelings. They must be checked against the reasons supporting them.

Moral judgment is in this respect unlike aesthetic judgment. When we disagree about the value of an artwork, all we can do is to point to features of the work, and perhaps its historical influence, and hope that the recognition of these features (sometimes complex relations) will lead to appreciation. Argument beyond such ostension becomes ad hominem: We can only lament the lack of training, impartiality, or sensitivity in those who oppose our judgments.[194] Reasoning itself has no place. But reasoning and argument are commonplace when it comes to moral judgment. This indicates that, unlike artworks, morally charged situations are not unique blends of properties that have the values they do only in those particular contexts. Take a phrase from a Mozart piano concerto and place it into some other work, and you have not perfect grace but aesthetic disaster. Morally relevant properties of actions and characters can be generalized more broadly than that, despite being context dependent in the way just indicated. If the fact that an act involves telling a lie counts against it in one context, it will count against other acts in other contexts as well, although it may not always do so.

There remains, however, a widespread assumption among moral theorists that the only way to support a particular moral judgment is by appeal to some fully general principle or rule.[195] I have emphasized that there are no rules that ordinarily determine priorities among conflicting values, precisely the sort of situation in which moral reasoning is required. Can we then honor Dancy's insight that these priorities can change with the context, while still allowing for reasoning to sort them out in particular cases? And how do we reason when we encounter genuinely novel circumstances that seem to constitute exceptions to any rules we might have considered? What sort of reasoning in the absence of rules can serve these functions and withstand metaethical scrutiny and criticism?

To be fair to particularists, we should note, first, forms of reasoning beyond Dancy's metaphors of salience and shape that are available to them. They need not simply trust to initial reactions or immediate perceptions, but can, first of all, check that their perceptions approximate to those of an "ideal observer," that they are what Rawls calls "considered" judgments. (This requirement does correspond to a similar one for art critics.) Such judgments are made with confidence, without hesitation; the judges are reflective, calm, and not under emotional stress; they have no personal interest at stake that might bias their judgment.[196]

One might well question these initial requirements. Why must moral judgments be calm, unbiased, and reflective?[197] Isn't moral outrage at some travesty a good source of evaluation of it? Shouldn't we be biased against the bad guys and in favor of the good? And might not our unreflective gut feelings be a reliable guide to the morality of various actions and policies if we ourselves are good or virtuous people? Aren't these requirements simply epistemological prejudices of an emotionless intellectual, themselves simply bald value judgments? The answer to these questions is that such requirements can be inductively supported. Experience teaches us that only judgments made in such conditions tend to be stable and consistent with each other and with other settled judgments. Only they therefore can be taken to reflect our stable values. (I make only this claim in order not to assume a realist goal that I will oppose later.)

In addition, those approximating to ideal moral judges must be sensitive to the interests and values at stake in the situations being evaluated. Sensitivity requires empathetic identification with other persons affected, and real agents may be sensitive to certain kinds of harms, discomforts, or wrongs and not to others.[198] We must learn to perceive all the morally relevant features of situations, and this involves training our affective as well as cognitive reactions. Such learning and training derive from the right kind of experience, both firsthand and secondhand, or vicarious, from encounters with literature, film, and other narratives.

Experience is necessary here as the only reliable source of information about what it is like to be in certain kinds of situations. And it must be experience of the right kind, that which sensitizes us to the feelings and interests of others instead of desensitizing, as some fictional art can.[199] Experience can correct our own desires, our thoughts about what we really want and do not want, by teaching us how acting on certain desires or values is likely to turn out. It also teaches us how others feel in various contexts, how they react and how we react to them. Narratives of much greater detail than we could provide ourselves can generate vicarious experience of the right sort in the absence of direct encounters, but their moral value will depend on their points of view. The goal here is always to broaden our own point of view, as our moral outlooks develop from identification with certain narrow groups and interests.

Experience provides us with a set of settled judgments and can also hone our ability to discriminate cases based on the interactions of values and interests at stake. Given this database and this ability, our particular judgments must be informed in other ways. In the situations in question, for example, we must be knowledgeable about all alternative actions and their probable consequences. Often a problem will remain unresolved because some acceptable solution has not been conceived as possible in the particular context or has been mistakenly thought to have certain consequences.

We can then add reasons to support our judgments by checking that our reactions are considered, sensitive, and informed. Just as prudential judgments must be backed by reasons that show our goals to be not merely desired, but desirable, so moral judgments must be backed initially by reasons of the same sort. Here we might therefore also borrow from the literature on desires, on rationally criticizing them and providing reasons in support of them. (Without such support, we lack reasons to pursue the objects of desires, as opposed to seeking to repress or eradicate them.) This literature is relevant also because suitably criticized desires constitute interests or values, and we are considering judgments in contexts of conflicting values. Among the authors on the subject are Richard Brandt and Elijah Millgram. Brandt argues that desires are rational only if they survive "cognitive therapy," repeated confrontation with vivid representation in imagination of relevant facts, including facts about the origins and objects of the desires.[200] Millgram emphasizes not the survival of desires, but their origin. Desires are supported by reasons if they originate in firsthand experience that teaches us what matters.[201] As mentioned previously, we learn what really matters by experiencing it firsthand (or, I would add, secondhand). Applying these criteria to the context of particular moral judgments, we seem to be led back to earlier considerations, however: Do judgments originate in properly informed, unbiased, and sensitive attention to the situations being judged, and do they survive calm reflection?

The criteria of Brandt and Millgram can also be criticized. Desires can survive Brandt's cognitive therapy for the wrong reasons – because they are deeply ingrained in childhood, by sheer force of habit, or because their subjects are too lazy to develop new interests.[202] Millgram's firsthand experience can mislead if it is based on a biased sample or influenced by extraneous associations, for example. What really matters is whether acting on particular desires results in ultimate satisfaction. This one might learn from further experience, but it is largely a matter of coherence with a broader set of first- and second-order desires. First-hand experience that generates immediate moral judgments can also be misleading. It can suggest superficial similarities to contexts of settled judgments that might mask relevant differences. To be justified, such judgments must really cohere with this core of settled or stable values, not simply immediately strike the observer as so cohering. I do not want to deny that the origin of moral judgments, their having resulted from calm, unbiased, sensitive, and informed consideration of the case, and their ability to survive further information and reflection, are relevant to their justification. But these features of ideal observers are important precisely for producing sets of coherent judgments based on stable values that qualify as moral. Thus we begin to move outside the domain of the particularist.

That we need to move outside that domain is clear as well from the fact that confident, informed, sensitive, unbiased, and reflective judgments can still conflict, especially when they concern priorities among recognized values. The only way to settle such disputes is for the opponents to reason to the judgment most coherent with that core of settled judgments on which they can agree. And, on the level of individual judgments, those with the previously mentioned attributes minus confidence can still leave us looking for further justification or confirmation. Once more, as individuals we must reason to the judgment that best coheres with those we take to be firmly settled. Such additional justification is still there to be had via the proper kind of reasoning, although not any kind available to the particularist. And disputes can still be rationally settled when particularists must part company, agree to disagree, or come to blows. If moral systems themselves exist to promote cooperation and settle disputes peaceably, then any further means to do so fairly and rationally must be welcome.

II. COHERENCE

I turn, then, to considerations of coherence among moral judgments as a source of justification for particular ones. "Coherence," of course, means many different things. In the domain of empirical knowledge or science, it refers mainly to causal explanatory connections: The more that explains or gets explained, the more coherent an empirical theory is. A similar criterion there determines the coherence of judgments with experience: A judgment regarding physical properties based on perceptual experience is warranted if it matches a natural inference to the best explanation of appearances to the nature of reality (although we most often make such perceptual judgments immediately and not by actually inferring them). But if sets of moral judgments do not arise from moral facts in the way that empirical judgments and theories are produced in reaction to empirical facts, then we will not be seeking the same sorts of causal connections here.

I have thus far avoided discussion of metaethical or metaphysical issues, since nothing in the previous chapters depended on the reality of moral properties. But here something must be said, since it is relevant to the method of reasoning, to objections that can be raised to my account of it, and to plausible answers to those objections whether such reasoning seeks to discover a truth independent of our moral beliefs and evaluations, or whether we aim only at coherent and informed sets of values that serve the social functions of moral norms. This is, of course, the topic of another book, and one that I among others have written, but a very brief summary of some of the main arguments in favor of the more plausible antirealist position is in order here. The arguments emerge from a comparison with the realm of empirical knowledge and the case for realism in regard to the physical world.[203]

Part of our justification for believing in real properties of independent physical objects is that we can specify the nature of those properties that help to explain causally how things appear to us, and we can understand the nature of these causal processes involving our sense organs. In the case of supposed moral properties of rightness and wrongness, by contrast, no one has succeeded in providing a natural reduction of these properties or an account of their nature if they are different from natural properties. The major historical attempts at reducing types of moral properties to types of natural properties – rational prudence, utility, or ability to will universally – all allow intuitively immoral actions to count as right (as we have seen in our discussion of similar proposed rules). Relational accounts, according to which being right is being such as to cause approval in suitably defined observers, can allow that the property is a unique type while allowing reduction of each token or instance. But here the problem is that ideal observers can seemingly disagree in their evaluations, which prompts a second and related argument against the realist.

156

This second argument appeals to the existence of incompatible but equally coherent moral frameworks or sets of judgments. The possibility of equally coherent but incompatible sets of empirical beliefs shows why coherence is not sufficient for truth in the empirical domain. Only if a set of empirical beliefs is anchored to the real world in the right way via experience can it make a plausible claim to truth. But in the moral realm we find fundamental disagreements between internally coherent frameworks – collectivist versus individualist (rights based), loyalist versus impartialist, egalitarian versus libertarian – none of which seems more anchored to the world or to experience than the others. Each is confirmed by experience in its own terms; none seems to rest on inaccurate predictions or ignorance of facts that, if brought to light, would cause its abandonment or resolve the disagreements. They seem to involve instead different fundamental values, different ways of balancing opposing interests, and distinct concepts of social flourishing, none of which mistakes or misperceives an independent property of rightness, as the realist must hold. The realist cannot tolerate disagreements that do not reduce to disputes over natural or nonmoral facts and that cannot be explained by appeal to ignorance on the part of one of the parties.

The argument here does not rely on differences across cultures to derive its relativist and antirealist premises. The problem with that argument is not that it posits too much disagreement, but instead too much agreement in taking cultures as homogeneous units.[204] The difficulty in finding impenetrable cultural diversity derives from the diversity within cultures, where dominant moral views do not determine the judgments of all members.[205] But the rejection of strong cultural relativism does not imply belief in one true morality, and the examples of fundamental differences between coherent frameworks listed earlier are all instantiated within our own culture. Indeed, fundamentally opposed theories such as Rawls's egalitarianism and Nozick's libertarianism claim as a common source the same basic pseudorule, the Kantian injunction against treating other individuals as means. Their opposition lies in interpretations of this norm in terms of very different paradigms of behavior in violation of it.

Nor does the argument rely on the idea of moral disagreements that are in principle irresolvable. The incompatibility of equally coherent frameworks does not imply the impossibility of resolving disputes within *or* across them. An important part of the method of reasoning to be described later is that it allows the resolution of any moral disagreement, given the willingness of the disputants to apply it to a common database. But the fact that such frameworks can jointly ascribe rightness and wrongness to the same actions or policies, and that there is no more objective or ideal viewpoint from which one of these frameworks must be mistaken, suffices to refute moral realism.

There are, of course, many other arguments on this topic to consider. I mention these not to convince the realist, but to excuse my not taking seriously objections to my account of moral reasoning that presuppose the truth of realism, those that fault the method for not demonstrating access to a moral truth independent of our fundamental values and evaluations. It can be similarly faulted for not capturing the revealed will of God. I assume, then, from this point that moral judgments reflect our values and not independent moral facts. That is why, in looking into the origins of moral judgments, we inquire not into causal connections to moral facts, but into the frames of mind in which the beliefs are formed and the social training that forms the background for these beliefs. And if the nonreductionist or antirealist is right, then the best candidate for moral facts lies in relations of coherence among moral judgments themselves. A moral judgment will be true, will correspond to a moral fact, if it coheres with others that count as moral in a maximally informed and coherent set. Such coherence cannot itself consist in causal connections to facts. The connection of such sets of beliefs to experience is required not to anchor them to an independent reality so as to ensure truth by a realist criterion, but because moral judgments require both information and sensitivity or empathy, and these are best acquired via experience.

The best-known model of coherence in ethics is that of Rawls, what he calls "reflective equilibrium." At its most basic level, equilibrium in Rawls's sense results from a set of mutual adjustments between rules and particular moral judgments, each having potential weight against the other when in conflict.[206] But we have noted that genuine rules fail to capture our considered judgments. From where, then, do they derive their independent weight? There are four possible sources for the belief that rules or principles must be weighed against particular judgments with which they conflict.

First, it might be assumed that judgments themselves cohere only when they can be subsumed under a set of universal norms. If that is so, then once we have inferred to a set of principles that capture a large set of our judgments and that we find plausible, we must adjust the recalcitrant judgments, since they cannot cohere with those captured by the principles. We adjust the particular judgments in light of the universal norms so as to create a coherent set of judgments. But we saw earlier that the initial assumption underlying this picture is false. Adhering to the weaker constraint of not judging cases differently without being able to state morally relevant differences between them renders judgments coherent without our being able to state sufficient conditions for our judgments or universal norms underlying them.

Second, one might think that the meanings of moral terms imply principles that must be weighed against particular judgments. This belief will most likely derive from the claim that moral judgments must be universalized, that this is part of the meaning of judging some action right, together with the belief that universalization requires stating a genuine rule or principle that underlies and implies the particular judgment. But this line of reasoning fails for a reason similar to that which defeated the previous one. We saw also in Chapter 1 that the most charitable interpretation of Kant's requirement identifies it precisely with the weaker constraint that governs analogical reasoning and renders sets of judgments coherent. Once more, universalizing – judging all similar cases alike – does not require following genuine rules. In addition to the requirement to universalize, the use of moral terms involves approval or disapproval on grounds that require restraint of narrow self-interest for the welfare of others or the collective, a weighing of opposing interests so as to promote peace and cooperation and reduce conflict. I have emphasized that different ways of weighing count as moral and that the most plausible ways do not apply rules as the norm.

Third, we might find moral rules or principles independently plausible because our having learned moral language and practice consisted initially in our having been taught to obey moral rules. But, it is first of all doubtful that we are taught genuine rules initially as opposed to learning paradigm reactions to various types of behavior in various contexts. I doubt that most of us were really taught never to lie, that is, intentionally utter falsehoods, as opposed to being taught when to tell the truth and when not to, when to bend the truth for the sake of courtesy, and so on. Even if we were taught moral requirements initially in the form of rules, we quickly learn that these are really rules of thumb admitting of open-ended exceptions.

Such rules, we noted, simply point to factors that must be weighed directly against others in controversial cases requiring reasoning. They cannot therefore have independent weight against particular judgments with which they conflict. Their having such weight might amount to counting certain judgments, those in accord with the rules, twice in a moral calculation that otherwise counted all particular judgments once. Or else rules of thumb simply stand in for the judgments in accord with them and are once more dispensable once those judgments, or the moral factors they reflect, come into play. We will not change a particular judgment to make it accord with a rule of thumb unless or until we are convinced that the case in question cannot be differentiated on moral grounds from the paradigm cases that the rule summarizes. The whole question will be whether the present case constitutes an exception to the rule as stated, which, being a rule of thumb, is acknowledged to admit of exceptions. If the present case is an exception, we will not weigh the rule against it.

But can't we (fourth) simply find some universal rule, such as the utilitarian principle, immediately intuitive, much as we might find some theory of personal identity, such as Parfit's theory (described in Chapter 2), plausible in itself and modify our view of morality and therefore some of our particular moral judgments accordingly? Or, to take a slightly narrower example, couldn't one reasonably alter one's negative moral judgment of homosexuality on the grounds that homosexual relations can be consensual and not harm anyone, and that even if one finds such relations offensive, mere offense is not sufficient for moral condemnation? Wouldn't this be to alter reasonably a particular judgment in light of intuitively plausible principles or rules? It may seem so, but the question here is whether the appeal to consent, lack of harm, and mere offense really is an appeal to genuine rules, whether it is most plausibly construed in that way. An alternative construal is that we appeal here to rules of thumb or, more perspicuously, to settled cases to which certain homosexual relations can be compared and from which they might or might not be differentiated.

If we do not begin with an antecedent faith that there must be genuine rules behind every sound particular judgment, then the interpretation in terms of settled cases becomes more plausible in light of the apparent counterexamples to the proposed rules. Sometimes offense *is* sufficient for condemnation (e.g., a flasher); sometimes consent is *not* sufficient for permissibility (e.g., slavery contracts); and harm is itself a normative notion generating only more pseudorules. Of course, we *could* dismiss all the counterexamples, but without the antecedent general faith in principles or rules, the particular judgments have more of the feel of primitives, from which theoretical laws derive all their support. This is not to say that moral judgments are observations of an independent reality, only that it is difficult to see in light of all of our previous discussion where proposed principles could derive independent weight against them.

As for the utilitarian principle, this will immediately lose all plausibility for one who takes individual rights seriously, once all the cases involving sacrificing one individual to many or greater interests to additions of lesser wants are revealed.

Thus, if our earlier discussion regarding rules is even mostly on the mark, then Rawls's conception of coherence must be replaced by a different conception that measures coherence only among the set of particular judgments. If the demand for coherence, which is to give us a way to reason to a correct judgment in a particular case, does not require subsuming the case under a rule, then it must require analogizing it to other particular judgments directly. As indicated, this involves the Kantian constraint whose violation generates *in*coherence among a set of moral judgments: One must not judge a case differently from a previously settled case unless one can cite a morally relevant difference between them, a difference that can be shown to make a difference in other cases as well. A set of judgments is coherent when there are no violations of this constraint.

The requirement for coherence in the practical realm derives from considerations different from those that ground the requirement for coherent beliefs about independent facts in the empirical realm. Coherence among empirical beliefs is necessary because contradictory beliefs cannot all be true and because we have less reason to believe in unexplained facts. It is not sufficient there because there can be coherent sets of fictional statements with little or no connection to reality. Since moral judgments need not capture an independent reality, it is no objection that mutually incompatible or incoherent sets cannot both do so. Disagreement between two such systems is no ground for suspicion of either, although such disagreements may need to be settled for the sake of peace or cooperation. Internal incoherence, however, the violation of the Kantian constraint, will first of all generate explanatory incoherence, as in the empirical realm: There will be no explanation for why a factor counts as morally relevant or overrides in one context but not in another.

More important here, coherence in the sense indicated is required among moral judgments because such judgments guide actions, and actions aim to fulfill purposes or realize values. It is a truism that, if I believe that two contexts for action cannot be distinguished by reasons for acting differently in them, I must, if rational, act the same way in both. (Of course, in nonmoral contexts, my reason for acting differently may be just to vary things a bit.) Since moral judgments guide moral actions, I must, if I aim to be moral, judge two situations in the same way if I cannot distinguish them morally. Otherwise, my judgments will be self-defeating in just the way that actions at cross-purposes are self-defeating. I will defeat an aim that I am committed to pursuing in just those circumstances at hand. Actions must be consistent not only with the purposes behind them, but also with other actions and the purposes and values they express, as these are prioritized in a stable ordering. In the moral sphere, it is perhaps a further requirement that I be able to cite or specify what the difference is between two cases that I judge differently, but this requirement follows from the use of moral judgment in reasoning and argument.

In both reasoning for oneself and arguing with another, the goal is to find the resolution of the controversial case that is most coherent with the database of settled judgments. In one's own case one begins, of course, with the seemingly most analogous cases in which one's judgments pass the tests described in the previous section (confident, etc.) and then seeks to find relevant differences from the case at issue. The same method under the same constraint allows for both genuine disagreement and resolution of disputes on particular issues between adherents of different and incompatible moral frameworks. No disagreement is in principle irresolvable. The possibility of resolution depends on a prior implicit agreement to limit the database from which argument proceeds to the set of shared paradigms. There will always be some shared paradigms at some level of generality between any frameworks recognizable as moral: To describe a set of judgments, or for that matter a disagreement, as moral is to point to some shared constraints that serve the social functions of moral systems. Furthermore, if you disagree with another and are willing to argue the point, then you are extending your judgment from your own framework to the other's; and this is some indication that you should be willing to suspend other disagreements and argue on the other's terms, that is, from the base of shared settled judgments, although only practical and not logical considerations can compel you to do so.

The disagreement itself in regard to a particular practice will likely derive from thinking of the practice under different paradigms – abortion as murder or as contraception or elective surgery, capital punishment as primitive revenge or as just deserts, affirmative action as discrimination or as compensation, equal opportunity, or justified diversity. It can be resolved by one party's (1) extending some shared paradigm to the new case when it is recognized that differences are not morally relevant, (2) coming to see relevant differences from a supposed paradigm where none were previously thought relevant, or (3) developing a new paradigm or modifying a previously settled one. Thus one might, for example, (1) extend civil rights to some previously excluded group, (2) come to agree that fetuses are indeed relevantly different from infants, or (3) come to agree that, although refusal of lifesaving medical treatment is indeed analogous to suicide, certain conditions might render suicide permissible. All these alterations might well be involved in changing one's mind under challenge, since coming to see relevant differences from one paradigm naturally precedes seeing closer analogies to another, possibly new or modified, one.

Argument on contested issues thus proceeds by proposing paradigms, coming to agreement on them, and examining similarities and differences between them and the case at issue. One must defend not only the internal coherence of one's judgment with one's paradigms, but the paradigms themselves. One can criticize another's settled judgments in the same way that one critically reflects on one's own, according to the criteria described in the previous section. Older paradigms may no longer fit practices they were thought to govern because of changed circumstances, for example, doctors practicing under health maintenance organizations may no longer fit the model of friends and trusted advisors (sometimes even taking on an adversarial role). The goal of such moral debate is not convergence on a single true moral framework, but the gradual adjustment of paradigms and recognized differences so as to achieve piecemeal resolutions of particular conflicts and thus introduce somewhat greater coherence across frameworks. Progress through peaceful resolution of conflicts will continue to allow frameworks to differ in those beliefs temporarily suspended in the particular debates resolved. So happens moral progress, not by radical shifts in moral concepts signaling the approach of universal agreement and certainly not by the discovery of real properties inhering in objects to which we were previously blind.

Such progress may be hard to come by on particular intractable issues. As noted, no argument can compel agreement if the parties are unwilling to suspend appeal to paradigms on which they disagree, unwilling to narrow the database to shared settled judgments, or unable to resolve different perceptions of relevant similarities and differences. While no issue is in principle irresolvable, some are in fact so and perhaps should remain so according to the central paradigms, the fundamental moral outlook, of the opposing parties. When argument does break down, this may or may not call for toleration of the opposing position. Much will depend on the internal coherence of the opposing framework, its qualification as moral, the extent of agreement of those governed by it, and the costs of various forms of opposition. From one's own point of view, even unresolved disagreement can be useful for prompting a reexamination of the coherence of one's moral beliefs and one's settled convictions, resulting in greater self-knowledge if not changes in commitments or self-identity.

Pursuing the goal of informed and sensitive coherence can fail to resolve issues within an individual's own framework as well. This might possibly happen because of an insufficient number of settled cases from which to reason; but the possibility is remote, since even a minimally developed moral framework will contain some quite general paradigms (involving stealing, lying, physically harming, and so on) to and from which new cases can be assimilated and differentiated. It is more probable that the settled convictions point equally by analogy to incompatible conclusions. This might well happen, for example, in regard to questions of killing some or letting some die in order to save others. There will most likely be settled cases at the extremes – we do not kill one to save one, and we would kill one to save the planet – but these judgments do not point either way in regard to many cases in between. Such situations can generate so-called moral dilemmas, which in turn have generated a medium-sized philosophical industry. Dilemmas are not unique to the method of reasoning described here and so are no objection to it.[207]

Let us return from this discussion of the method of seeking coherence to the nature of coherence itself. There are two parts to the central requirement: One must find morally relevant differences between cases judged differently, and these differences must be relevant more broadly, must distinguish other cases as well. Can particularists accept the full constraint? Dancy's main argument for particularism – that context can eliminate the moral relevance of a factor, or even change its valence or direction – is compatible with the first clause of this constraint. We can reason from case to case despite his point, from the case at hand not to all cases with the same features relevant in that one, but to all cases with those features and no relevant differences. If there are no relevant differences from one case to the next, then nothing can change the values of the factors in the first case, and so we can generalize its judgment to the second case. My second clause marks the point at which I part company

164

with Dancy. Without it the first clause becomes trivial, since there will always be some differences between cases to which one can point. A claim of unique relevance fails to state a moral aim to be consistently pursued or a value to be maintained. It is a mere bald assertion. A claim that some such difference is morally relevant in the present case will lack the possibility of challenge and the need for genuine defense if one can respond to a challenge by simply claiming that one sees its unique relevance here. Argument will again break down too soon.

If, for example, one can distinguish abortion from infanticide by arguing that infants and fetuses breathe in different ways and that the manner of respiration is morally relevant here, although nowhere else, this would reduce the constraint of coherence to triviality. All sets of judgments would be coherent as long as all cases differ in some respect that their evaluators could claim to see as relevant. An opponent would have no way of responding to this alleged perception of uniquely instantiated relevance. I think the constraint is not trivial. So although I agree with Dancy that we cannot argue from something's making a difference here to its making the same difference everywhere, or from its not making a difference here to its not making a difference anywhere, I think we can argue from its making a difference here to its doing so elsewhere. The value of something need be neither a brute particular fact nor an instance of a universally valuable property. It can be an instance of a generally valuable property. Then we can explain its value in a given case by pointing to similar value in another context that is not relevantly different. It is then up to one who judges cases differently to produce a morally relevant difference and to show that it makes a difference in other cases.

You may still think that Dancy's point, which I accept, is damaging to the method of argument I wish to defend and to its requirement that morally relevant differences be generally, if not universally, so. If other values at stake in a context can nullify the relevance of some factor that counts as a value in some other context, why can't the latter be relevant only that once? The possibility of relevance unique to a single context or situation may seem to be entailed by the ever-present possibility of nullification or reversal. How can the actualization of that possibility be limited? Isn't the requirement that it be so simply wishful thinking or at best ad hoc?

Part of the answer is indeed that we simply do not allow this move, the appeal to a uniquely relevant factor, in a moral argument, as the abortion example and others show. Only generalized factors or differences function as reasons in argument. According to rule theorists, they do this by instantiating rules that state invariably relevant conditions for moral judgments. According to the view advocated here, they function in reasoning by analogy: If a factor is relevant in another case, and there are no relevant differences between that case and this one, then it must be relevant in the same way here. The requirement that relevant factors not be unique to a particular context could be viewed as part of the normative conventions we adopt to settle disputes by argument instead of combat and to prolong the possibility of peaceful settlement. Nevertheless, if the requirement forced us to violate our rational orderings of values (in all their complexity), then its irrationality certainly would not recommend it as such a convention and would probably override its useful function in argument.

But this requirement accords with rational value orderings rather than violating them. A factor that is relevant in one context may be canceled in another, but it won't count only once unless it is always found elsewhere together with its defeaters. On the face of it, this is highly unlikely even if we consider only contexts that have occurred in the real world. The things we value are things that satisfy our instincts or things that we have learned to value. In both cases, these sources of value recur, or we would not learn, adopt, or continue to value them. The preceding questions once more seem to presuppose a realism in regard to values. They presuppose that values are simply out there in the world and then wonder why they could not be out there in only one place, just as some extremely rare mineral might be found at only one source. But if instead it is a question of what we value, what values we have developed and continue to maintain, then the mystery of why values must recur disappears. It is then predictable that I cannot think of a single property that makes something valuable or disvaluable but that does so for nothing else. I may value persons or artworks as unique individuals, but in moral judgment we cite relevant properties as reasons, not individuals.

And in moral reasoning, we are not limited to appeal to actual cases; instead we appeal to reasons and value orderings that could be instantiated in conceivable cases, a much broader class. We may learn from testimony and experience from actual cases what to value, but we can then argue and reason from imaginary cases as well, in which these valued factors figure in new combinations analogous to the controversial contexts being decided. The requirement that we show moral relevance elsewhere if we are to claim it in the instant case is made easier to satisfy when we can appeal to fictional cases, but it is not thereby trivialized.

For one thing, the fictional cases themselves must lack relevant differences from the case at hand if we are to show that the factors that count in them count in the case at hand as well. It is not easy, although it is possible, to invent new contexts in which priorities are both clearer than but analogous to actual cases under dispute. For example, Judith Thomson's case of unhooking your kidneys from a famous violinist to whom you have been connected in order to keep him alive does seem to show that in the normal case the right to life does not extend to the right to use the bodies of others.[208] There is a danger in such highly fictionalized cases that one would not really react as imagined; but here we generalize in the opposite direction as well: from our knowledge or experience of how people do react in somewhat similar circumstances.

There is another feature of moral judgment that is relevant to this argument. I pointed out earlier that individuals can act to realize one value in a particular context and act to realize another that competes with it in a later context simply because they have already realized or secured some of the first value on the previous occasion. Trivially, I will read for a while tonight and then watch some TV. The same may be true of a whole society. One way to compromise among competing claims is to sometimes honor or pursue one and sometimes the other, even when the situation is otherwise the same. Equally trivially, we spend some money on education and then some on police protection (usually in the reverse order). But the case of moral judgment is different.

As Ronald Dworkin pointed out in an example cited earlier, we do not compromise on the abortion issue by allowing half of the women who seek abortions, say those born on odd days of the month, to obtain them.[209] That is largely because the issue of fairness is central in the moral domain, as it is not in the prudential one (even the collective prudential one), and fairness involves comparative justice more than absolute justice. In order to avoid comparative injustice, we do not need to act according to genuine rules or principles, as Dworkin and others seem to think. We need only obey the weaker constraint that I am defending. Odd versus even birth dates are not relevant in candidates for abortions, and we would not allow, with good reason, that they could be relevant in this context only.

An objector might claim that an odd-numbered birthday is relevant here in many cases: for those born not only on the first, but also on the third, fifth, and so on.[210] But this is to misinterpret the requirement that differences make a difference in different moral contexts. The objector would need to show that odd-numbered birth dates affect the values at stake in abortions, as well as in other contexts involving similar values or interests (life versus choice) or others that may compete. I see no way to do this or even to claim it sincerely. Thus, we can allow and should recognize that value A trumps value B in context x, while B trumps A in y, but only if we can point to a difference δ between x and y that also makes a difference between some w and z. W and z need not involve values A and B, but they must involve some values whose priorities are altered because of δ.

III. THE REASONING PROCESS REVIEWED

We can now review the steps at which we have pointed or hinted thus far in describing moral reasoning without rules. First, we must specify those factors that are morally relevant in a case. If the case is controversial, as it will be if reasoning about it is required, these factors will involve competing values or interests that must be prioritized in choosing the appropriate action. Their recognition requires both information about the context at hand and unbiased but empathetic identification with the interests of those individuals involved or affected. We must know how the situation developed, which alternative actions are available to us in it, how they are likely to realize or frustrate the competing values at stake, and how the individuals involved are likely to feel and react to our possible actions. The correct description of the situation and its history may, of course, itself be a matter of considerable dispute, and the specification of alternative actions may require imaginative ingenuity. If the nature of the situation is ambiguous, for example in regard to what goes under the name of affirmative action, we may need to decide what is permissible or required under different characterizations. And sometimes disputes cannot be settled until someone finds a possible action that compromises among the competing values in a way that had not been conceived before, as when we allow a risky activity with strict liability and a guarantee of insurance or compensation for harm.

Second, at the point at which agreement is reached as to relevant factors or values at stake, but at which there is still disagreement about their ordering in the present context, when particularists await gut feelings or perceptions of what to do or how to judge, when they hope that the correct priorities just take shape as if by magic, we must instead look to previously settled cases in which priorities among these values were determined in a way that would be acceptable to the parties to the present dispute. Here we must first identify either real or fictional situations in which similar interests compete but our judgments are more confident. In evaluating certain preferential affirmative action programs, for example, we look to other contexts in which claims to compensation oppose distributive claims to goods, or in which the goal of diversity is allowed partially to determine the award of positions, or in which the promotion of equal opportunity requires temporary departures from considerations of merit that are fair grounds for distributing positions only in the context of equal opportunity.[211] At the same time we must review these settled judgments, their origins, implications, and so on, to make sure they should remain settled.

In regard to compensation, we must decide when groups can be owed for past injustices, what kinds of groups can be owed and what distinguishes them from other collectives, and how compensation is distributed or paid to the former groups. In regard to diversity, we must decide whether, for example, it is agreed to be unproblematic to balance diversity against other desiderata for applicants to entering classes in colleges, for which characteristics it is legitimate to seek diversity, and why it is fair or legitimate to aim at (rough) quotas in regard to these characteristics. We might choose this as our exemplary practice because it is long-standing and might be assumed to be deemed acceptable to parties to a dispute over more controversial appeals to diversity. If this assumption proved false, we would need a different paradigm. In regard to equal opportunity, we must think of lower levels in the education system, for example, where resources are justifiably aimed at equalizing opportunities for future benefits by nullifying initial social disadvantages (instead of being distributed on the basis of, say, test scores). We identify such contexts and the reasons for the primacy of considerations of equality within them in order then to compare them with the award of benefits at higher levels in the educational system and in job markets, where the weight of the value of equality is more controversial. In regard to all these potential arguments on this and other controversial moral and social issues, the first step is always to find paradigms in which the parties to the present dispute can intelligently agree on the priorities among the same competing interests or values.

After we have found appropriate analogous cases, an equally important third step is to seek to identify disanalogies between the context at issue and these less problematic cases and to determine whether these disanalogies are morally relevant (whether they affect the values at stake or add others). In the same critical spirit, we must (fourth) attempt to find yet more similar cases in which our judgments may come down on the other side. Sticking with the affirmative action example, that diversity in background is a reasonable goal in a college class as a measure of probable diversity in opinions and outlooks that fosters fruitful discussion does not mean that it is a reasonable goal for the faculty, where diversity in opinion, if that is desirable, can be measured more directly from published work or interviews. That equality in educational resources is important for creating equal opportunities to compete for later desirable positions through productive efforts does not imply that the chances for those positions themselves must be equal. That groups whose members closely interact in pursuit of common goals can be harmed as units, and hence collectively or commonly compensated, does not imply that groups as diverse and dispersed as that of women can be so harmed or should be so compensated.

To take another example mentioned earlier, when Judith Thomson shows us a case in which a person is not obligated to let another person use her body in order to stay alive as an analogy to the rights at stake in the abortion issue, we should point out that obligations to strangers differ from obligations to one's own children and that, if one grants that the fetus is a person (as she is willing to grant in this argument), a closer analogy may lie in the extreme sacrifices that parents are sometimes obligated to make for their children. If the fetus is the child of its mother, then parents' stringent duties to preserve their children's lives seem to constitute a more analogous case, despite other differences between fetuses and infants. The fourth step in our sequence naturally follows the third, since finding disanalogies to proposed cases naturally leads one to seek closer analogies.

Accurate identification of differences is as crucial to coherence as the recognition of analogies. Just as we must not judge cases differently without being able to identify a generally morally relevant difference between them, so we must not judge them the same way when such a difference calls for the opposite judgment. To do so is to fail to bring values to bear that one recognizes to make a difference among other relevantly similar cases, again a form of incoherence. Perhaps the most common error in analogical reasoning is to focus on superficial similarities, ignoring differences relevant to the values implicit in the comparison of cases.[212] Just as both parties to a dispute can often trot out rules supporting their positions, so both might be able to claim some analogy with a favored paradigm: Hawks in regard to any potential armed conflict always have Munich and doves Vietnam. In fact, the error of relying on superficial analogies without noting relevant differences is equivalent to applying a rule whose conditions prohibit consideration of factors that would otherwise defeat them and should defeat them in the case at hand. Its remedy lies in a thorough search for differences as well as similarities (for exceptions in the context of rules).

Of course, just as rules and superficial analogies can lead to oversimplification or overassimilation, so can the search for differences, now being urged as a further discrete step in moral reasoning, lead to overcomplication or false distinctions. Perhaps, for example, diversity in a student body is of value not solely for generating a diversity of opinions, in which case the difference between faculty and students in this regard (that one knows the opinions of faculty in advance) may not be as significant as indicated earlier. Perhaps the goal of diversity among students is instead itself a means to enable them to live more easily in diverse environments outside the university, in which case diversity among faculty will further serve this function for students, despite other differences between faculty and students. Perhaps the differences between women and more closely knit groups does not matter in arguments for collective compensation if women share common interests that are affected by overt discrimination against some of them or if all have been harmed by more subtle injustice. Whether differences, such as those between faculty and students that matter in some contexts, matter in the context at issue depends on how they affect the values at stake and the ways they are at stake. Some differences that matter generally are simply irrelevant in differentiating particular cases. When they are nevertheless thought to be relevant, we have overcomplication. The difference, however, between this occasional overcomplicating effect of case reasoning and the oversimplifying effect of applying rules to ordinary contexts is that it is in the nature of rules to oversimplify in those contexts, while the method of reasoning described here need not involve either type of error.

The skills needed for this kind of reasoning nevertheless exceed by far those involved in knowing a set of rules and being able to apply them to cases that fall under their stated conditions of application. The former skills include, first of all, the ability to empathize in an unbiased way with various interests and concerns and with possible harms to various agents. They also include a knowledge of or ability to imagine numerous morally charged contexts in which specified values compete against one another. Moral knowledge, according to this account, consists not in knowing a set of rules, but in knowing how to act consistently with coherent orderings of norms or competing values as ex-

171

pressed in settled judgments in a large variety of cases or contexts. This knowledge must be brought to bear on problematic present cases through an appreciation not only of its areas of similarity, but also through an ability to discriminate, to discern differences among superficially similar cases, and to determine whether these differences matter in the end, whether they affect the values at stake in such a way as to alter their priorities. In short, the sort of skill required by a moral reasoner is not unlike that of a good lawyer or medical diagnostician, except that here the knowledge base is largely unwritten (at least the annals of sound applied ethics are both less required as a database and less routinely consulted). All these skills – the ability to empathize, to bring to bear a large base of settled judgments, and to discriminate morally relevant properties – develop only in relation to sufficiently broad firsthand and secondhand experience of the right, sensitizing kind.

We may close this section by considering, in outline, a final example of how the full method might be applied to a contemporary unsettled issue. Should doctors allow their patients to die, and should they aid in bringing about less painful and prolonged deaths? First, we must identify the competing values at stake – from the patient's side, life versus avoidance of suffering and freedom of choice; from the doctor's side, the possible effects on character and on medical practice of allowing or causing death versus allowing preventable prolonged suffering and blocking informed patient choice. Fortunately, we have never experienced terminal illness firsthand. But many have experienced it secondhand with relatives or friends, and we all have some personal experience of major life choices and decisions in medical contexts, as well as knowledge of fictional narratives depicting such choices. Thus, it is not difficult to identify the competing values, although disagreements may result from identifying more with those on one side or the other.

Second, we need relevant factual information and estimates of probabilities. We must identify what is possible in the situation in question, for example whether we can produce safeguards that will guarantee that alleged choices of patients really are their choices in these contexts. How much influence do relatives typically exert (and should such influence be discounted)? How rational are patients in terminal conditions (and can we determine which of them are rational in these contexts aside from their choice to refuse life-prolonging medical treatment)? We must also seek out information about outcomes of various policies where these data are available: How has legalized euthanasia in other societies affected the medical profession there (and how similar to ours was medical practice there otherwise)? We must also estimate the probability that a rule allowing euthanasia in specified cases could be followed without being abused or leading to a broader unwarranted practice (assuming what also needs arguing, that a rule is preferable to discretion on the part of doctors to decide cases in the absence of a rule). All this information and estimation is relevant to the next step, producing paradigm cases for comparison to this context.

Third, then, we must canvas the relevant analogies and look for differences as well. In the case of "passive" euthanasia, perhaps the closest model derives from a seemingly absolute right of patients to refuse medical treatment in other contexts. This right appears to be part of settled social practice: Unauthorized treatment of alert and competent patients is legally classified as battery. But opponents of patient choice in terminal contexts will see the imminent threat of death as a relevant difference from other medical situations. In light of this difference, they are likely to see as a closer analogy attempts at suicide, intentional choices to end life, and the right of doctors to intervene in order to prevent such attempts from succeeding. The model of patient choice can be extended to the case at hand, therefore, only if doctors at least sometimes lack the obligation or right to intervene and prevent attempted suicides from succeeding. Defenders of the model must point to some relevant difference between some intentional choices of death and the case of persons rushed unconscious to hospitals with overdoses of barbiturates who are then saved. The latter is again part of accepted practice. The defender of choice for terminal patients must then differentiate attempted suicide in the context of known resolve from other attempts. Informed and known resolve can be shown to differentiate many situations in which paternalistic interference is contemplated on grounds of perceived harm to the agent. Does it override the fact that death, unlike other harm, is irreversible?

If we accept passive euthanasia, a prohibition against forced life-prolonging medical treatment for competent patients (and if such patients can be reliably identified), then we encounter James Rachels's argument that there is no relevant difference between killing and letting die, and that active euthanasia must therefore be accepted as well. But he argues this by producing one case in which the difference between killing and letting die is irrelevant,[213] and I have agreed with Dancy that we cannot argue from one case or context to all. Factors that make differences must count more than once, but they need not always count. It follows that not counting in one context does not imply not counting in all. In fact, in other contexts this particular difference between killing and letting die does seem relevant. If I am wrong to let a starving person in Africa die instead of contributing the money to save him, it seems more wrong, given a choice between killing that person and losing the same amount of money, to choose the former. Letting the person die, if a moral crime, is one of which we are almost all guilty; killing the person is hopefully a crime of which few would be guilty if the situation occurred.

Thus, instead of attempting to assimilate active to passive euthanasia, we might do better to consider cases of acceptable active euthanasia, for example killing wounded animals that cannot be saved in order to prevent prolonged suffering. Here, of course, we must consider differences between animals and humans. The differences are, of course, enormous, but their general moral significance, especially when it comes to relieving or preventing suffering, is a matter of considerable debate. The capacity for rational choice does seem to be a relevant difference in the context we are presently considering, but its relevance may be limited to the capacity to opt for life or death itself. The capacity for other choices may not be relevant in the context of terminal illness, where the prolongation of life with only very limited rational or moral agency may alone compete against the alleviation of suffering. This context may, however, relevantly differ from other requests for doctor-assisted suicide, in part because of the capacity for other autonomous choices or changes of mind if the agent survives. Thus, doctor-assisted suicide may be permissible for the terminally ill who choose that course, but not for others (assuming that we can draw a line for terminal illness). But doctors may also have the right to refuse such aid, especially if they have a right to refuse to provide other permissible medical services of which they disapprove, such as abortions.

In this final stage of the reasoning process, the key to sound reasoning lies in the search for the closest analogies and the subsequent attempt to identify relevant differences that remain. The relevance of differences once more depends on their being so elsewhere and on how they affect the values at stake here. Examples of such reasoning on current social issues could, of course, be multiplied, and I shall have occasion to consider a few more in the next section. My purpose here, however, is not to argue fully for particular solutions to any of these problems, but to indicate how such argument might proceed, to illustrate how the method is applied and how commonly it is used without being explicitly conceptualized. Complex concrete issues rarely admit of resolution or even intelligent discussion by appeal to rules (although weak rules may sometimes enter the calculations). But a survey of the better literature in applied ethics would reveal the ubiquity of at least partial use of the method described here.

IV. OBJECTIONS

In this last section, I shall briefly consider some objections to the account of moral reasoning I have been defending. The first arises from the description of moral knowledge and reasoning skills offered earlier. It might be objected that this description ties moral capacities too closely to cognitive skills and intelligence, while moral behavior depends more on good character, which is largely a matter of benevolent motives and sensitive feelings. If correct moral judgment is so much a matter of close analysis of cases in the search for complex analogies and subtle differences, then how are relatively unsophisticated people who are not trained in such analysis so often able to do the right thing?

In response, I certainly do not wish to downplay the importance of emotion, and I included among the skills required of the moral agent the ability to identify empathetically with the concerns of others and a sensitivity to the factors that might adversely affect their interests. Such affective capacities are necessary to generate proper inputs or information from which the cognitive reasoning process can appropriately begin. At the end of the process, it is certainly true also that the will to do what is right is as important as the knowledge of what is right. That is one reason why we might not find a strong correlation between moral behavior and general intelligence. Another reason is that skill in the area of moral reasoning and the sort of experience that often generates the database for such reasoning may not correlate closely with success in other domains of intelligence: Cognitive skills sometimes come apart in surprising ways. As for unsophisticated people doing the right thing, most need not solve such difficult issues as abortion, capital punishment, or affirmative action. Most paradigms and the cases they govern are quite straightforward, and real moral reasoning is the exception. When ordinary people do need to act on issues like abortion, or when they voice their opinions on issues like capital punishment or affirmative action, it is not at all clear that they, whether generally virtuous or not, most often do (or say) the right thing.

I do wish to deny that moral judgment itself is best seen as an affective reaction, that we do better in the face of real moral problems by trusting

175

to gut feelings than to the outcomes of complex reasoning processes.[214] There are at least two problems with gut feelings in this domain. One is that they are often based, in the absence of preliminary reasoning, on misleading or irrelevant similarities, as when we react to what looks like a fetus screaming in an antiabortion film, based on a likeness in visual appearance that may mask relevant differences between fetuses and infants. Another problem was noted earlier: Gut feelings or immediate perceptions are not suitable moves in an argument, not part of the methods by which we attempt to resolve disputes peaceably, which is a central function of moral systems. Such feelings are the stuff of disputes, not part of their resolution.

The second objection to our method concerns the move from settled cases to problematic ones. It again derives from Dancy's particularism[215] and in my version takes the form of a double dilemma, as follows. Either the problematic case is more complex than the settled case or it is not. If, on the one hand, it is more complex, then it will have possibly relevant properties in addition to the morally relevant properties of the first case. If these additional properties are relevant, then we cannot assimilate the judgment of the second case to that of the first, and the latter will be of no help. But in order to know that these additional properties are not relevant in the second context, we must already know how to judge the second case. So once more, the first case will be of no use. If, on the other hand, the second case is not more complex than the first, then it will be just as easy to judge the second case directly, and yet again we will have no need to appeal to the first. Hence a settled case cannot force a judgment in a problematic one; as particularists maintain, we must always perceive the right answer in each case directly.

But we need only think again of the force of certain arguments in applied ethics to know that there is something wrong with this argument. These arguments show us first of all that, without thinking of analogous settled cases, the problematic nature of the case at hand can blind us to the ordinary priorities among the competing values. As Judith Thomson pointed out, if we think of the value of life versus that of choice (or control over one's body) only in the abstract, then the former may seem more important. Concrete examples show us that it can be otherwise.[216] Similarly, until we think of concrete contexts in which debts of compensation are owed and take precedence over further distributions of goods on other grounds, we might well think that merit criteria should not be sacrificed to make up for past wrongs in the award of desirable positions.

But how can we move from the settled cases to the problematic ones in light of Dancy's claim that we cannot know whether additional properties in the latter cases alter the values or priorities of the former unless or until we know how to judge the problematic cases in themselves? According to him, we cannot assimilate the cases without knowing which properties are relevant in the controversial ones, and this knowledge amounts to knowing how to judge those cases. It is this second horn of the second (embedded) dilemma that we must seize here. Its main claim has force only if we lack an independent test for the moral relevance of various properties, and specifically the properties that controversial cases have in addition to those of settled cases.

I emphasized earlier that this is precisely where I part company with Dancy. In his account, we must determine in each separate case whether each of its properties is morally relevant. A property may be relevant in a particular context and nowhere else. Hence we cannot know which properties are relevant prior to judging the case itself; determining the ways they are relevant just is judging the case. No other cases can help us to do this precisely because no generalization at all is possible. But in my view, defended earlier, we can know that if properties are not relevant elsewhere, then they are not relevant in the case at hand. If they are relevant elsewhere, then they are relevant here in the absence of other relevant differences. Hence we can decide whether they are relevant in the case at hand prior to deciding that case. In the absence of differences that seem relevant and that cannot be eliminated in this way, we assimilate the problematic case to the settled one, and these two independent steps complete the judgment of the former. Dancy's objection applies only if one already accepts his particularist framework. It cannot be used to establish that framework against my alternative.

The final objections concern the status of the settled cases themselves and are typically raised against any coherentist methods in ethics. The method I advocate takes cases that remain controversial after fully informed, unbiased, and sensitive reflection and seeks to assimilate them to settled judgments. It is therefore only as reliable as the set of settled judgments themselves. Some of these judgments may have been settled by the coherentist method of appealing to those settled earlier. But the typical charge is that such judgments, when pushed back far enough, represent only old or stale intuitions – moral beliefs acquired from one's parents, religion, or personal prejudices or derived from ancient social taboos or from brute economic forces or power relations. In our society, for example, it seems settled that lawyers may do almost anything for their clients and that enormous inequalities in wealth are allowed to stand. Coherence with such judgments is worth only as much as the judgments themselves, which is not much at all if we cannot provide them better credentials than in these instances.

The answer to this objection is that we can provide better credentials. In fact, it is precisely here that the (re)application of the initial steps of our methodology is most important, subjecting the judgments to fully informed reflection, especially aimed at their origins and outcomes. The later steps can be applied here as well, since we might find some apparently settled judgments and practices to be incoherent with others. We might find that some apparently settled cases are judged differently from others without our being able to specify generally relevant differences between them. The initial and later steps can be combined in calling into question, that is, unsettling, what were previously taken to be settled judgments. These must cohere with each other, but our set of judgments as a whole, our full moral framework, must also cohere with the facts, as reflected in experience, with the social aims of moral systems and with the psychologies of individuals to be governed by it.

In regard to the first requirement, settled judgments must not be based on factual error that, if revealed, would prompt changing them or on false predictions of experience that results from acting on them and the values they reflect. Here, as with empirical beliefs, coherent moral judgments must be grounded in broad experience of the right kind. For an individual, much of this experience can be secondhand, derived from fictional and nonfictional narratives as well as from life, but ultimately moral frameworks, like scientific theories, must be confirmed by first-hand experience. In regard to the second requirement, the moral framework must promote peaceful, cooperative relations and reduce hostility and conflict. In regard to the third, it must not make impossible demands of individuals, demands that are too stringent or that call upon some to suffer intolerably at the hands of others. Demands that are too stringent to be met by less than angels or saints are mostly irrelevant as guides to action.

These tests of narrower and broader coherence can lead us to unseat some judgments that we previously considered settled. For example, when we find that fully zealous advocacy of their clients' interests by lawyers without significant moral limits is out of line with moral limits to partisanship in other areas of conduct (coherence); when we find that some of the relevant differences that distinguish some legal contexts from partisan behavior elsewhere (e.g., the criminal defendant facing the pros-

178

ecutorial powers of the state) do not obtain in other legal contexts (e.g., corporate law – coherence); when we see the heightened conflicts and harms that result to innocent third parties from this practice (outcome); and when we find that many of the provisions of the legal code that underwrite this practice appear to originate from the economic advantages they confer on the legal profession (origin), we should be less likely to take this legally settled practice to be morally settled.[217] At least we will not allow such extreme partisanship in other areas of conduct to be defended by appeal to the legal model.

When, by contrast, settled judgments withstand such additional reflection, we can trust that they express stable priorities among our values. And, of course, it is relevant that they need to capture only our coherent collective value orderings, not some independent realm of objective fact. That we acquire some of these values and judgments from our parents is therefore not as damaging as it would be if it were our knowledge of nuclear physics in question (assuming our parents are not nuclear physicists). Indeed, some of these judgments, for example that we should not torture sentient beings for fun, express priorities that approach being foundational, not because of some immediate apprehension of fact, but because it is very hard to see how, given our values, they could require revision in light of other judgments, as opposed to the reverse. No judgment in this domain is genuinely foundational, however, because none is in principle immune from revision.

That settled judgments represent stable orderings of our own values means that we need not fear error in any fully coherent and informed set of them. We can accept not only influence from parents or tradition, but also genuinely conventional aspects of our system of moral norms. Just when the aforementioned distinction between harming and not helping (or killing and letting die) is relevant, for example, is partly a function of how our society happens to set needed limits to moral demands on individuals. But even our own values are suspect if they originate from misinformation, ignorance, or some irrational frame of mind, or if they ultimately conflict and hence generate self-defeat or frustration.

That we seek to capture only our own values also explains why we can trust intuitions regarding generally relevant differences between cases. However, if relevant differences are simply those we take to generally make a difference, the question can be raised of how this central constraint can have any real bite. Our willingness to generalize may not seem sufficient if generalized differences still exist wherever we

179

seem to find them. But the constraint does have bite. Differences are only those that sincerely count as reasons for different actions, that affect the values at stake, and these must be moral values, those that in some sense count the interests of all on the same scale and thereby promote peaceful cooperation. Being named Alan Goldman, for example, fails to count as a reason for action, and being who I am fails to count as a moral reason. Differences that I do take to matter generally must make differences regardless of the particular individuals involved (in the absence of other relevant differences between them), no matter who is on the receiving or acting end. This is why the constraint is an interpretation of Kant's requirement of universalizability.

That values are ultimately subjective does not mean that they are a matter of whim or even choice. Ultimately our instincts and the nature of the environment cause us to value what we do; and our social instincts, our deep-seated need to identify with certain groups, underlie our moral values and obligations. To this we might add prudence, where prudence and moral requirement coincide in opposing temptation. Given these sources, we cannot change our obligations by simply choosing to change our paradigms or the differences between cases that we recognize as morally relevant. Moral obligations and the judgments that reflect them have their source outside the individual, certainly outside the individual's immediate desires, and even groups can be mistaken in their shared judgments if, for example, they are based on misinformation about the objects valued or about the long-range consequences of acting on them.

Properly informed and criticized settled judgments, as well as convictions about what differentiates new cases from them, can, by contrast, be trusted. But now the question can again be raised of whether there will always be settled judgments from which to reason by analogy to the right answer in a new case. I mean really new – novel circumstances in which we must acquire new judgments or orderings from new experiences. Old aims and interests may not fit future situations; we do sometimes acquire new interests or values in contexts that seem relevantly different from all previous cases.[218] This has been cited as one reason why genuine rules fail as a general guide to behavior: We cannot predict exceptions generated by genuine novelty. But if we cannot predict new exceptions to previously accepted rules, can we nevertheless always assume a base of settled judgments that will provide suitable analogies to genuinely novel cases? The two claims are indeed consistent. We need not simply rely on gut feelings in the face of novelty. There may indeed arise new kinds of threats or new ways of satisfying interests that at some level of specificity are different from anything that came before. But at the same time, at some level of generality, similar values and interests will have competed in the past.

Some illustrations will help here. Until the development of stock markets, there could have been no such thing as insider trading, and so it might seem that an entirely new kind of wrongdoing emerged with stock market trading. Until the development of automobiles and roads for them, there could have been no road hogging, tailgating, or passing on the right, again new forms of wrongdoing in the twentieth century. And now we might seem to need new moral categories by which to classify various kinds of genetic engineering and Internet invasions of privacy. But while insider trading, Internet intrusions, and the various automotive transgressions were at some point new, as just described, their wrongness could be seen to derive from similarities to more traditional forms of cheating, monopolizing public goods, placing others in danger, or invading their privacy. This is not to imply, however, that there are any genuine rules to the effect that cheating, or placing others in danger, or passing on the right, or . . . is always wrong. Hence, as claimed earlier, our inability to predict all exceptions to rules in the face of genuine novelty is compatible with our always being able to find paradigms from which to reason.

Indeed, paradigms are now available by which to judge parents' future wishes to alter the genes of their embryos in order to avoid diseases or enhance the physical or mental capacities of the future children. In one sense, nothing remotely like these possibilities has existed until now. But we have been able to make choices that enhance the chances of our children in the genetic lottery, and, more often, we have made choices in regard to their health and the training of their mental capacities without their informed consent. In regard to the former, some people avoid choosing spouses with inheritable diseases; fewer (and perhaps odder) people choose spouses specifically for inheritable characteristics. In regard to the latter, we have our children inoculated against diseases; some of us buy them educational advantages that permanently affect their future chances, and so on. Gene altering, it is true, presents new dangers, especially in regard to susceptibility to harmful agents, and there are important distinctions to be drawn between choices within the existing gene pool and new variations. But once again, new dangers can

181

be compared to older ones, and distinctions must be sought, as always, between the settled cases, if indeed they are settled, and the new controversial ones.

If indeed there are always settled convictions as paradigms from which to reason, it might next be objected that the method of reasoning defended here is too conservative in requiring controversial questions to be settled always by assimilation to these previously decided issues or orderings. The main alternative to such assimilation seems to be decision by gut feeling or, less pejoratively, particular perception, which I have rejected as a generally reliable method of moral judgment. We must also recognize the possibility that novel experience will lead to changes in priorities, either directly or via some judgment that later is seen to conflict with ones taken previously to be settled. When this happens, when there come to be different judgments in contexts that cannot be relevantly distinguished, then coherence must be restored. But in accomplishing this revision, there is always the choice of which judgments, values they reflect, and behavior patterns they produce, to change.[219]

The search for coherence by attempting to assimilate judgments to precedents is therefore not conservative in ethics in the way that it is in the legal system. In law, a judge cannot as easily change the past as conform present judgment to it. There, the rejection of past decisions or the overturning of rules by courts generally requires showing that those past decisions were incoherent or mistaken at the time they were made. But in the realm of moral judgment, we can, in light of new experience, change our minds about judgments that were coherent and not clearly based on false factual information when made. In fact, the constraint that guides the search for coherence is as much forward-looking as backward-looking: We must be willing to generalize recognized differences to distinguish new cases that will arise.

Thus, the recognition that no judgment is in principle immune from revision allows us to answer this final objection. But haven't I now contradicted myself by rejecting experience as a reliable immediate source of moral judgment in favor of assimilation of new judgments to paradigms and then admitting that supposed paradigms themselves can be legitimately revised in light of judgments that arise directly from experience? These claims are compatible when properly interpreted or expanded. Experience does not typically provide immediate answers to difficult moral issues because it can easily mislead; we often react to morally irrelevant but perceptually salient features of situations bearing superficial analogies to settled judgments. But experience does sometimes teach us that differences thought to be relevant do not generalize (especially when based on experientially unsupported stereotypes) or that cases thought analogous are relevantly different. These lessons often occur as experience broadens our outlook from the narrow groups with which we initially identify and from which we derive our initial paradigms. When new judgments lead us to revise older ones, we must make sure that the former have arisen from experience in the right way. They must again be based on the type of experience that sensitizes us to the feelings and interests of all involved and that reveals similarities and differences that reflect that sensitivity better than our prior frameworks.

That such revision occurs, requiring as it does reasoned reflection on its overall effects on the ways we lead our lives, is further evidence for the pervasiveness of the method of non-rule-based, but non-particularist, coherentist reasoning described earlier.

Notes

INTRODUCTION

1. Jan Narveson pointed this out to me. See Henry Sidgwick, *The Methods of Ethics* (London: Macmillan, 1907), pp. 379–80.
2. R. M. Hare, *Moral Thinking* (Oxford: Clarendon, 1981); Joseph Raz, *Practical Reason and Norms* (Oxford: Oxford University Press, 1999); Frederick Schauer, *Playing by the Rules* (Oxford: Clarendon, 1991).
3. Thomas Hobbes, *Leviathan* (London: Penguin, 1985), Ch. 15 (first published 1651).
4. John Stuart Mill, *On Liberty* (Chicago: Gateway, 1955) (first published 1859).

CHAPTER 1

5. This justification for rules is emphasized by Edward McClennen, "Pragmatic Rationality and Rules," *Philosophy & Public Affairs* 26 (1997): 210–58.
6. Two prisoners are given the choice of confessing or not. If one confesses and the other does not, the first will be given immunity and the second will receive five years in prison. If both confess, they will receive three-year sentences, and if neither does, they can be convicted only of a lesser crime carrying a two-year sentence. Both are better off confessing no matter what the other does, but by doing so, they receive three- instead of two-year sentences.
7. I will deny, after considering the question in a later chapter, the Hobbesian claim that moral reasoning reduces to long-range prudential reasoning.
8. Cass R. Sunstein, "Political Conflict and Legal Agreement," *The Tanner Lectures on Human Values* 17 (1996): 137–249, pp. 203–5.
9. Sunstein, "Political Conflict," p. 219
10. Jon Elster, *The Cement of Society* (Cambridge: Cambridge University Press, 1989), p. 15.
11. Elster, *Cement of Society,* pp. 110, 124.
12. Schauer, *Playing by the Rules,* p. 49.
13. H. L. A. Hart, *The Concept of Law* (Oxford: Oxford University Press, 1994).
14. Once more, the best way to weigh opposing reasons rationally, in my view, is

to reason in terms of analogies and disanalogies to cases in which the weights go one way or the other.

15. Donald Regan, "Authority and Value," *Southern California Law Review* 62 (1989): 995–1095, p. 1027.
16. Edward McClennen has emphasized the function of rules to make certain optimal patterns of behavior possible. See "Pragmatic Rationality and Rules."
17. This claim might still have to be hedged in light of considerations to be discussed later. Whether the rule should be given extra weight, i.e., be more than a rule of thumb, will depend on our estimation of fallibility in identifying exceptions.
18. We could, however, imagine end-of-the-world scenarios in which exceptions might abound.
19. This principle was suggested by an anonymous referee.
20. An example is Stephen Stich, "Moral Philosophy and Mental Representation," in edited by Michael Hechter, *The Origin of Values* (Hawthorne, NY: Aldine De Gruyter, 1993), pp. 221–2.
21. See Geoffrey Brennan and James Buchanan, *The Reason of Rules* (Cambridge: Cambridge University Press, 1985), p. 67, for example.
22. See, for example, Michael S. Moore, "Authority, Law, and Razian Reasons," *Southern California Law Review* 62 (1989): 829–96, p. 847.
23. Scott Shapiro, "The Difference That Rules Make," in *Analyzing Law,* edited by Brian Bix (Oxford: Clarendon Press, 1998), pp. 39, 47.
24. Shapiro, "The Difference That Rules Make," p. 46; see also his "Judicial Can't," *Philosophical Issues* 11 (2001).
25. McClennen, in "Pragmatic Rationality and Rules," emphasizes this rational justification of rules. I disagree with his general account only in speaking of a global improvement instead of a global optimum. In the cases I shall emphasize later, rules are not simply solutions to coordination problems, but second-best solutions to collective action problems when global optima cannot be attained.
26. Michael Robbins objected in this way to Shapiro in a talk at the American Philosophical Association, 1999.
27. Shapiro, "The Difference That Rules Make," p. 62.
28. Jonathan Dancy, *Moral Reasons* (Oxford: Blackwell, 1993), p. 56.
29. This difficulty is emphasized by Russ Shafer-Landau, "Moral Rules," *Ethics* 107 (1997): 584–611
30. This objection was raised by Jonathan Adler.
31. Shafer-Landau, "Moral Rules," p. 590.
32. Shafer-Landau recommends this strategy in "Moral Rules," p. 594.
33. See Michael Stocker, *Plural and Conflicting Values* (Oxford: Clarendon, 1990), pp. 270–2; John Kekes, *The Morality of Pluralism* (Princeton, NJ: Princeton University Press, 1993); Dancy, *Moral Reasons,* pp. 120–3.
34. Among the best extended discussion of these issues is Stocker, *Plural and Conflicting Values.*
35. Contrast Michael Slote, *Beyond Optimizing* (Cambridge, MA: Harvard University Press, 1989), Chs. 1–3. See also David Schmidtz, *Rational Choice and Moral Agency* (Princeton, NJ: Princeton University Press, 1995), Ch. 2.
36. I will decide among these alternatives later.
37. See Schauer, *Playing by the Rules,* pp. 86–7, 100.

38. Brennan and Buchanan, *The Reason of Rules,* p. 8. They emphasize the function of rules in providing information necessary for coordination.
39. See Sunstein, "Political Conflict and Legal Agreement," p. 201.
40. Schauer, *Playing by the Rules,* p. 98
41. Hare, *Moral Thinking,* Ch. 3.
42. Schauer, *Playing by the Rules,* p. 229.
43. A rights-based theory also avoids another potential problem for the skeptical position on rules. Rule-skeptical persons who accept such a theory and who sign contracts will not always try to look for better ways to spend their time or money than by fulfilling them, as they might if they are utilitarians. The reason is that contracts almost always create the strongest rights when they apply. This point is compatible with the admission of unspecifiable possible exceptions that have to be weighed directly against contractual claims when they arise.
44. See, for example, Alan Goldman, *The Moral Foundations of Professional Ethics* (Totowa, NJ: Rowman & Littlefield, 1980), Ch. 1; and J. L. Mackie, "Can There Be a Right-Based Moral Theory?", *Persons and Values* (Oxford: Clarendon, 1985).
45. According to this conception, rights pretty much equate with the morally relevant factors of which I have been speaking throughout. Although I favor a rights-based moral theory and have defended this view elsewhere, I continue to use the more general term in order to indicate that much of the discussion of rules, and even of moral reasoning, does not depend on the adoption of this sort of moral theory.
46. Conrad Johnson, *Moral Legislation* (Cambridge: Cambridge University Press, 1991), Ch. 3.
47. Johnson, *Moral Legislation,* p. 60.
48. Johnson, *Moral Legislation,* p. 26.
49. Ronald Dworkin argues against "checkerboard" solutions to issues such as abortion that divide society. We should not, for example, compromise on this issue by allowing abortions for women born on odd days of months. He concludes that law must embody principles and links this to the demand for communal integrity. This is not the place to decide what he means by "principle." The sort of compromise he rightly condemns here can be dismissed as unfair because it is in violation of the Kantian constraint. Thus its wrongness has no implications regarding the interpretation of law as a set of rules, which Dworkin has also notoriously attacked and which will be the subject of a later chapter. See *Law's Empire* (Cambridge, MA: Harvard University Press, 1986), pp. 178–84.
50. Gerald Postema calls it "rule-sensitive particularism" in "Positivism, I Presume," *Harvard Journal of Law and Public Policy* 14 (1991): 797–822.
51. See Donald Regan, *Utilitarianism and Cooperation* (Oxford: Clarendon, 1980), p. 62.
52. Compare Philip Petit, "Free Riding and Foul Dealing," *The Journal of Philosophy* 83 (1986): 361–79, p. 370.
53. This is formally the reverse of the oligopolists' case, in which each is tempted to lower prices in order to seize a larger market share, resulting in a worse situation for all. When antitrust laws block a solution in the form of an explicit agree-

ment to this generalized prisoners' dilemma, this leads to a coordination problem. See Edna Ullmann-Margalit, *The Emergence of Norms* (Oxford: Clarendon, 1977), pp. 128–9.

54. Margaret Gilbert has argued that even if there is a unique best pattern of behavior, all know what it is and know that all others are rational and know this, it still may not be irrational not to act so as to realize that pattern. In the absence of communication or a shared rule, a maximin strategy can be rational if there is a high risk to aiming and failing to optimize. In my example, maximin would call for the adoption of a strong rule for all judges. See Gilbert, "Rationality, Coordination, and Convention," *Synthese* 84 (1990): 1–21.

55. Schauer, in *Playing by the Rules,* emphasizes this point in his account as well, p. 49.

56. See Geoffrey Brennan and Loren E. Lomasky, "Large Numbers, Small Costs: The Uneasy Foundations of Democratic Rule," in *Politics and Process* (Cambridge: Cambridge University Press, 1989).

57. For more philosophical treatments see, for example, Russell Hardin, *Collective Action* (Baltimore: Johns Hopkins University Press, 1982); Mark Lichback, *The Cooperator's Dilemma* (Ann Arbor: University of Michigan Press, 1996).

58. In a groundbreaking philosophical work, Edna Ullmann-Margalit argued that norms in general arise as solutions to prisoners' dilemmas and coordination problems. This is an incomplete explanation, since many norms fail to arise that would solve major problems of this sort – we continue to have overpopulation and traffic jams. It is nevertheless an important thesis and related to mine, but also very different. First, my topic is moral rules and not norms. Second, I am interested not in when rules exist or are in effect, but in when they are warranted, not in explanation but in justification. Norms, generally followed prescriptions often backed by sanctions, do not ordinarily take the form of genuine rules; and prudential prisoners' dilemmas, the typical ones, do not justify the adoption of moral rules, I have argued. See Ullmann-Margalit, *The Emergence of Norms.*

59. Anarchists and libertarians disagree. An analysis of the potential of free markets in this regard is beyond the scope of this work. But in a nutshell, I believe lack of knowledge of where the greatest needs turn up, as well as lack of motivation on the part of individuals, favors government solutions to these collective action problems.

60. Compare Elster, *Cement of Society,* p. 110.

61. Goldman, *Moral Foundations of Professional Ethics.*

62. See Colin Strong, "What If Everyone Did That?", *Durham University Journal* 53 (1960): 5–10.

63. Joseph Raz, *The Morality of Freedom* (Oxford: Oxford University Press, 1986), pp. 47, 53, 67, 75.

64. Raz, *Morality of Freedom,* p. 42.

65. Joseph Raz, "Facing Up," *Southern California Law Review* 62 (1989): 1153–1235, p. 1194.

66. Raz, *Practical Reason and Norms,* pp. 41–5, 75.

67. Raz, *Practical Reason and Norms,* p. 79.

68. Raz, "Facing Up," p. 1169.

69. Raz, *Practical Reason and Norms,* p. 141.

70. Compare Moore, "Authority, Law, and Razian Reasons," pp. 850, 863, 872, 895. He also holds that rules introduce new reasons, but without an analysis of my kind of reason.

71. Contrast Raz, *Morality of Freedom,* pp. 50–1.

72. Raz, *Practical Reason and Norms,* p. 185.

73. Raz, "Facing Up," p. 1159.

74. Compare Regan, *Utilitarianism and Cooperation,* p. 1030.

75. Given that I have recognized the need for weak genuine rules, one might object to the order of my presentation here, to my having introduced this category so late in the discussion. One might think that, had I introduced it at the beginning, the argument that rules do not figure in ordinary moral reasoning would have been less convincing. But it is not so. As mentioned previously, weak genuine rules require the concept of "extra weight." Extra weight must be defined in contrast to ordinary moral reasoning and the normal weights it assigns to various relevant factors. Hence weak genuine rules cannot by definition figure in such reasoning. Their introduction had to await the explanation of rules as second-best strategies.

76. Perhaps the closest to a rule on the metaethical level is "Don't expect neatness or simplicity."

CHAPTER 2

77. Robert Nozick, *The Nature of Rationality* (Princeton, NJ: Princeton University Press, 1993), Ch. 1.

78. See Jon Elster, *Ulysses and the Sirens* (Cambridge: Cambridge University Press, 1979), Ch. 2.

79. Nozick, *Nature of Rationality,* p. 30.

80. Nozick, *Nature of Rationality,* p. 36.

81. See, for example, Alfred Mele, "Recent Work on Self-Deception," *American Philosophical Quarterly* 24 (1987): 1–14.

82. Muriel Spark, *The Prime of Miss Jean Brodie* (New York: HarperPerennial, 1994).

83. Kent Bach, "(Apparent) Paradoxes of Self-Deception and Decision," in Jean-Pierre Dupuy, ed., *Self-Deception and Paradoxes of Rationality* (Stanford, CA: CSLI, 1998).

84. Annette Barnes, *Seeing Through Self-Deception* (Cambridge: Cambridge University Press, 1997).

85. Barnes, *Seeing Through Self-Deception,* p. 21.

86. Compare Brennan and Buchanan, *The Reason of Rules,* pp. 78–80.

87. Compare Graham Oddie, "Act and Maxim: Value-Discrepancy and Two Theories of Power," *Philosophy & Phenomenological Research* 53 (1993): 72–92.

88. McClennen, "Pragmatic Rationality and Rules," p. 231.

89. See Michael Bratman, *Intention, Plans, and Practical Reason* (Cambridge, MA: Harvard University Press, 1987), pp. 33–4. Since in my view intentions are often akin only to rules of thumb, lacking independent weight or exclusionary force, this also leaves it open for one to change one's mind without good reason but also without being irrational. I may plan to take one road home from work

and then simply change my mind when the time comes to make a turn onto that road without being irrational.

90. Another difference between the two contexts relates to the issue of fairness, related to free riding as mentioned earlier. While it is not unfair to different temporal stages of oneself to snack at some times and not at others, it is unfair for some individuals to have their legal cases decided one way while others in similar legal contexts have their cases decided another way, or for some to have to pay taxes but not others in similar financial situations. Thus, certain compromise strategies in the intrapersonal context are ruled out in the interpersonal context.

91. On the other side, if each act of abstinence raises the probability of staying below the threshold and thus avoiding long-term harm, then this expected utility may outweigh that from indulgence in the single case. (See Oddie, "Act and Maxim," p. 75.) But if, in the normal case, the acts are causally independent and occur on numerous occasions (as in the snacking and smoking examples), then the effect of each act on this probability will again be negligible.

92. A similar example was provided by Frederick Schauer in commenting on a shorter version of this chapter.

93. See my *The Moral Foundations of Professional Ethics,* Ch. 2.

94. Nozick, *Nature of Rationality,* p. 10.

95. Nozick, *Nature of Rationality,* pp. 12–13.

96. Mark Halfon, *Integrity* (Philadelphia: Temple University Press, 1989), pp. 5, 39.

97. Gabriele Taylor, "Integrity," *Proceedings of the Aristotelian Society* 55 (1981): 143–59, p. 143.

98. Compare Halfon, *Integrity,* pp. 9, 18, 37, 85.

99. Slote, *Beyond Optimizing.*

100. Slote, *Beyond Optimizing,* p. 72.

101. Slote, *Beyond Optimizing,* pp. 78–9.

102. Slote, *Beyond Optimizing,* p. 19.

103. See Mark Overvold, "Self-Interest and the Concept of Self-Sacrifice," *Canadian Journal of Philosophy* 10 (1980): 105–18.

104. See Stephen Darwall, "Self-Interest and Self-Concern," in E. Paul, F. Miller, and J. Paul, eds., *Self-Interest* (Cambridge: Cambridge University Press, 1997).

105. Brad Hooker, "A Breakthrough in the Desire Theory of Welfare," in John Heil, ed., *Rationality, Morality and Self-Interest* (Lanham, MD: Rowman & Littlefield, 1993).

106. Both Philip Pettit and David Schmidtz note the conceptual link between choice and evaluation in also arguing against Slote. See Philip Pettit, "Satisficing Consequentialism," *Proceedings of the Aristotelian Society* 58 suppl. (1984): 165–76, p. 172; Schmidtz, *Rational Choice and Moral Agency,* p. 39.

107. Allan Gibbard, *Wise Choices, Apt Feelings* (Cambridge, MA: Harvard University Press, 1990), pp. 18–19.

108. David Sobel, "Full Information Accounts of Well-Being, *Ethics* 104 (1994): 784–810; Don Loeb, "Full-Information Theories of Individual Good," *Social Theory and Practice* 21 (1995): 1–30; J. David Velleman, "Brandt's Definition of 'Good'," *The Philosophical Review* 97 (1988): 353–71; Connie Rosati, "Per-

sons, Properties, and Full Information Accounts of the Good," *Ethics* 105 (1995): 296–325.

109. Connie Rosati, "Brandt's Notion of Therapeutic Agency," *Ethics* 110 (2000): 780–811, p. 806.

110. Derek Parfit, *Reasons and Persons* (Oxford: Clarendon, 1984), Chs. 4, 6, 7.

111. See Darwall, "Self-Interest and Self-Concern."

112. Contrast Evan Simpson, "Prudence and Anti-Prudence," *American Philosophical Quarterly* 35 (1998): 73–86.

113. This objection was raised by Christopher Gowans.

114. For expansion, see Alan Goldman, "Reasons and Personal Identity," *Inquiry* 28 (1985): 373–98.

115. Hobbes, *Leviathan,* p. 122.

116. Gregory Kavka, *Hobbesian Moral and Political Theory* (Princeton, NJ: Princeton University Press, 1986), p. 347.

117. Hobbes, *Leviathan,* p. 114.

118. David Gauthier argues on similar grounds that, given reasonable epistemic assumptions, an individual is predictably better off being a "constrained maximizer," cooperating when others are and when the payoff is better for all with cooperation than without it, than being a straightforward maximizer. See *Moral Dealing* (Ithaca, NY: Cornell University Press, 1990), p. 4, and *Morals by Agreement* (Oxford: Clarendon, 1986), pp. 182–4.

119. Kavka, *Hobbesian Moral and Political Thought,* p. 301.

120. See G. Sayre-McCord, "Deception and Reasons to Be Moral," *American Philosophical Quarterly* 26 (1989): 113–22, pp. 118–19.

121. David Hume, *An Inquiry Concerning the Principles of Morals* (Indianapolis: Bobbs-Merrill, 1957), especially pp. 99–103.

122. See, for example, Schmidtz, *Rational Choice and Moral Agency.*

123. We should also note that even genuine altruism toward other individuals does not guarantee moral treatment of them, as is clear from how men have traditionally treated the women they loved.

124. For a very good recent review of this tradition, see Steven Luper, *Invulnerability* (Chicago: Open Court, 1996).

125. See Alfie Kohn, *No Contest* (Boston: Houghton Mifflin, 1986).

126. The latter consideration – whether, for example, it is possible for individuals to make themselves noncompetitive – depends also on social inputs and therefore on the structure of their society. Ironically, perhaps, our society has risen to the economic level at which scarcity no longer makes cutthroat competition inevitable only through pervasive encouragement of fierce competition.

127. Stephen Darwall, *Impartial Reason* (Ithaca, NY: Cornell University Press, 1983), especially pp. 222–5.

128. David Copp, "The Ring of Gyges," in Paul, Miller, and Paul, eds., *Self-Interest,* pp. 101–2. Copp holds that the same argument applies to reasons for belief, e.g., epistemic versus self-interested or pragmatic reasons (p. 104). Here there is a simple counterargument against him. To believe a proposition is to believe it to be true. If epistemic reasons are the only ones linked to probable truth, then they must trump others as reasons for belief. It requires self-deception to

believe contrary to one's grasp of the epistemic reasons or evidence, and self-deception is not a rational ground for belief.

129. Compare Mark Overvold, "Morality, Self-Interest, and Reasons for Being Moral," *Philosophy & Phenomenological Research* 44 (1984): 493–507, p. 495.

CHAPTER 3

130. Frederick Schauer, "Rules and the Rule of Law," *Harvard Journal of Law and Public Policy* 14 (1991): 645–94, pp. 675, 677.
131. *Regents of University of California v. Bakke,* 438 U.S. 265, 98 S.Ct. 2733 (1978).
132. Schauer, "Rules and the Rule of Law," p. 660.
133. See Pierre Schlag, "Rules and Standards," *UCLA Law Review* 33 (1985): 379–430, pp. 381–3; Larry Alexander and Ken Kress, "Against Legal Principles," in Andrei Marmor, ed., *Law and Interpretation* (Oxford: Clarendon, 1997), p. 280.
134. Shapiro, "Judicial Can't."
135. Some of this skepticism derives from mistaken interpretations of Wittgenstein's discussion of rules in the *Philosophical Investigations* (New York: Macmillan, 1958). All competent interpreters agree that Wittgenstein did not doubt that we can follow clear rules, that we can be correct or incorrect in our applications. They may disagree on what Wittgenstein held to be the grounds on which we get it right or wrong, or whether there are such grounds at all.
136. See Alan Goldman, *Aesthetic Value* (Boulder, CO: Westview, 1995), Ch. 4.
137. Compare Martin Stone, "Focusing the Law: What Legal Interpretation Is Not," in Marmor, ed., *Law and Interpretation,* p. 36.
138. Lon L. Fuller, "Positivism and Fidelity to Law," in Joel Feinberg and Jules Coleman, eds., *Philosophy of Law* (Belmont, CA: Wadsworth, 2000), p. 90.
139. *Riggs v. Palmer,* 115 N.Y. 506, 22 N.E. 188 (1889).
140. At least on the first level. Hart allows that law identified by sources specified in the rule of recognition can then build moral criteria into the identification of other law.
141. Hart, *The Concept of Law,* postscript, p. 261. This is another way to specify how rules that are not strong in the sense defined earlier may be given extra weight against other moral considerations. Hart's specification is narrower and clearer than Schauer's in that rules may be overridden only by other rules that apply. His rules therefore appear to be stronger than Schauer's presumptive rules.
142. Hart, *The Concept of Law,* p. 263.
143. Stephen Macedo, "The Rule of Law, Justice, and the Politics of Moderation," *Nomos* 36 (1994): 148–77, pp. 152–3; Steven Burton, "Particularism, Discretion, and the Rule of Law," *Nomos* 36 (1994): 178–201, p. 187.
144. Contrast Lawrence Solum, "Equity and the Rule of Law," *Nomos* 36 (1994): 120–47, p. 120.
145. See Ruth Gavison, "Legal Theory and the Role of Rules," *Harvard Journal of Law and Public Policy* 14 (1991): 733–70, p. 735.
146. Dworkin, *Law's Empire,* pp. 350–4.

147. J. L. Mackie, "The Third Theory of Law," *Philosophy & Public Affairs,* 7 (1977): 3–16.

148. In the case of statutory rules, however, Dworkin seems to think that such principles as legislative supremacy will require judges to treat them normally as if they were genuine rules. But weighing that principle against others in context shows otherwise.

149. This criticism is made by Alexander and Kress, "Against Legal Principles."

150. Schauer, "Rules and the Rule of Law," p. 647.

151. Postema, "Positivism, I Presume?"

152. Jeremy Waldron, "Precommitment and Disagreement," in Larry Alexander, ed., *Constitutionalism* (Cambridge: Cambridge University Press, 1998), pp. 283–5. See also Jon Elster, *Ulysses Unbound* (Cambridge: Cambridge University Press, 2000), pp. 167–8.

153. Waldron, "Precommitment and Disagreement," p. 280.

154. Schlag, "Rules and Standards," p. 391.

155. Schauer, remember, claims it should be read as presumptive.

156. We may speak of a continuum here: rules have strength to the degree to which they override consideration of factors not mentioned in them.

157. See Robert Bork, *The Tempting of America* (New York: Touchstone, 1990), pp. 163–4.

158. Michael Perry, "What Is 'the Constitution'?", in Alexander, ed., *Constitutionalism*, p. 100.

159. Richard Kay, "American Constitutionalism," in Alexander, ed., *Constitutionalism,* p. 36.

160. Macedo, "Rule of Law," p. 164.

161. Ronald Dworkin, *Freedom's Law* (Cambridge, MA: Harvard University Press, 1996), pp. 10, 13.

162. Bork, *Tempting of America,* pp. 329–30.

163. Margaret Radin, "Presumptive Positivism and Trivial Cases," *Harvard Journal of Law and Public Policy* 14 (1991): 823–37, pp. 835–6.

164. Dworkin, *Freedom's Law,* pp. 35–6.

165. Frank Easterbrook, "Statutes' Domains," *University of Chicago Law Review* 50 (1983): 533–52, p. 536.

166. For a popular critique of such rules, see Philip Howard, *The Death of Common Sense* (New York: Random House, 1994).

167. Frederick Schauer, "Precedent," *Stanford Law Review* 39 (1987): 571–605, p. 575.

168. For a recent discussion of these options, see M. A. Eisenberg, *The Nature of the Common Law* (Cambridge, MA: Harvard University Press, 1988).

169. For further discussion of this, see Cass Sunstein, "Norms in Surprising Places: The Case of Statutory Interpretation," *Ethics* 100 (1990): 803–20.

170. *United Steelworkers v. Weber,* 443 U.S. 193 (1979).

171. One good discussion of this case along these lines is William Eskridge, "Dynamic Statutory Interpretation," *University of Pennsylvania Law Review* 135 (1987): 1479–1555, pp. 1488–94.

172. Easterbrook, "Statutes' Domains."

173. Meir Dan-Cohen, "Decision Rules and Conduct Rules: On Acoustic Separation in Criminal Law," *Harvard Law Review* 97 (1984): 625–77.

174. Warren Lehman, "Rules in Law," *The Georgetown Law Review* 72 (1984): 1571–1603, p. 1585.

175. Douglas Baird and Robert Weisberg, "Rules, Standards, and the Battle of the Forms," *Virginia Law Review* 68 (1982): 1217–62, pp. 1227–37.

176. Lehman, "Rules in Law," p. 1580.

177. Schauer, "Rules and the Rule of Law," pp. 673–4; *Playing by the Rules*, p. 203.

178. Dworkin, *Freedom's Law*, p. 37.

179. For example, Eisenberg, *The Nature of the Common Law*, p. 86.

180. Dworkin, *Law's Empire*, pp. 178–84.

181. As pointed out earlier, by "second best" I do not mean that better mechanisms are necessarily available, only that rules, as a second-best strategy, cannot achieve perfect justice, the optimal outcome.

182. Antonin Scalia, "The Rule of Law as a Law of Rules," *University of Chicago Law Review* 56 (1989): 1175–88.

183. Scalia, "Rule of Law," p. 1177.

184. Scalia, "Rule of Law," p. 1178.

185. This point is argued by Randy Barnett, "Can Justice and the Rule of Law Be Reconciled?", *Harvard Journal of Law and Public Policy* 11 (1988): 597–624, p. 606.

186. Scalia, "Rule of Law," p. 1179.

187. Scalia, "Rule of Law," p. 1180.

188. Radin, "Presumptive Positivism," 823–37.

189. For more complete discussion, see Goldman, *The Moral Foundations of Professional Ethics*, Ch. 2.

CHAPTER 4

190. Alan Goldman, "Legal Reasoning as a Model for Moral Reasoning," *Law and Philosophy* 8 (1989): 131–49.

191. Dancy, *Moral Reasons*, pp. 111–16.

192. W. D. Ross, *The Right and the Good* (Oxford: Clarendon, 1930), Ch. 2.

193. Compare Elijah Millgram, *Practical Induction* (Cambridge, MA: Harvard University Press, 1997), p. 57.

194. For a full account, see my *Aesthetic Value*.

195. See, for example, Nozick, *The Nature of Rationality*, pp. 3–5.

196. John Rawls, *A Theory of Justice* (Cambridge, MA: Harvard University Press, 1971), p. 47.

197. These questions are raised in slightly less strong terms by Michael DePaul, *Balance and Refinement* (London: Routledge, 1993), p. 17.

198. This point is emphasized by Lawrence Blum, *Moral Perception and Particularity* (Cambridge: Cambridge University Press, 1994), pp. 46–7.

199. DePaul, *Balance and Refinement*, p. 15.

200. Richard Brandt, *A Theory of the Good and the Right* (Oxford: Clarendon, 1979), Ch. 6.

201. Millgram, *Practical Induction*, pp. 27, 43–4.

202. Compare Stephen Nathanson, "Brandt on Rationality and Value," in Brad Hooker, ed., *Rationality, Rules, and Utility* (Boulder, CO: Westview, 1993), pp. 1–16.

203. For much fuller discussion, see Alan Goldman, *Moral Knowledge* (London: Routledge, 1988).

204. This point is made convincingly by Michele Moody-Adams, *Fieldwork in Familiar Places* (Cambridge, MA: Harvard University Press, 1997).

205. Moody-Adams, *Fieldwork,* p. 43.

206. Rawls, *Theory of Justice,* pp. 48–51.

207. For my discussion, which essentially sees each of the opposed actions as permissible, if regrettable, see *Moral Knowledge,* pp. 140–4.

208. Judith Thomson, "A Defense of Abortion," *Philosophy & Public Affairs* 1 (1971): 47–66.

209. Dworkin, *Law's Empire,* pp. 178–81.

210. This may seem an odd objection, but an anonymous (no wonder) referee for a journal, probably born on an odd day of a month, actually raised it.

211. For an extended example of such reasoning on this topic, see Alan Goldman, *Justice and Reverse Discrimination* (Princeton, NJ: Princeton University Press, 1979).

212. See Keith Holyoak and Paul Thagard, *Mental Leaps* (Cambridge, MA: MIT Press, 1995), p. 131.

213. James Rachels, "Active and Passive Euthanasia," *New England Journal of Medicine* 292 (1975): 78–80.

214. The view opposed to mine here is suggested by Stuart Hampshire, *Morality and Conflict* (Cambridge, MA: Harvard University Press, 1983), pp. 105–10.

215. Jonathan Dancy, "The Role of Imaginary Cases in Ethics," *Pacific Philosophical Quarterly* 66 (1985): 141–53, pp. 146–7.

216. Thomson, "Defense of Abortion."

217. For a full discussion of this issue, see Goldman, *Moral Foundations of Professional Ethics,* Ch. 3.

218. This is a main theme of Millgram, *Practical Induction,* especially pp. 6, 97–8.

219. Despite this choice, the method of coherence remains viable as a means to settle disagreements. While there may be more than one way to make an incoherent set of judgments coherent, there will not be more than one way to make a specific judgment coherent with a base of settled judgments that are agreed to remain for the present unchanged.

References

Alexander, Larry, and Kress, Ken, "Against Legal Principles," pp. 279–327 in *Law and Interpretation,* ed. Andrei Marmor. Oxford: Clarendon, 1997.

Bach, Kent, "(Apparent) Paradoxes of Self-Deception and Decision," pp. 163–89 in *Self-Deception and Paradoxes of Rationality,* ed. Jean-Pierre Dupuy. Stanford, CA: CSLI, 1998.

Baird, Douglas, and Weisberg, Robert, "Rules, Standards, and the Battle of the Forms," *Virginia Law Review* 68 (1982): 1217–62.

Barnes, Annette, *Seeing through Self-Deception.* Cambridge: Cambridge University Press, 1997.

Barnett, Randy, "Can Justice and the Rule of Law Be Reconciled?", *Harvard Journal of Law and Public Policy* 11 (1988): 597–624.

Blum, Lawrence, *Moral Perception and Particularity.* Cambridge: Cambridge University Press, 1994.

Bork, Robert, *The Tempting of America.* New York: Touchstone, 1990.

Brandt, Richard, *A Theory of the Good and the Right.* Oxford: Clarendon, 1979.

Bratman, Michael, *Intention, Plans, and Practical Reason.* Cambridge, MA: Harvard University Press, 1987.

Brennan, Geoffrey, and Buchanan, James, *The Reason of Rules.* Cambridge: Cambridge University Press, 1985.

Brennan, Geoffrey, and Lomasky, Loren E., *Politics and Process.* Cambridge: Cambridge University Press, 1989.

Burton, Steven, "Particularism, Discretion, and the Rule of Law," *Nomos* 36 (1994): 178–201.

Copp, David, "The Ring of Gyges," pp. 86–106 in *Self-Interest,* eds. E Paul, F. Miller, and J. Paul. Cambridge: Cambridge University Press, 1977.

Dan-Cohen, Meir, "Decision Rules and Conduct Rules: On Acoustic Separation in Criminal Law," *Harvard Law Review* 97 (1984): 625–77.

Dancy, Jonathan, *Moral Reasons.* Oxford: Blackwell, 1993.

"The Role of Imaginary Cases in Ethics," *Pacific Philosophical Quarterly* 66 (1985): 141–53.

Darwall, Stephen, *Impartial Reason.* Ithaca, NY: Cornell University Press, 1983.

"Self-Interest and Self-Concern," pp. 158–78 in *Self-Interest,* eds. E. Paul, F. Miller, and J. Paul. Cambridge: Cambridge University Press, 1997.

DePaul, Michael, *Balance and Refinement.* London: Routledge, 1993.

Dworkin, Ronald, *Freedom's Law.* Cambridge, MA: Harvard University Press, 1996.
Law's Empire. Cambridge, MA: Harvard University Press, 1986.

Easterbrook, Frank, "Statutes' Domains," *University of Chicago Law Review* 50 (1983): 533–52.

Eisenberg, M. A., *The Nature of the Common Law.* Cambridge, MA: Harvard University Press, 1988.

Elster, John, *The Cement of Society.* Cambridge: Cambridge University Press, 1989.
Ulysses and the Sirens. Cambridge: Cambridge University Press, 1979.
Ulysses Unbound. Cambridge: Cambridge University Press, 2000.

Eskridge, William, "Dynamic Statutory Interpretation," *University of Pennsylvania Law Review* 135 (1987): 1479–555.

Fuller, Lon F., "Positivism and Fidelity to Law," pp. 76–90 in *Philosophy of Law,* eds. J. Feinberg and J. Coleman. Belmont, CA: Wadsworth, 2000.

Gauthier, David, *Moral Dealing.* Ithaca, NY: Cornell University Press, 1990.
Morals by Agreement. Oxford: Clarendon, 1986.

Gavison, Ruth, "Legal Theory and the Role of Rules," *Harvard Journal of Law and Public Policy* 14 (1991): 733–70.

Gibbard, Allan, *Wise Choices, Apt Feelings.* Cambridge, MA: Harvard University Press, 1990.

Gilbert, Margaret, "Rationality, Coordination, and Convention," *Synthese* 84 (1990): 1–21.

Goldman, Alan, *Aesthetic Value.* Boulder, CO: Westview, 1995.
Justice and Reverse Discrimination. Princeton, NJ: Princeton University Press, 1979.
"Legal Reasoning as a Model for Moral Reasoning," *Law and Philosophy* 8 (1989): 131–49.
The Moral Foundations of Professional Ethics. Totowa, NJ: Rowman & Littlefield, 1980.
Moral Knowledge. London: Routledge, 1988.
"Reasons and Personal Identity," *Inquiry* 28 (1985): 373–98.

Halfon, Mark, *Integrity.* Philadelphia: Temple University Press, 1989.

Hampshire, Stuart, *Morality and Conflict.* Cambridge, MA: Harvard University Press, 1983.

Hardin, Russell, *Collective Action.* Baltimore: Johns Hopkins University Press, 1982.

Hare, R. M., *Moral Thinking.* Oxford: Clarendon, 1981.

Hart, H. L. A., *The Concept of Law,* 2nd ed. Oxford: Clarendon, 1994.

Hobbes, Thomas, *Leviathan.* London: Penguin, 1985 (first published 1651).

Holyoak, Keith, and Thagard, Paul, *Mental Leaps.* Cambridge, MA: MIT Press, 1995.

Hooker, Brad, "A Breakthrough in the Desire Theory of Welfare," pp. 205–13 in *Rationality, Morality and Self-Interest,* ed. John Heil. Lanham, MD: Rowman & Littlefield, 1993.

Howard, Philip, *The Death of Common Sense.* New York: Random House, 1994.

Hume, David, *An Inquiry Concerning the Principles of Morals.* Indianapolis: Bobbs-Merrill, 1957 (first published 1751).

Johnson, Conrad, *Moral Legislation*. Cambridge, Cambridge University Press, 1991.

Kavka, Gregory, *Hobbesian Moral and Political Theory*. Princeton, NJ: Princeton University Press, 1986.

Kay, Richard, "American Constitutionalism," pp. 16–63 in *Constitutionalism*, ed. Larry Alexander. Cambridge: Cambridge University Press, 1998.

Kekes, John, *The Morality of Pluralism*. Princeton, NJ: Princeton University Press, 1993.

Kohn, Alfie, *No Contest*. Boston: Houghton Mifflin, 1986.

Lehman, Warren, "Rules in Law," *The Georgetown Law Review* 72 (1984): 1571–603.

Lichback, Mark, *The Cooperator's Dilemma*. Ann Arbor: University of Michigan Press, 1996.

Loeb, Don, "Full-Information Theories of Individual Good," *Social Theory and Practice* 21 (1995): 1–30.

Luper, Stephen, *Invulnerability*. Chicago: Open Court, 1996.

Macedo, Stephen, "The Rule of Law, Justice, and the Politics of Moderation," *Nomos* 36 (1994): 148–77.

Mackie, J. L., *Persons and Values*. Oxford: Clarendon, 1985.

"The Third Theory of Law," *Philosophy & Public Affairs* 7 (1977): 3–16.

McClennen, Edward, "Pragmatic Rationality and Rules," *Philosophy & Public Affairs* 26 (1997): 210–58.

Mele, Alfred, "Recent Work on Self-Deception," *American Philosophical Quarterly* 24 (1987): 1–14.

Mill, J. S., *On Liberty*. Chicago: Gateway, 1955 (first published 1859).

Millgram, Elijah, *Practical Induction*. Cambridge, MA: Harvard University Press, 1997.

Moody-Adams, Michele, *Fieldwork in Familiar Places*. Cambridge, MA: Harvard University Press, 1997.

Moore, Michael S., "Authority, Law, and Razian Reasons," *Southern California Law Review* 62 (1989): 829–96.

Nathanson, Stephen, "Brandt on Rationality and Value," pp. 1–16 in *Rationality, Rules, and Utility*, ed. Brad Hooker. Boulder, CO: Westview, 1993.

Nozick, Robert, *The Nature of Rationality*. Princeton, NJ: Princeton University Press, 1993.

Oddie, Graham, "Act and Maxim: Value-Discrepancy and Two Theories of Power," *Philosophy & Phenomenological Research* 53 (1993): 72–92.

Overvold, Mark, "Morality, Self-Interest, and Reasons for Being Moral," *Philosophy & Phenomenological Research* 44 (1984): 493–507.

"Self-Interest and the Concept of Self-Sacrifice," *Canadian Journal of Philosophy* 10 (1980): 105–18.

Parfit, Derek, *Reasons and Persons*. Oxford: Clarendon, 1984.

Perry, Michael, "What Is 'the Constitution'?", pp. 99–151 in *Constitutionalism*, ed. Larry Alexander. Cambridge: Cambridge University Press, 1998.

Pettit, Philip, "Free Riding and Foul Dealing," *The Journal of Philosophy* 83 (1986): 361–79.

"Satisficing Consequentialism," *Proceedings of the Aristotelian Society* 58, suppl. (1984): 165–76.

Postema, Gerald, "Positivism, I Presume," *Harvard Journal of Law and Public Policy* 14 (1991): 797–822.

Rachels, James, "Active and Passive Euthanasia," *New England Journal of Medicine* 292 (1975): 78–80.

Radin, Maragret, "Presumptive Positivism and Trivial Cases," *Harvard Journal of Law and Public Policy* 14 (1991): 823–37.

Rawls, John, *A Theory of Justice*. Cambridge, MA: Harvard University Press, 1971.

Raz, Joseph, "Facing Up," *Southern California Law Review* 62 (1989): 1153–235.

The Morality of Freedom. Oxford: Oxford University Press, 1986.

Practical Reason and Norms. Oxford: Oxford University Press, 1999.

Regan, Donald, "Authority and Value," *Southern California Law Review* 62 (1989): 995–1095.

Utilitarianism and Cooperation. Oxford: Clarendon, 1980.

Regents of University of California v. Bakke, 438 U.S. 265, 98 S.Ct. 2733 (1978).

Riggs v. Palmer, 115 N.Y. 506, 22 N.E. 188 (1889).

Rosati, Connie, "Brandt's Notion of Therapeutic Agency," *Ethics* 110 (2000): 780–811.

"Persons, Properties, and Full Information Accounts of the Good," *Ethics* 105 (1995): 296–325.

Ross, W. D., *The Right and the Good*. Oxford: Clarendon, 1930.

Sayre-McCord, G., "Deception and Reasons to Be Moral," *American Philosophical Quarterly* 26 (1989): 113–22.

Scalia, Antonin, "The Rule of Law as a Law of Rules," *University of Chicago Law Review* 56 (1989): 1175–88.

Schauer, Frederick, *Playing by the Rules*. Oxford: Clarendon, 1991.

"Precedent," *Stanford Law Review* 39 (1987): 571–605.

"Rules and the Rule of Law," *Harvard Journal of Law and Public Policy* 14 (1991): 645–94.

Schlag, Pierre, "Rules and Standards," *UCLA Law Review* 33 (1985): 379–430.

Schmidtz, David, *Rational Choice and Moral Agency*. Princeton, NJ: Princeton University Press, 1995.

Shafer-Landau, Russ, "Moral Rules," *Ethics* 107 (1997): 584–611.

Shapiro, Scott, "The Difference That Rules Make," pp. 33–62 in *Analyzing Law,* ed. Brian Bix. Oxford: Clarendon, 1998.

"Judicial Can't," *Philosophical Issues* 112, in press.

Sidgwick, Henry, *The Methods of Ethics*. London: Macmillan, 1907.

Simpson, Evan, "Prudence and Anti-Prudence," *American Philosophical Quarterly* 35 (1998): 73–86.

Slote, Michael, *Beyond Optimizing*. Cambridge, MA: Harvard University Press, 1989.

Sobel, David, "Full Information Accounts of Well-Being," *Ethics* 104 (1994): 784–810.

Solum, Lawrence, "Equity and the Rule of Law," *Nomos* 36 (1994): 120–47.

Spark, Muriel, *The Prime of Miss Jean Brodie*. New York: HarperPerennial, 1994.

Stich, Stephen, "Moral Philosophy and Mental Representation, pp. 215–28 in *The Origin of Values,* ed. M. Hechter. Hawthorne, NY: Aldine de Gruyter, 1993.

Stocker, Michael, *Plural and Conflicting Values*. Oxford: Clarendon, 1990.

Stone, Martin, "Focusing the Law: What Legal Interpretation Is Not," pp. 31–96 in *Law and Interpretation,* ed. Andrei Marmor. Oxford: Clarendon, 1997.

Strong, Colin, "What if Everyone Did That?", *Durham University Journal* 53 (1960): 5–10.

Sunstein, Cass, "Norms in Surprising Places: The Case of Statutory Interpretation," *Ethics* 100 (1990): 803–20.

"Political Conflict and Legal Agreement," *The Tanner Lectures on Human Values* 17 (1996): 137–249.

Taylor, Gabrielle, "Integrity," *Proceedings of the Aristotelian Society* 55 (1981): 143–59.

Thomson, Judith, "A Defense of Abortion," *Philosophy & Public Affairs* 1 (1971): 47–66.

Ullmann-Margalit, Edna, *The Emergence of Norms.* Oxford: Clarendon, 1977.

United Steelworkers v. Weber, 443 U.S. 193 (1979).

Velleman, J. David, "Brandt's Definition of 'Good'," *The Philosophical Review* 97 (1988): 353–71.

Waldron, Jeremy, "Precommitment and Disagreement," pp. 271–99 in *Constitutionalism,* ed. Larry Alexander. Cambridge: Cambridge University Press, 1998.

Wittgenstein, L., *Philosophical Investigations,* trans. G. E. M. Anscombe. New York: Macmillan, 1958.

Index

ambivalence, moral, 58–9
abortion issue, 32, 139, 145, 162–3, 167–8, 170, 176
abstract vs. concrete moral arguments, 176–7
addiction: example of, 74–5, 76, 85; weakness of will distinguished from, 76–7
aesthetic judgments, 29; "art critic" analogy, 151–2
affirmative action issue, 32, 162–3, 169
alcohol prohibitions, 15, 47
altruism, 97–8. *See also* self-sacrifice
ambiguous situations. *See* novel or controversial cases
analogical reasoning, 32, 105, 119, 138, 159, 169–71. *See also* legal precedents; novel or controversial cases; settled cases
anarchism, 188n.59
antirealist position, 156–8
antitrust laws, 187–8n.53
Aristotle, 1, 86
authority: legal, 142, 144–5; moral, 33, 47, 58–60. *See also* moral judgment; public sphere
autonomy, 29, 33

Bach, Kent, on self-deception, 70

Bakke v. Regents of the University of California, 106
balance of reasons, 38–9, 51; equilibria, 44–5, 50, 53, 56; "metarules" given extra weight (*See also* metarules), 117; moral reasoning and, 23–4, 52; rules having independent moral weight when genuine, 158–61; weak genuine rules having moral weight, 55–6, 60–1, 102, 106–7, 150, 189n.75; the weighing of legal principles, 114–15. *See also* moral reasoning
bank foreclosure case, 43–4, 65, 94, 104, 146
Barnes, Annette, on self-deception, 70
baseball manager (example), 27–8, 33, 37
Brandt, Richard, on desires, 154–5
Bratman, Michael, on intentions, 73–4
Buddhist detachment, 84, 88

capital punishment issue, 162
cases. *See* novel or controversial cases; paradigm cases; settled cases
causal independence assumption, 68, 71–2, 74–5
censorship, 51. *See also* freedom of speech

203

8, 163–4. *See also* novel or controversial cases

diversity: cultural or racial, 157; as a value, 32, 169, 171

dog control regulations (example), 21, 109

driving rules (example), 18, 28, 53–4

"due process" clause, 129, 142

duress, defense of, 135

Dworkin, Ronald: on "checkerboard solutions, 139, 187n.49; on interpreting cases, 109, 133–4, 138; on legal principles as genuine rules, 114–16, 118

egalitarianism: sharing rules as (Johnson), 30–3; Rawls on, 157

egoism: as narrowly defined self-interest, 99–100; self-interest as (Slote), 81, 82–3

equal opportunity as a value, 169

equal protection clause (Fourteenth Amendment), 123, 125, 128, 140

euthanasia issue, 172–5

exclusionary reasons (Raz), 56–8, 73, 106; critique of, 58–60

experience, moral judgment and, 153–4, 182–3

fairness issue, 167–8, 190n.90

fallibility of judges, 35, 42–3, 47–8, 115, 130–2

fallibility of moral judgment, 36, 39, 42; as a justification for moral rules, 35, 43

fictional cases, 69, 166–7, 168–9

First Amendment: interpretation of, 127–8; as a weak genuine rule (Schauer), 107, 119

force of law, 95, 117

Fourteenth Amendment, equal protection clause in, 123, 125, 128, 140

freedom of speech, 31, 123–4, 127–8. *See also* First Amendment

freedom as a value, 29. *See also* autonomy

free markets, 102, 188n.59

free riding, 67, 71

Fuller, Lon F., war memorial example, 108, 109, 133, 134

Gauthier, David, on the "constrained maximizer," 191n.118

genetic alteration issues, 181–2

genuine moral rules. *See* Moral rules

Gert, Bernard, 31

Gibbard, Allan, on rational optimization, 83–4

Gilbert, Margaret, 188n.54

goodness as object of rational desire, 83–6

Hare, R. M., 4, 36–7, 37–8

harm: cumulative (*See* collective action problem(s)); as a normative notion, 160; self-defeating behavior, 12–13, 49–50, 162; threshold of harm, 72, 121, 190n.91

Hart, H. L. A., 31; legal positivism in theory of, 112–15, 133; on metarules, 117; on "penumbra" areas of moral judgment, 16, 108–9

Henningson v. Bloomfield Motors, 136

Hobbes, Thomas: on avoiding death as paramount value, 29; on observance of rules, 4, 5, 12, 92–5; response to "the Fool," 93–4; on the threat of punishment, 94, 95–6

homosexuality, negative view of, 160

Hume, David, 97–8, 114

immorality, 96

incest ban (example), 21

individuals, relevant differences between, 100–1

insider trading, 181
institutional constraints, 21, 42
integrity, 40–1, 77–9
intentions, 73–4, 189–90n.89
internet invasions of privacy, 181
intuitionism, 150

"Jean Brodie" (fictional character), 69
Johnson, Conrad, on shared rules as
egalitarian, 39–42
judges: bound to the rule of law, 104;
cumulative effects of rulings to be
considered (*See also* bank foreclosure case), 145–8; fallibility of, 35,
42–3, 47–8, 115, 130–2; personal
values of, 125–6, 137, 138–9;
scope of decision-making, 129–30,
142, 144–5; shielding from unpopular decisions (Scalia), 142, 145.
See also justice; moral judgment
jurisprudence, normative theory of,
116–17
justice: the "appearance" of, 141–3;
the justice system, 42–7; as a value,
29. *See also* judges
justification for moral rules, 11, 18,
33, 36, 42; consistency, 33–4; efficiency, 33; fallibility, 35, 43; predictability, 33, 34–5, 108, 141–2,
143; rules opaque to justification,
107

Kant, Immanuel, 1, 157; concept of
moral autonomy, 29, 33; on moral
reasoning, 22, 100–1, 180
Kantian constraint, 3, 9, 22, 159, 161;
adhering to, 41, 79, 139, 167;
characterized as the "weaker constraint," 2, 22, 159; ignoring the,
138, 140, 143–4
Kavka, Gregory, 93
killing (example), 17, 21–2, 26–7

legal cases cited: *Bakke v. Regents of
the University of California*, 106;
*Henningson v. Bloomfield Motors,
Inc.*, 136; *Plessy v. Ferguson*, 145;
Riggs v. Palmer, 109, 134, 136; *Roe
v. Wade*, 145; *Weber v. Kaiser Aluminum and Chemical Corporation*, 134–
5
legally relevant differences, 137–8,
139
legal positivism, 112–15
legal precedents, 42, 113, 130–2, 132,
137–8, 140; as determinant of future decisions, 144–5. *See also* settled cases
legal principles: based on core (settled) cases, 116–17, 119, 128; as
genuine rules (Dworkin), 114–16
legal rules: defined and characterized,
7–8, 108–9; design and wording of
important, 109–10, 127–30, 133–
4, 135, 140–1, 142; the rule of law,
42, 46–7; whether to be read or
written as genuine, 104–5, 108,
112–16, 118–20, 125, 130, 134–8,
140, 145–8. *See also* judges; justice
legal standards: broadly stated, 113,
128–9; evolving into genuine rules,
129–30; as pseudorules, 107–8, 110–
12, 124, 135; requiring interpretation, 108–10, 110–12, 126–9
legislative intent, 111, 127, 133; original intent doctrine, 124–7, 134–5.
See also Constitution, U. S.
legislative rule-making, 35–6, 120
libertarianism, 188n.59; Nozick on,
157
loopholes/technicalities, 33, 136
loyalist versus impartialist paradigm,
157

McClennen, Edward, 73, 186n.25
metaphysics, 156, 158

206

metarules, 117, 130–1
Millgram, Elijah, on the source of desires, 154–5
Mill, J. S., 12, 33, 51
moral disputes. *See* novel or controversial cases
moral judgment: cognitive skills vs. character in, 175; experience and, 153–4, 182–3; fallibility of, 36, 39, 42; as moral knowledge, 8–9, 131, 171–2; sensitivity and, 153–4, 164. *See also* judges
morally relevant factors: contextuality and, 25–6, 63, 149, 164; in settled cases, 116, 164, 168–9; strong rules and, 27–8, 37
moral outrage, 153
moral reasoning, 4; in the absence of moral rules, 63, 149–54, 162–4, 168–71; analyzing/criticizing moral paradigms in, 162–3, 169–70; compared to legal reasoning, 149, 182, 194n.190; 181; first-order vs. second-order reasons, 57; self-interest encompassing, 101–2; whether moral properties are real, 156–8. *See also* analogical reasoning; balance of reasons; ordinary moral reasoning
moral rules: advocated as necessary, 4, 5, 12, 36–7; broadly/nonnormatively descriptive when genuine, 10–11, 13, 19, 20–1, 82–3, 105; defined, 2, 10, 25, 63, 105, 158–61; interpretation rarely required of genuine, 108–10; justification for using, 11, 18, 42–5, 47–51, 53–5, 64; rules of thumb distinguished from genuine, 14–16, 20, 54, 73, 76; as second-best strategies, 4–5, 11, 19, 72, 150; whether and when they are necessary, 1–2, 10, 20–1, 50–1. *See also* justification for

moral rules; strong rules; weak genuine rules

normative theory of jurisprudence, 120–1
novel or controversial cases, 108–10, 168; finding data bases for, 149, 158, 162; analyzing moral paradigms in, 162–3, 169–70, 181; innovation-based, 181–2; reasoning from settled cases to resolve, 132–4, 137, 151, 166, 169–70, 172, 177, 180–2
Nozick, Robert: on libertarianism, 157; on the necessity of prudential rules, 62, 65–6, 72, 75, 77–9; on the symbolic transference of utilities, 67–9, 70–1, 75

optimal pattern of behavior, 13, 19, 30, 44–5, 191n.118
optimization, 30, 83–4; global vs. local, 72–3, 186n.25; as "greed," 80–1; maximization of goods as, 83, 90; prudential rationality and, 86, 87, 102; rational optimization, 83–4, 87–90; strategies of, 79–80, 90–1. *See also* self-interest
ordinary moral reasoning, 19–20, 22–3, 28, 149; moral rules and, 149. *See also* contextuality; morally relevant factors; moral reasoning
original intent doctrine, 124–7, 134–5. *See also* legislative intent

paradigm case(s), 19, 34, 44, 104, 105, 119, 131, 134. *See also* bank foreclosure case; settled cases
paradigms, moral, 52, 175; analyzing/criticizing, 162–3, 169–70
Parfit, Derek: on personal identity, 87–9, 160; on "present-aim" reasons, 86–9

particularism: "art critic" analogy, 151–2; morality as context-dependent (Dancy), 25–6, 150–3, 164–5, 173, 176; particularist account of moral reasoning, 8, 11; Ross's account of moral reasoning, 3–4, 150–1; "rule sensitive" (Postema), 118–19, 187n.50; the unique relevance claim, 165–6

past/present/future. *See* time

personal identity, Parfit's theory of, 87–9, 160

pet regulations (example), 21, 109

Platonic moderation, 83

plea bargaining, 135

pleasure/satisfaction, 25–7, 30. *See also* desire

Plessy v. Ferguson, 145

political ideology, 145

pollution regulation, 55, 74

Postema, Gerald, on "rule sensitive particularism," 118–19, 187n.50

Powell, Justice, 106

practical reason, 2. *See also* Kantian constraint; moral reasoning

predictability: contextuality and, 35; as justification for rules, 33, 34–5, 108, 141–2, 143

presumptive rules. *See* weak genuine rules

prima facie rules, 26–7; vs. rules of thumb, 20

prisoners' dilemma cases, 44, 45–6, 49, 64, 76–7; defined, 5, 185n.6; model case, 3; moral-moral prisoners' dilemmas, 5, 48, 53; prudential-moral prisoner's dilemmas, 12–13, 49, 91–2; prudential-prudential dilemmas, 12–13

problematic cases. *See* novel or controversial cases

property rights, 52

prudential rationality, 96–7; optimization and, 86, 87, 102

prudential rules: being personal/intrapersonal rules, 5, 6, 6–7, 48, 121; disanalogies with interpersonal rules, 62; as necessary in normal conduct (Nozick), 62, 65–6, 72, 75, 77–9; rules of thumb and, 76–7, 91, 97; the rule to act morally, 63, 66–7, 88, 91–2, 99–100, 102–3; whether needed, 75, 88–9, 102–3

pseudorules, 16–17, 105

public sphere, 42, 47, 49–51; institutional constraints, 21, 42. *See also* legal rules

punishment, ban against cruel and unusual, 128–9

"quasi-rule following," 43

Rachels, James, 173–4

rational optimization, 83–4, 87–90

Rawls, John: on egalitarianism, 157; on higher-level desires, 86; on "reflective equilibrium," 158, 161–2

Raz, Joseph, 4; critique of exclusionary account, 58–60; on exclusionary reasons, 56–8, 73, 106

relativist position, 156

religious rules (example), 23–4

resoluteness, 73–4

"respecting others" (example), 21–2

Riggs v. Palmer, 109, 134, 136

rights-based theory, 38, 38–9, 187n.43 and 45; constitutional interpretation and, 126; property rights, 52; rights as moral rules, 51–2. *See also* affirmative action issue; Civil Rights Act of 1964; due process clause; equal protection clause

Roe v. Wade, 145

Ross, W. D., intuitionist account of moral reasoning, 150–1

rule of law, 42, 46–7; judges bound to, 104

rule makers. *See* judges; legislative rule-making

rules: classification of, 13–14, 38; concept of, 10–11, 33; vagueness or "penumbra" re: application of, 16; when content requires definition, 21–2, 28. *See also* legal rules; moral rules; pseudorules

rules of thumb, 14–15, 49, 160; counterexamples and, 17–18; prima facie rules distinguished from, 20; prudential rules and, 76–7, 91, 97; strong rules distinguished from, 15–16

"salient" factors (Dancy), 150–1, 152

same actions requirement, 64

sanctions/punishment, 34; Hobbes on the threat of, 94, 95–6

satisfaction of desires, 30, 79–81, 90–1

Scalia, Antonin, 141–3

Schauer, Frederick, 4, 36–7; on the First Amendment as a weak general rule, 107, 119; on weak genuine rules as presumptive, 118, 136–7, 147

second-best strategies, 6–7; genuine moral rules as, 4–5, 11, 19, 44–5, 72–3, 150; genuine moral rules essential to, 32–3, 150. *See also* optimal pattern of behavior

seeing-eye dogs, 109

self-deception, 69–70, 71, 128–9n.128

self-defeating behavior, 162; when self-interest is, 12–13, 49–50

self-interest, 128–9n.128; broad vs. narrow definition of, 93, 97–9, 101–2; as egoistic (Slote), 81, 82–3; vs. collective interest, 48–9; vs. moral action, 37, 48; when it is self-defeating, 12–13, 49–50. *See also* optimization

self-respect, 97

self-sacrifice, 59–60, 82. *See also* altruism

Sensitivity, moral judgment and, 153–4, 164

settled cases: morally relevant factors in, 116, 164, 168–9; reasoning from (*See also* analogical reasoning), 132–4, 137, 151, 166, 169–70, 172, 177, 180–2. *See also* legal precedents; paradigm cases

Shapiro, Scott, interpretation of rules as strong, 23–5

Sherman Act, 133

simplification argument, 4, 36–7, 57

Slote, Michael, on optimization, 79–83, 86, 89

snacking between meals (example), 65–6, 70, 71–2, 75–6, 79–80

social morality, 137

social welfare as a value, 29–30, 98

sophistication, 73

standards. *See* legal standards

stocks, insider trading in, 181

strategies: desires as, 98–9; genuine rules flowing from, 73; of optimization, 79–80, 90–1

strong rules: defined and characterized, 15–17, 28, 30–2, 106; and morally relevant factors, 27–8; novel cases and, 149; as second-best strategies, 45–7; Shapiro's interpretation of, 23–5. *See also* moral rules

superrogatory acts, 57–8

Supreme Court, U. S., 122

tax evasion (example), 50, 64–5, 74

terminal illness, patients with, 172–5

theft (example), 53, 95

Thompson, Judith, 170, 176

threshold of harm, 72, 121, 190n.91

Tibetan monk example, 84

time: collective identity/political majorities over, 121, 125, 126, 139; personal identity over, 86–9, 160, 190n.90; "present-aim" reasons (Parfit), 86–9

Title VII of the Civil Rights Act, 134–5

trade laws, 133

trust, mutual, 31–2, 33–4

Ullmann-Margalit, Edna, on the origin of norms, 188n.58

"universal" values, 30–2

utilitarian account of moral reasoning, 1, 81, 156, 161; moral utilities and disutilities, 37–8, 67; the symbolic transference of utility (Nozick), 67–9, 70–1, 75

values: competing, 109–10; diversity of, 3, 29–30, 114, 149; interpersonal, 30–1; monolithic or homogeneous, 116, 117, 137; moral paradigms and, 137–8, 175; moral rules and, 28, 31–2; rational ordering of, 166; "universal," 30–2

voting, example of a collective action rule, 48–9, 68

war memorial example (Fuller), 108, 109, 133, 134

"weaker constraint": Kantian constraint as the, 2, 22, 159; ignoring the force of the, 138, 140, 143–4. *See also* Kantian constraint

weak genuine rules: having moral weight, 55–6, 60–1, 102, 106–7, 150, 189n.75; moral reasoning and, 150. *See also* moral rules

weakness of will, 33, 65–6, 76–7

wealth, redistribution of, 52

Weber v. Kaiser Aluminum and Chemical Corporation, 134–5

welfare law, 136

welfare of others as a value, 29–30, 98

will: resoluteness, 73–4; weakness of will, 33, 65–6, 76–7

Wittgenstein, Ludwig, 192n.135

working conditions, 52